EDINBURGH
PORTRAITS

EDINBURGH PORTRAITS

MICHAEL TURNBULL

JOHN DONALD PUBLISHERS LTD
EDINBURGH

To my family

ISBN 0 85976 135 5

Exclusive distribution in the United States of
America and Canada by Humanities Press Inc.,
Atlantic Highlands, NJ 07716, USA

Phototypesetting by Newtext Composition Ltd., Glasgow
Printed in Great Britain by Bell & Bain Ltd., Glasgow

Contents

Introduction

In the waist of Scotland, where the Forth river swells into the open sea, lies the City of Edinburgh, born out of one of the many volcanic crags in which the eastern tracts of the Lothians abound. From the stronghold of the rock, 440 feet above sea-level, a determined garrison could successfully dominate the approach by land or water. Few traces of early occupation remain, for the oldest building still standing in the city is Queen Margaret's Chapel, constructed around 1090 on what is now the Castle Rock.

The ground slopes away from the Castle in a mile-long 'crag and tail' ridge towards the east, and it was along the spine of this ridge (now the High Street) that the ancient burgh grew in the protection of the Castle, defended to the 'north by the deep water of the Nor' Loch. In this small medieval city the burghers kept their crofts, a handful of cattle, pigs or sheep, and wrested a precarious living from the soil. With the building of Holyrood Abbey and St Giles parish church, Edinburgh followed the traditional medieval pattern of Castle, Burgh and Abbey. After Flodden in 1513, when the burgh had been nearly destroyed, a strong defensive wall was constructed to replace the earlier King's Wall. For the next two hundred years the Flodden Wall marked the boundaries of the Old Town.

There were now four main points of entry to the burgh: the Netherbow Port (gate), the Cowgate Port, Bristo Port and the West Port. Below, to the east, at the foot of the ridge, lay the new burgh of Canongate, granted by the King to the Augustinian Canons in the Abbey of Holyrood. Until 1690 the Canongate remained an independent burgh; in that year Edinburgh bought it over.

Until around 1550 most houses in the High Street were constructed on a timber framework with brightly coloured plaster or clay infilling; the roofs were of thatch or slate.

After 1550 the danger of fire led to more houses being built of locally quarried stone, roofed with red clay pantiles. So many people wanted to live inside the protection of the Flodden Wall that storeys were piled one on top of another to as many as nine – or in one instance (now demolished) behind Parliament Square, fourteen! – producing the characteristic 'lands' (medieval tower-blocks). It has even been said that seventeenth-century Edinburgh, not New York, invented the skyscraper. Often the gable-ends were built to face the street, and 'closes' (blind alleys) or 'wynds' (open alleys) were needed to allow access to the front doors or to the 'courts' (courtyards). Sometimes a close was framed by an arch wide enough to allow a cart through and would then be known as a 'pend'. Merchants conducted their daily business below the Mercat (market) Cross in the centre of the High Street until 1753, when the Royal Exchange (later known as the City Chambers) was built. Proclamations were made at the Mercat Cross.

At first, burghs were the only place where trade and commerce could be carried on in accordance with Royal Charter. This enabled the King to keep a close control over trade and collect revenue regularly in the form of taxes.

There were specific selling-points for other commodities: a weekly grain and livestock market was held in the Grassmarket; a wool and linen sale was held once a week in the part of the High Street known as the Land or Lawn Market. Other necessities such as meat or butter were to be had in special walled markets. As the town grew and spread, so did the places of commerce and trade.

Next to the Kirk of St Giles in the High Street was the Old Tolbooth which served as a meeting-place for the Town Council, for the Burgh Council, the supreme courts and even the Scottish Parliament, and it served as the central tax collection office. The virtue of the Tolbooth was that it was secure, and this explains its notoriety as the town jail. The Old Tolbooth was demolished in 1817.

Further down the High Street at the Tron stood the weigh-beam where that indispensable commodity, salt, was measured and sold. Throughout the burgh were a number of wells which quenched the burgh's thirst and in which the citizens could wash themselves. The ruling body of the town from medieval times to 1832 was the Town or Burgh Council composed of merchants and members of the exclusive craft guilds. By 1600 there were fourteen incorporated trades; below them in the social scale came the journeymen, servants, labourers and the beggars, the 'outland' folk from outside the burgh, the 'unfreemen', the vagabonds and the gypsies. The skilled trades such as bakery, butchering, shoemaking, goldsmithing or tailoring were almost exclusively in the hands of the guilds and the merchants. Whereas the guilds were permitted to manufacture the finer articles, only the merchants could conduct trade on an international basis. The Luckenbooths (permanent enclosed shops built up against the Old Tolbooth) housed the goldsmiths, jewellers, watchmakers and booksellers in the precincts of the Kirk of St Giles after the Reformation, but by 1830 such permanent structures were done away with and the booths sold only cheap toys, sweets, shoes or second-hand clothes. The Krames (open stalls erected against the buttresses of St Giles) were used by the unfreemen to sell their goods on market days, which were the only occasions on which they could lawfully do so in the early history of the burgh. Between 1790 and 1830 the draining of the Nor' Loch and the construction of two bridges and an earthen Mound linking the High Street with the New Town accelerated the development of the New Town to the north of the Old. The Treaty of Union between England and Scotland in 1707 signalled the end of the Old Town's siege mentality and its community spirit, and heralded the arrival of a more leisurely and cosmopolitan style of living. Like Topsy, the Old Town 'just grew' in an exciting and often chaotic huddle. The New Town, however, was based on the logical grid-iron design of the twenty-three year old architect James Craig, who in 1766 won the competition organised by the Town Council. Craig's design was an orderly and severely geometric one, freed from the constraints imposed on Old Town architecture by the slope of the High Street and by the confines of the Flodden Wall. Further development of the New Town by the architects Robert Adam and William Playfair added to the classical elegance and dignity of the site with spacious terraces and stately columns, but what perhaps got lost along the way was the Old Town's lively 'democracy of the common stair'.

The maintenance of law and order in the city had at first been the duty of the burghers ('watching and warding'). In

1689 a Town Guard was established which quickly gained a reputation for cowardice, incompetence and cursing which earned its members the scornful nickname of 'The Town Rats'. During the execution of a criminal in 1736 the Guard panicked and fired into the crowd. The disturbances which followed were later known as the Porteous Riots after the trigger-happy officer in command.

The Highland Clearances drove crofters in large numbers south into the Lowland towns to look for work. The Industrial Revolution at the same time forced many agricultural workers from all parts of the country into the same towns. Both factors increased overcrowding, insanitariness and the poverty of many of the population of cities such as Edinburgh.

As the New Town was built, the gentry moved out of the Old Town, leaving it to decay into tenement slums crammed with poorly paid labourers, artisans and the destitute. Robert Louis Stevenson, writing of the Old Town as he knew it in the 1870s, gives a striking picture of its degeneration and mystery:

> In one house, perhaps, two score families herd together, and, perhaps, not one of them is wholly out of the reach of want. The great hotel is given over to discomfort from the foundation to chimney-tops, everywhere a pinching, narrow habit, scanty meals, and an air of sluttishness and dirt. In the first room there is a birth, in another a death, in a third a sordid drinking-bout, and the detective and the Bible-reader cross upon the stairs. High words are audible from dwelling to dwelling, and children have a strange experience from the first; only a robust soul, you would think, could grow up in such conditions without hurt. And even if God tempers his dispensations to the young, and all the ill does not arise that our apprehensions may forecast, the sight of such a way of living is disquieting to people who are more happily circumstanced. Social inequality is nowhere more ostentatious than at Edinburgh ... to the stroller along Princes Street, the High Street callously exhibits its back garrets. It is true there is a garden between. And although nothing could be more glaring by way of contrast, sometimes the opposition is more immediate, sometimes the thing lies in a nutshell, and there is not so much as a blade of grass between the rich and the poor. To look over the South Bridge and see the Cowgate below full of crying hawkers, is to view one rank of society from another in the twinkling of an eye.

Between 1770 and 1800 the population of Edinburgh doubled to 80,000 and continued to rise meteorically till the end of the nineteenth century. Crimes of a minor variety were on the increase and the Town Guard, and later the police force, were kept busy. In 1847, for example, there were 176 known housebreakings in the City, 257 cases of carters riding furiously on carts, 1,472 cases of begging and 5,573 persons found drunk in the streets and taken into the police office for protection.

Gradually the traditional diet of oatmeal gave way to imported wheat, poor in minerals and vitamins. The low wage earner in the town received only an inadequate supply of fresh fruit, vegetables and milk. The high tenements cut off sunlight, and the pall of smoke over the City absorbed the ultra-violet rays. Rickets and tuberculosis became the scourge of the labouring poor.

Until the end of the eighteenth century there was no organised cleansing of the town. At 10 o'clock every morning in the Old Town a drum sounded and housewives in the tenements shouted 'Gardyloo' (Gardez l'eau or Garde à l'eau – Watch out for the water) as they threw down slops and waste into the street below, adding to the accumulated piles of decaying rubbish whose peculiar stink was known at home and abroad as 'The Flowers of Edinburgh'. The New Town also had its share of embarrassment in the failure of the National Monument on Calton Hill, overlooking Princes Street. Begun with insufficient funds, modelled on the Parthenon of Athens and designed to commemorate the fallen of the Napoleonic War, the National Monument was never completed. The few solitary pillars of the Monument are a permanent reminder of the ingratitude of Edinburgh's citizens, the City's Folly and her Disgrace. Nevertheless, Edinburgh's history and geographical location provided a many-levelled stage for the actors in the human drama which we shall now share in the pages which follow.

Artists, Architects and Others

Artists

During his convalescence at Craiglockart Hospital following shellshock in the trenches of the First World War, the poet Wilfrid Owen described Edinburgh and its castle as reminiscent of an Earl's Court scenic backdrop. There are those who have tried to point to the geographical similarities between Edinburgh and Rome, and there are even those who have seen the City as a carbon copy of Jerusalem. What can be said with some conviction is that Edinburgh, with its windswept fortress, has long been an inspiration to artists.

Allan Ramsay (1713-1784), the portrait painter, and the son of the author of *The Gentle Shepherd*, signed indentures with the Edinburgh School of St Luke in 1729. He travelled on the Continent in 1736 and later formed the Select Society with the philosopher David Hume and the economist Adam Smith. Ramsay was highly thought of by Dr Johnson, who said of him, 'You will not find a man in whose conversation there is more instruction, more information and more elegance...' He became the friend and correspondent of Voltaire and of Jean-Jacques Rousseau, and when the latter sought asylum in England in 1766, Ramsay painted his portrait for David Hume. Horace Walpole observed that 'Mr Reynolds seldom succeeds in women, Mr Ramsay is formed to paint them'.

Alexander Nasmyth (1758-1840) is honoured with the title of 'father of Scottish landscape'. He was originally an apprentice coach-painter in Edinburgh, but Ramsay had met him and persuaded his master to cancel Nasmyth's indentures. As well as painting easel-pictures, Nasmyth completed many pieces of theatrical scenery for theatres in London and Glasgow.

Of considerable merit also is the wickedly accurate cartoonist **John Kay,** whose etchings of a host of Edinburgh notables with

John Kay

accompanying text have delighted generations and have now become collectors' items. Kay began life as a surgeon-barber but from 1784 to 1826 devoted himself to his 'Portraits', which give an invaluable picture of life in the Capital during that period. Kay is buried in Greyfriars Kirk.

Probably Scotland's best-known painter of this period, **Sir Henry Raeburn** (1756-1823), was born the son of an Edinburgh yarn-boiler. Orphaned at the age of six, the boy was

Sir Henry Raeburn

educated at Heriot's Hospital and apprenticed at 15 to a jeweller and goldsmith. However, one day a seal-engraver and etcher called to see Raeburn's master and surprised the apprentice working on a portrait. The seal-engraver, David Deuchar, gave Raeburn lessons in painting and introduced him to David Martin, the leading portrait painter in Scotland at the time. Raeburn established himself in turn as the foremost

portrait painter, working from his studio in George Street,
acquired in 1787. On his visit to Scotland in 1822, George IV
knighted Raeburn at Hopetoun House, and thus set the seal on
his career. Raeburn was a man of wide interests, fascinated by
mechanical science and archaeology, building and gardening,
as well as taking a keen practical interest in archery and golf.

Walter Geikie was born in 1795. His father, a perfumer and
hairdresser, lived at 1 Charles Street. At the age of two Geikie

Walter Geikie's etching 'Very Fou'

became deaf and dumb as a result of an illness. His education
was effected by Thomas Braidwood, the founder of the deaf
and dumb academy in Dumbiedykes Road. Geikie was admitted in 1812 to the Drawing Academy of the Board of Trustees
for the Encouragement of Scottish Manufactures (one of the
forerunners of the Edinburgh College of Art). He became a
Scottish Academician in 1834 and died three years later. In
1841 his etchings 'Illustrative of Scottish Character and Scenery' were first published, and it is by these that he is best known
today, with their intimate knowledge of the common man and
the ordinary way of life of his time, the 'characters' of the
streets and their pawky humour.

Photographers

The two pioneers of photography, **David Octavius Hill** (1802-1870), and his associate, **Robert Adamson** (1820-1860), worked for a large part of their career in Edinburgh, recording its scenes and its people, its dignitaries and luminaries, and its ordinary working men and women.

Dr Thomas Keith, born in Aberdeenshire in 1827, was apprenticed in 1845 to Sir James Young Simpson in the old Edinburgh Infirmary. He became house-surgeon to Professor James Syme three years later, and, after a spell abroad, returned to join his brother's medical practice in Edinburgh. His chief claim to fame, however, grew out of his skill as an amateur photographer. He experimented with a waxed paper process which gave photographs with finer detail and better quality and enabled unexposed slides to be stored for a considerable time (which had not been possible before). Secondly, he recorded, in a series of studies made between 1855 and 1856, many of the fast-disappearing parts of the Old Town of Edinburgh, his photographs providing an invaluable complement to the views of the Old Town made by artists in oil, water-colour or pencil sketches.

Probably the modern artist with the greatest contemporary reputation who originated from Edinburgh is **Eduardo Paolozzi.** He was born in the City in 1924, the son of an ice-cream shop proprietor in Leith. After attending evening classes at the Edinburgh College of Art, he entered the Slade in London where he studied for three years. At the age for military service he joined the Pioneer Corps for the period 1943-44. After the end of the War he went to L'Ecole des Beaux Arts in Paris and made contact with the celebrated Italian sculptor Alberto Giacometti and some or the original Dadaists such as Tristan Tzara. In 1952 he was chosen as an exhibitor in the prestigious Venice Biennale and five years later in the São Paulo Biennale. He taught sculpture at St Martin's Art School in London and later taught design at the Central School. In 1967 he won the $2,000 sculpture prize at the Pittsburgh International Art Exhibition and was visiting professor at the University of Berkeley and in Hamburg, as well as taking up an appointment as lecturer in ceramics at the Royal College of Art. His work as an artist has revolved around sculpture but has embraced many other media, from textiles to lithography. His sculpture has been described as being composed of salvaged scrap, crushed and pressed into idiosyncratic monoliths which combine the monumentality of Celtic standing stones and the impersonality of modern technology.

Richard Demarco graduated from Edinburgh College of Art in 1954 and after a spell in teaching became one of the directors of the Traverse art gallery. By 1972 he had set up the

Richard Demarco

Demarco Gallery, which injected an element of international modernism into the Edinburgh art scene. A reflection of this was his award of the Gold Order of Distinction by the Polish government in 1976 for outstanding contributions to cultural co-operation between Poland and Scotland. Demarco has the drive and the awareness to cut through traditional areas of demarcation and the flair to make people sit up and take notice. 'Art is for everyone,' he once said: 'Paint, like a piece of music, is the most international thing I know.' Recently awarded the OBE, Richard Demarco's own work ranges from a sixty-foot mural of St Andrews Old Course for a golf club in Japan to drawings illustrating the Edinburgh & Lothians telephone directory.

A heartening contemporary story is that of **Richard Wawro.**

Severely mentally-handicapped, with defective eyesight, he was born in Tayport, Fife in 1952, the son of a Scottish mother and a Polish-born father. He attended a number of occupation centres from the age of six. In 1960 he and his family moved to Edinburgh. They had been advised to 'put him in a home and forget him'. Nevertheless he showed an extraordinary aptitude for art and within a number of years was brought to the attention of Richard Demarco, who gave him his first one-man show in the Richard Demarco Gallery in 1970. Shows followed in London, Paris and the Edinburgh Festival where Richard's pictures (over three hundred of them), chiefly in wax crayons and based on images from books and television, attracted great interest. Exhibitions followed in 1973 at the YMCA Gallery, Kensington Gardens in London, in the High Street, Edinburgh (1975), and in 1978 came the turning-point in Richard's career when Laurence Becker of Maine, USA saw a ten-minute BBC Nationwide documentary on Richard and began an association which was to lead to visits to America and a full-length documentary film. Mr Becker was awarded a doctorate for the thesis he completed on Richard Wawro and his gift for the graphic arts. Today Richard Wawro has drawn and coloured some two thousand pictures, some of which are in the possession of the Pope, Mrs Thatcher and Mrs Nancy Reagan. His vivid and vigorous images are the product of a baffling imagination and an unbelievable talent.

The Dovecot Studios at Corstorphine take their name from a neighbouring sixteenth-century dovecot. The idea of setting up a tapestry workshop was first mooted in 1898 when the third Marquess of Bute and Sir Rowand Anderson were considering using tapestries as decoration for the grand hall at Mount Stuart on the Isle of Bute. The third Marquess died before the idea could come to fruition, and it fell to his son, the fourth Marquess, to have the studios specially designed. They opened in 1910, their purpose being to make tapestries for the Marquess's family. In due course tapestry panels were produced for the English Law Courts and prestige industrial concerns such as Rolls-Royce. In 1954 the Bute family withdrew from full-time control, while retaining a family representative on the board. Designer Sax Shaw continued to work for what was now the Edinburgh Tapestry Company Ltd. In 1963

Archie Brennan became Director, having set up the Tapestry Department at Edinburgh College of Art in the previous year. The earliest tapestries produced by the Dovecot Studios had been exhibited in 1939 at the Royal Scottish Museum. These included 'The Time of the Meeting' which was based on a description of an early Highland gathering contained in a manuscript belonging to the Marquess of Bute. Others were 'The Lord of the Hunt' (which took five men five years to complete) and 'The Duchess of Gordon' and 'The Admirable Crichton'.

Many of Britain's finest artists have designed for the Dovecot weavers (some of whose looms belonged to early Soho craftsmen working in 1690). Sir Frank Brangwyn RA presented two cartoons. Paul Gauguin's 'Ia Orana Maria' proved a challenge, but the Edinburgh Tapestry Studio has developed skills which have enabled it to render the work of contemporary artists in a centuries-old medium. Among their tapestries have been designs by Ivon Hitchens, Eduardo Paolozzi, Graham Sutherland and David Hockney, which contrast with the coat of arms commissioned by the Queen on her visit to the Studios in 1946, which now hangs in Buckingham Palace. The largest commission came in 1984, when the Pepsi-Cola Company commissioned eleven large tapestries designed by the American artist Frank Stella for its headquarters in New York, and these were the subject of an exhibition at the Scottish National Gallery of Modern Art in 1986.

Sculptors

Up to the end of the eighteenth century there were only two public statues in Edinburgh: that of Charles II, cast in lead and made in Holland in 1685 (now the oldest surviving statue of its kind in Britain) and Roubiliac's statue of Lord President Forbes in Parliament House.

Edinburgh now boasts upwards of fifty public statues. Ten of these are the work of the Aberdeen-born sculptor, **Sir John Steell** (1804-1891). Most of Steell's major works are to be found in the City, including the Albert Memorial in Charlotte Square for which Steell was knighted. His first public sculpture in

Edinburgh was that of Alexander and his horse Bucephalus, originally placed in St Andrew Square but removed to the City Chambers in 1917. There followed the large statue of Queen Victoria on the pediment of the Royal Scottish Academy, after which (in 1838) Steell was created Her Majesty's Sculptor for Scotland. Other works came in quick succession: Sir Walter Scott, Lord Jeffrey, the Second Viscount Melville, Allan Ramsay, John Wilson, and Dr Chalmers. His fine portrayal of the Duke of Wellington astride his charger was unveiled in 1852 in the middle of a violent thunderstorm and gave rise to the following verse:

> Mid lightning's flash and thunder's echoing peal,
> Behold the Iron Duke, in bronze, by Steell!

The Iron Duke, in bronze, by Steell

Old soldiers of all ranks attended the ceremony, many of whom had not seen each other since Waterloo. When the band began to play 'The Garb of Old Gaul' and 'The British Grenadiers', the soldiers cheered their hearts out.

C. D. Pilkington Jackson (1887-1973) was born in Cornwall and educated at Loretto School in Musselburgh. He was responsible for eighty-three statuettes finished in the 1930s for the United Services Museum in Edinburgh Castle and also has work in the Scottish National War Memorial, Paisley Abbey, and the Imperial War Museum. His most famous work, however, is the magnificent equestrian statue of King Robert the Bruce at Bannockburn, the head modelled on Bruce's skull.

Architects and Engineers

Robert Adam (1728-1792), although born in Kirkcaldy, lived a good proportion of his early life in Edinburgh's Canongate, was educated for three years at the High School, and matricu-

Robert Adam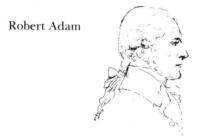

lated at the University at the age of 15. Some of the finest glories of the City are his, including the north and south sides of Charlotte Square, Register House and the Old Quad of the University.

Thomas Telford was born in Dumfriesshire in 1757. He trained as a stonemason before coming to Edinburgh in 1779. He spent two years working on the New Town and Princes Street and used his time in the City to study its architecture with a view to improving his knowledge of civil engineering. He writes of Edinburgh: 'The grandeur of its general situation is perhaps unrivalled, and is best seen from the walks which now encompass the Calton Hill, the view comprising a great extent of fertile and well-cultivated country, a large city of romantic appearance'. Telford was to carry out a number of road surveys on the Edinburgh to London route with the intention of improving communications between the cities. His most striking achievement in Edinburgh is the magnificent Dean Bridge, with its ninety-foot span, the greatest of the stone bridges built by Telford, still standing and still in use. Known as the Colossus of Roads for his achievements in building

The Dean Bridge

roads, docks, canals, and bridges of stone and iron, he died in 1834 and was buried in Westminster Abbey.

Sir Robert Lorimer (1864-1929) was born in Edinburgh and studied at the University. He deserves mention here for having designed the Scottish National War Memorial, within Edinburgh Castle.

Sir Robert Matthew, Dux of Melville College, Edinburgh was born in 1906 and trained at the Edinburgh College of Art. He became the Chief Architect of the Royal Festival Hall in 1951 and ten years later, while Professor of Architecture at Edinburgh University, he designed the new national capital for Pakistan at Islamabad and, among Edinburgh buildings, the Royal Commonwealth Pool.

Sir Basil Spence, born in Edinburgh in 1907, is best known for his brilliant and controversial design for the new Coventry Cathedral. He was responsible for the sea and ships pavilion at the Festival of Britain and, in Edinburgh itself, the headquarters of the Scottish Widows company. He died in 1969.

John L. Paterson was born in Australia where his father, a civil engineer from Bonnyrigg, had emigrated. After a period living in Shanghai, he came to Edinburgh and was educated at the Royal High School. He gained a diploma in Architecture from the Edinburgh College of Art in 1957 and won a scholarship to the University of Pennsylvania. Instead of going to America, Paterson began working for Robert Matthew, Johnson Marshall and Partners, engaged on projects such as the redevelopment of the Gorbals in Glasgow. Six years later he came to the Edinburgh College of Art as a lecturer in Architecture. In 1972 he was appointed head of the School of Design and Crafts, and twelve years later became Principal of the College. Successful as his academic career has been, Paterson's greatest success has been in putting his ideas into practice: he designed the Landmark Visitor Centre at Aviemore which won a Building of the Year Award in 1969; he drew up the plans for the Fruitmarket Gallery in Edinburgh, converted the former West End Church into the Scottish Experience, and designed the 1967 New Town Bicentenary Exhibition, the Diaghilev Memorial Exhibition and the exhibition on the life and work of Patrick Geddes; he designed the sun clock in the grounds of the new Gallery of Modern Art and the Camera Lucida exhibition on the Calton Hill. His design for the Tron Kirk as a heritage centre gave promise of being every bit as exciting and informative as his other achievements.

Sir Patrick Geddes (1854-1932), a great individual, has been described as 'Edinburgh's greatest all-round citizen', 'the Father of British Townplanning', and an 'academic maverick'. He was

Sir Patrick Geddes

born in Ballater and brought up in Perth where he went to school and later worked for a time in a bank. He soon left for London, where he studied for five years with the biologist T. H. Huxley, and also in Brittany and at the Sorbonne in Paris. Although he had given up studying in the Department of

Botany in Edinburgh after a week and had shown his impatience with the School of Mines in London (where Huxley taught) by betting that he could pass both elementary and advanced courses in a week (which he did after swotting through the textbooks), he was appointed demonstrator and lecturer in Zoology at Edinburgh University (despite having no degree).

In 1886 he married and took a house at 81a Princes Street but quickly moved into the Old Town, whose slums appalled him. His new home at 6 James Court was speedily renovated at the University which were managed by the students themselves without a warden. He was passed over for promotion at Edinburgh, however, but was given the Chair of Botany at Dundee.

Geddes bought Ramsay Lodge at the top of the Royal Mile at Castlehill and extended it. He called it 'a seven-towered castle built for his beloved', and proceeded to build a number of other Ramsay Garden flats. Next to Ramsay Lodge was Short's Observatory with its camera obscura. Geddes bought the building in 1892 (which was known as the Outlook Tower) and turned it into what he called a 'training ground for citizens'. The Outlook Tower was arranged as an 'index-museum' of the universe as seen from Edinburgh. Below the camera obscura was a hollow planetarium; in the Scotland Room below was a large floor-map of the country, and below it again the Edinburgh Room, followed by surveys of Britain as a whole, Europe and the other continents, and finally the World Room with two great globes, one geological and one showing vegetation. What Geddes showed were the improvements which needed to be made in the environment and how to carry them out. The Outlook Tower was 'the world's first sociological laboratory'. The effects of the work of the Outlook Tower were to be seen in the first town-planning exhibitions held around 1910.

The debt Edinburgh owes to Geddes can be seen in the list of properties which he renovated by his own efforts, among them four University residences housing 120 students, and eighty-five flats or apartments reconditioned or built by him in slum areas for working families. He also helped to plan Edinburgh Zoo and, having already made notable contributions to town-planning in India, he drew up the layout for the University of

Jerusalem. In 1924 he moved to Montpellier in the South of France where he established a Scots College (with an Outlook Tower).

In Geddes' view the besetting sin of Edinburgh was respectability, and its culture was 'frozen as if in an ice-pack'. He also detested the lure of imperial London and its 'Cockneyfication' of culture.

The City Art Centre

The impetus for a City Art Centre came from a decision in early 1961 (largely influenced by Lord Provost Duncan Weatherstone) to appoint a sub-committee to help local groups interested in the arts. In July of that year the City received a generous financial gift from Miss Jean F. Watson to finance the building of a civic collection of painting and sculpture eventually to be housed in a municipal art gallery. First purchases made for this purpose were of J. D. Fergusson's (1874-1961) painting 'The Blue Hat' and of Jacob Epstein's (1850-1959) sculpture 'Kathleen'. Further works were acquired by the City when most of the collection belonging to the Scottish Modern Art Association came its way in 1964, comprising paintings and sculpture by Scottish artists from around 1890 to 1960. In 1971 the Old Royal High School below the Calton Hill was opened as the first City Art Centre.

By 1975 the City Art Centre had become part of the Museums and Art Galleries Department of Edinburgh District Council, and a Keeper of Fine Art was appointed. The purchase of the Royal High School building for the proposed Scottish Assembly made a new home for the collection a priority, and in 1980 a million-pound Art Centre was opened in former warehouses in Market Street. The new City Art Centre contained four floors of galleries plus studios for rental, and was designed by the Department of Architecture of the City of Edinburgh District Council. The building opened during the Edinburgh Festival with a major exhibition, 'The Legacy', contributed by the Provincial Museum of British Columbia which was devoted to historic and contemporary Canadian/Indian art. One of Edinburgh's six twin cities, Vancouver, sent over a partially carved totem pole, and the carving of this traditional monument was continued in the City Art Centre during the period of the exhibition. Other important and stimulating exhibitions have followed: Piranesi Drawings and Etchings; American Abstract Expressionists; Scottish Football: A History; and in 1984/85 the unique Treasures of the Edinburgh Room which explored many facets of Edinburgh life through the collection of artefacts, photographs and other memorabilia held by the City's Central Library in George IV Bridge.

The First Christmas Card

To conclude with a historic tailpiece: Edinburgh can lay claim to having originated the Christmas card. The laughing face of a curly-headed man was first engraved by an Edinburgh man, Alexander T. Aikman, for the cover of one of the ever-popular Victorian jest books. A Leith printer, Charles Drummond, added the words 'A Guid New Year an' Mony o' Them' and published it for Christmas 1841, also including two outspread hands indicating a table groaning with fruit and wine. This was several years before the first Christmas card appeared in England.

Business

George Heriot – 'Jinglin' Geordie' as he was known – was born in Edinburgh in 1563. His father was a prosperous jeweller and goldsmith who was Deacon-Convener of Incoporated Trades and had represented the City in the Scottish Parliament.

George Heriot

George was trained by his father in the most lucrative trade in the kingdom, and after his marriage in 1586, his father set him up in business in a shop off the north-east corner of St Giles Kirk. In the course of time his son transferred his business to a site on the west side of the Kirk. This second shop existed in Parliament Close till 1809 when the extension to the Advocates' Library meant it had to be demolished. Until that date visitors could still see the forge and bellows and the hollow stone fitted with a stone cover for putting out the embers from Heriot's furnace when the shop was closed at night. The shop was tiny: only about seven feet square.

As a goldsmith George Heriot wore the uniform of that skilled craft: a scarlet cloak with a cocked hat and a cane. But there was another side to his business which was just as financially rewarding. In 1597 he was appointed goldsmith to James VI's consort, Anne of Denmark. The appointment was proclaimed to the sound of trumpets at the Mercat Cross of Edinburgh.

Heriot drove a hard bargain with his suppliers: he bought precious stones from Spain and Portugal at low prices, and such was the passion of the Queen for jewellery that she often handed over her most precious personal pieces to Heriot as security against the purchase of new necklaces, rings and brooches. In 1601 Heriot was appointed Jeweller to the King and received large fees for both royal patronages. He was now acting as cashier and banker to the King and Queen, but such was his patriotism and loyalty that he is said to have torn up and burnt a Royal bond for thousands of pounds before the King's eye as a gesture of his confidence.

It is estimated that, during the ten years before the accession of James VI to the throne of Great Britain, Heriot's bills for the Queen's jewels alone were not less than £50,000 in the money of the time. When James had his farewell procession down the High Street, Heriot supplied the rings and other jewels to the Scottish nobility. Two months before she joined her husband in London, Queen Anne ordered Heriot to supply her with many costly items such as a pendant with diamonds, and a silver chafing dish. Heriot in return also charged her for lambskins to keep her jewels in. When the whole court moved to London, Heriot followed and increased his fortune.

When he died in London in 1623 his will was found to contain instructions for the founding of a children's home for the education, nursing and upbringing of poor orphans and fatherless children of burgesses and freemen of the City of Edinburgh who had fallen on hard times. The Provost, Baillies and the Council and their successors were made governors of the children's hospital, which was the forerunner of what is now George Heriot's School.

Along with another Scot, William Paterson (who founded the Bank of England), **John Law** was a pioneer of modern banking and founded an institution which paved the way for a national bank in France. Born in 1671, he attended the Edinburgh High School and at his father's death was left very well off with a goldsmith's business, the rents of a number of properties and money owed to his father by various debtors. John's consuming interest was banking and the exchange and accumulation of wealth. He was an active sportsman also, playing tennis in the old court at the Water Gate near Holyrood. His head for figures gave him a great talent for cards and dice, and he soon acquired the nickname 'Beau' Law. When he left Edinburgh

John Law

for London, he gambled but also studied games of chance scientifically and was able to calculate the odds against a player in every game. But gambling was for the nights, and he spent his days studying banking methods in the City.

He became involved in a mysterious dispute over a lady, killed a man in a duel and was imprisoned and condemned to death in 1694. Subsequently Law was pardoned, but his opponents appealed and Law was again imprisoned. He cut through four bars of his cell window with a file but was discovered and put in irons. The trial was postponed and he managed to escape with some help in 1695, dropping thirty feet from his cell and spraining his ankle. He quickly left England for Holland, where it is thought he next took a post as a secretary to the British representative there, the poet Matthew Prior. Law visited Amsterdam to learn more about Dutch banking methods and then travelled to Paris, whence he eloped with a married lady, whom he married, through Switzerland to Genoa, where he settled. In Genoa, a great Italian banking centre, Law soon made money by speculating in foreign exchange and securities and then took himself off to Venice to make some more. Returning to Edinburgh in 1703, he settled with his wife and young son at Lauriston Castle, the family home. He petitioned the new monarch, Queen Anne, to be allowed to return to England, but was refused. In 1705 he wrote an essay containing proposals for the encouragement of the Scottish economy which was debated by the Scottish Parliament. Law's plan of issuing bank notes was discussed, but his proposals were rejected, and he left Edinburgh in the following year for Brussels, going on to Paris in 1701, to a France groaning under the weight of taxation and very great financial and economic problems. Law tried to persuade the French Minister of Finance to introduce bank notes into circulation. Again no success, so he returned to Genoa and wrote another work on political economy. All this time he was working out his 'System' for saving the economies of nations. He proposed the setting up of a state bank to Duke Victor Amadeus in Turin. His finances had been so well managed that Law was said to be worth around £100,000 at this time.

Law developed a scheme for paying off the French national debt, which he submitted to the French Foreign Minister, but it was rejected by King Louis XIV on the grounds that Law was not a Catholic and could not therefore be fully trusted. He was nothing if not persistent. He announced that he had found the Philosopher's Stone, his 'System'. When asked what it was, Law replied, 'I can tell you my secret: it is to make gold out of paper'. Finally in 1716 his proposal for a joint-stock bank was accepted by the French Government, and as a token of his commitment to France, Law became a naturalised Frenchman. This was the period of his greatest successes. A Company of the West was set up to represent French commercial interests in North America. The new company had exclusive trading rights with Louisiana (as well as mineral rights), and transported some 6,000 white and 13,000 coloured settlers to the new territory. Louisiana at that time included much of the centre of North America: the present Louisiana, Mississippi, Arkansas, Missouri, Illinois, Iowa, Wisconsin and Minnesota, lands stretching from the Gulf of Mexico to Canada.

The Company of the West was amalgamated with the French East India Company and the China Company, and Law ordered the construction of a new town, the future New Orleans. A colossal boom in Mississippi shares now followed. Law became the first 'millionaire'. He acquired over twenty landed properties in France (some carrying the title of Marquis), he had collections of jewels, a library of 45,000 books, and wine cellars, held the position of King's Secretary, was elected a member of the French Academy, and also received the Freedom of the City of Edinburgh. He was generous too, for he gave much to charity and emptied the Paris prison of debtors.

Realising that only his religion was against his being appointed to high office, Law became a Roman Catholic and in 1720 was appointed Controller-General of Finance for the Kingdom of France. In the same year, however, an edict was issued which resulted in the devaluation of the French currency, and Law's 'System' collapsed. He was exiled, going first to Venice and then England, where he persuaded Walpole to send him on a secret mission to Bavaria in 1721. He retired to Venice in 1726, spending his time attending Mass, drinking coffee, writing, reading his mail from France, gossiping, visiting old picture dealers, going to masquerades and travelling gracefully through the canals by gondola. The philosopher Montesquieu visited Law and observed that 'He was still the same man, with small means but playing highly and boldly, his mind occupied with projects, his head filled with calculations'. Saint-Simon, the scientist and socialist, had this to say: 'There was neither avarice nor roguery in his composition. He was a gentle, good respectable man whom excess of credit and fortune had not spoiled . . .' Law died in Venice in 1729.

In 1749 **William Younger** from West Linton, who had trained in the village brewery, moved to Leith at the age of sixteen and four years later was an exciseman. His son Archibald by 1778 had his own brewery in Holyrood Abbey Sanctuary; this location meant he avoided the Town Council's

William Younger

two pence impost and also had easy access to fine wells and springs which gave him a good strong ale which he supplied to customers in taverns such as John Dowie's in Libberton's Wynd. Dowie's Regulars like Adam Smith or visitors like Robert Burns found the ale 'wholesome and invigorating'. Robert Chambers writes that 'Johnnie Dowie's was chiefly celebrated for ale – Younger's Edinburgh Ale – a potent fluid, which almost glued the lips of the drinker together, and of which few, therefore, could despatch more than a bottle'.

By 1802 William Younger's was shipping ale to the Edinburgh Ale vaults in London and had moved its premises out of the Sanctuary into the Canongate proper. Four years later the firm was brewing porter. William McEwan started business in 1856 in Fountainbridge and after his death in 1913 only seventeen years passed before McEwan and Younger's amalgamated.

Edinburgh, it is often said, is a City eternally in gratitude to the brewing industry: the sale of beer financed the building of the McEwan Hall, the Usher Hall and numerous other projects. When Hugo Arnot, in his *History of Edinburgh,* wrote that in 1779 there were over 2,000 houses in Edinburgh retailing spirituous and other liquors, with eight licensed and four hundred unlicensed stills, he pointed to the changes in public drinking habits. The gentlemen drank claret because there was no import tax on it, and the working classes gradually threw over twopenny ale for tea and whisky. Today, Edinburgh still has more than half a dozen brewers and more than that number of distillers.

As well as being a centre of the publishing and printing industry since the eighteenth century, Edinburgh has an honourable record in the production of quality newspapers. The earliest, the *Edinburgh Courant,* began in 1705 and was edited for a time by Daniel Defoe. It became the *Daily Courant* in 1860 but ceased publication in 1886. The *Caledonian Mercury* was founded in 1720. Six years later it became a five-times-weekly paper and in 1806 an evening paper until 1867 when it was bought by the *Scotsman*. The *Scotsman* was started by a lawyer, **William Ritchie,** and **Charles MacLaren,** a clerk in the Edinburgh Custom House, in 1817. Its circulation rocketed from 1,700 in 1830 to 100,000 in 1861. In 1953 the *Scotsman* was bought over by the Canadian **Roy Thomson,** who also bought control of Scottish Television. The *Scotsman's* evening paper, the *Edinburgh Evening News*, began production in 1873 under the direction of three men from Morayshire. The *Scotsman* is the only quality daily newspaper produced in Edinburgh, rivalling the *Glasgow Herald*.

One of Edinburgh's most distinguished firms is **Craig and Rose.** Founded in 1779, the firm as we know it today has its base in a partnership between James Craig and Hugh Rose in the sale of oils and colours, and later whale oils and sherry. In 1874 Craig and Rose began to focus on the manufacture of paints, for which it is famous today. The position it enjoys is largely as a result of winning the contract for painting the Forth Railway Bridge (that is, for devising and supplying Forth Bridge Oxide or Iron Paint). Craig and Rose, among their many contracts, painted the 1050-foot BBC TV mast at Bilsdale, Yorkshire, and also supplied the paint for the interior decoration of the restored Inveraray Castle and the Georgian House in Charlotte Square, Edinburgh.

The first Leith Walk glassworks is recorded in 1798 making flint glass. In the 1840s the Edinburgh Flint Glass Works were in operation, and by 1872 Alex Jenkinson from East Lothian (1821-80) worked in the China Pottery and Glass Merchant at 10 Princes Street, later becoming a glass manufacturer in Leith Walk. He was the leading figure in the development of the Edinburgh and Leith Flint Glass Company and also took a very active part as superintendent of the Sunday School at the Carruber's Close Mission in the High Street. The Company was already making a name for itself in 1862 for its ornamental glass which was cut and engraved at the Norton Park works. The fine Edinburgh light-blown table glass was awarded a gold medal diploma at the 1886 International Exhibition of Industry, Science and Art held at the West Meadows. During the First World War the Company turned to making light bulbs, tubing and laboratory glass. In 1921 the Norton Park works were taken over by Webb's Crystal Glass Company Ltd and were soon supplying Holyrood Palace with fine crystal for the royal banquets held there. In 1955 the name of the Company was changed to the **Edinburgh Crystal Glass Company.** Many of Edinburgh's finest glass engravers used the Company's blanks: Alison Kinnaird, Alison Geissler, Norman Orr and Helen Munro (who founded the Glass Design Department of the Edinburgh College of Art). Edinburgh Crystal has been exported all over the world for many years (to Tiffany's and Gimbels of New York, for example); the Thistle pattern was gifted to Princess Margaret by the Glasgow and Ayrshire Regiment on her marriage in 1960, while the Mayor of Florence (one of Edinburgh's twin cities) was given Thistle pattern decanters and glasses by Lord Provost Herbert Brechin. The Lochnagar pattern, dating from Victorian times, was used by Edinburgh Corporation in their regular gifts of glassware on the occasion of royal weddings: to King George V and Queen Mary, to Princess Margaret, and to the present Queen while she was Princess Elizabeth. The Star pattern was chosen in 1982 as the service for use on board the US Presidential yacht, USS *Sequoia*. Since 1974 Edinburgh Crystal have been established at a new factory in Penicuik, some miles outside Edinburgh, but their links with the City are as strong as ever.

James Thompson was an Edinburgh builder with an interest in Italian marble for the houses of the well-to-do. He and his two sons set up as shipbrokers at Leith in 1825. Their first ship was called, appropriately enough, the *Carrara* (after the world-famous quarries used by Michelangelo). From 1839 she was used to carry marble from Leghorn to Leith. In time a regular trade developed taking Alloa coal from Leith to Canada and bringing timber back. A small fleet was established, the ancestor of the **Ben Line.** Voyages to the Chinese and Japanese ports followed in the 1850s; two ships sailed to Australia during the Gold Rush, and others were involved in the tea trade. With the advent of steamships runs were made to Chile with coal, or with guano from the Chinchas to Mauritius, where sugar was loaded on board for the journey back to Leith. In the mid-1890s the practice of naming ships after Scottish mountains began. Some of the fleet was requisitioned during the First World War; in the Second, fourteen Ben Line ships were sunk, and one was deliberately scuttled on the Normandy coast on D-Day as part of a Mulberry harbour. In 1943 the head office of Ben Line Steamers Limited moved from Leith to Edinburgh. By the 1970s ownership of bulk carriers came; and

B

so to the present, with an offshore drilling company with a self-propelled drillship and two semi-submersible rigs to meet the challenge of the North Sea Oil bonanza.

John Menzies (1808-79) was born in Edinburgh and educated at the Royal High School, where one of his best friends was the future inventor of the steam-blast the engineer James Nasmyth. In the early nineteenth century Edinburgh possessed some ninety booksellers as a result of the City's intellectual and cultural prominence during the Enlightenment and the Romantic Revival led by Scott and other writers North of the Border. Edinburgh was also a centre for publishing and printing. As an apprentice with Sutherland the bookseller in the Calton district of Edinburgh, John Menzies had to supply his own share of the coal required for the daily fire in the shop. He would be in early to wash the stairs, sweep the pavement and clean the windows before prayers at eight in the morning. He had to work till nine o'clock at night, eating on the hoof, with only Sundays and New Year's Day off. After he had finished his apprenticeship his father gave him ten pounds and put him on a ship for London, sailing from Leith. In London he found work with Charles Tilt, a Fleet Street bookseller, and made extremely good progress.

In 1833 his father died. Menzies returned to Edinburgh and set up his own business at the corner of Princes Street and Hanover Street. In future years the headquarters of the firm would always be known as Hanover Buildings. Soon he acquired the rights to sell the works of Charles Dickens in the East of Scotland (it is said that he was a close friend of the author, who often visited Edinburgh). He became sole agent for the new satirical magazine, *Punch,* and began to sell the *Scotsman* (normally newspapers had to be bought direct from the publishers by subscription). The mid-nineteenth century saw John Menzies follow the lead of W. H. Smith by moving into railway bookstalls. After the death of the founder in 1879, the Company changed its title to John Menzies and Co Ltd (1906). In 1948 they branched out into new fields by establishing the first of their airport bookstalls at Turnhouse, Edinburgh's airport. In 1962 the Company went public with 63 depots, 330 bookstalls and 117 shops. As John Menzies (Holdings) Ltd. (later plc), the Company has six divisions: Wholesale, Retail, Commercial, Financial, Personnel and Property, diversification which no doubt the original John Menzies would have approved of, in what is still a family firm.

In 1851 **Christian Fredrik Salvesen,** a young Norwegian, left Norway for Charlotte Street, Leith. His brother Theodor had arrived in Scotland some years before in 1841. He had spent a year in a Glasgow merchant's office, then started his own shipbrokering business and branched out into shipowning and the timber trade in Grangemouth, later setting up in Leith. Into this established enterprise came his brother. The firm expanded into carrying pitwood and sawnwood cargoes, into the coal trade, into salt and Norwegian herrings and Icelandic ponies for Scottish collieries. In 1859 Christian Salvesen was appointed Hanoverian vice-consul in Leith. One of his sons, Edward, Lord Salvesen (1857-1942), became Solicitor-General for Scotland in 1905, a Senator of the College of Justice and a Privy Councillor.

By 1900 there were twelve Salvesen merchant vessels sailing to the Baltic, the Mediterranean and the Black Sea. They carried stores and equipment to the southern whaling stations. By this time Salvesen's had established bases on New Island in the West Falklands (1907), constructing a whaling-station there and killing 227 whales in their first year of operation. In 1909 they had opened a base at Leith in South Georgia. In 1913 they shipped the first of over 800 penguins from South Georgia to Edinburgh Zoo. Lord Salvesen was active in the founding of the Royal Zoological Society of Scotland and was its first President. During the Second World War sixteen of the Salvesen ships were lost, and twenty-three of their officers and men received decorations. Today Christian Salvesen, operating out of their East Fettes Avenue headquarters, have diversified into food services (with a freeze-at-sea fish factory fleet); a USA vegetable refrigerating division; a marine division with bulk-carriers; seafoods; oil services; and even into the house-building business.

In 1985 Ogilvy & Mather, the second biggest advertising agency in the world, opened their 201st office, in Edinburgh. **David Ogilvy** was educated at Fettes in Edinburgh, trained as a chef in Paris, sold Aga cookers in Scotland, and saw war service

David Ogilvy

with the OSS. In 1948, taking the bull by the horns, he founded Ogilvy & Mather in New York, and among the better-remembered of his slogans has been: 'At 60 miles an hour the loudest noise in this new Rolls Royce comes from the electric clock'. Dubbed 'The Creative King of Advertising', he has written an autobiography, *Blood, Brains and Beer,* and two books about advertising, *Confessions of an Advertising Man* and *Ogilvy on Advertising.* He is also a trustee of the World Wildlife Fund. Interestingly, the agency made further Scottish headlines when in 1986, to mark his wife's 60th birthday, a former chairman, Mr John Elliott, an American, put up most of the purchase price to enable the National Trust for Scotland to acquire the island of Staffa with its world-famous Fingal's Cave.

Classical Music

Edinburgh, as capital of Scotland (and seat of the monarchy till the Union of the Crowns in 1603), has always been rich in music, both instrumental and vocal. During the Middle Ages the demands of the Church's liturgical year meant that boys and clerics would be trained by religious orders to perform plain chant and, later, polyphony; and the study of approved musical instruments (such as the organ) would also be undertaken.

The structure of this educational tradition in sacred music was changed by the Reformers, anxious to wipe the slate clean so far as they were able. However, iconoclasm did not entirely win the day, and in due course singing schools were set up by the Reformers to maintain an acceptable standard in church music. As the Renaissance took root in Scotland, Edinburgh set the pace of the new learning and of the revived interest in secular music and secular instruments.

The year 1682 is generally reckoned to be a turning point in the secular musical life of the City, for in that year the Duke of York held the first of his many revels in the tennis court at Holyrood Palace. In 1693 the first public concert was organised by Beck, whose ensemble was the first of its kind in Scotland.

Two years later came the famous St Cecilia's Day Concert at which nineteen gentlemen amateurs and eleven professional masters of music performed. Over the following ten years many private concerts were held. It was not however until 1728 that the inauguration of the Musical Society of Edinburgh (and its private concerts at **Patrick Steil's** tavern, the Cross Keys, near Parliament Close) provided focus and organisation for the development of classical music in Edinburgh.

Steil (a popular singer of Scots songs and a violin-maker) and his circle of amateur and professional musicians contributed to the setting up of the Musical Society with a membership of seventy. Private concerts were also organised by the Society at St Mary's Chapel in Niddry Wynd, which remained the meeting-place of the Society until 1762 when **St Cecilia's Hall** was built.

During the 1750s the first open-air concerts were held at Lauriston Gardens and also at Heriot's Gardens, where they were administered by the German Johann Friedrich Lampe, said to have been Handel's favourite basoonist. A school for church music was opened in 1755, and a steady influx of German and Italian performers, both vocal and instrumental, arrived in the City.

Among these foreign guest performers may be singled out Giusto Ferdinando Tenducci, a hard-living Italian castrato from Siena, who was nevertheless briefly married to an Irish girl, and was frequently in and out of the debtors' prison. The poet Fergusson, who shared a berth in the Tolbooth with the singer, wrote songs for Tenducci to sing in Arne's *Artaxerxes,* and Tenducci also performed in Germany for Mozart in later years, thus forging an interesting connection between Mozart and Edinburgh.

Domenico Corri and his brother Natale made their mark on the Edinburgh musical scene. The former was a composer and teacher who got himself into all sorts of matrimonial tangles. His brother was equally unfortunate, despite his having opened Corri's Concert Rooms and his dealership in sheet music and musical instruments. Both brothers seem to have had a facility for losing money.

Among the Scottish musicians who made a special contribution to music in Edinburgh, 'Fiddler Tam' (**Thomas Alexander Erskine, 6th Earl of Kellie**) must be singled out. Born at Kellie Castle in Fife, but educated at the Royal High School, the Earl of Kellie was a composer whose works were widely played at home and attained some popularity on the Continent. By 1750 the Earl was a full member of the Musical Society of Edinburgh and a committee member seven years later. Since his father had come out in support of Bonnie Prince Charlie, entry was not easily found for a career in many of the professions normally open to men of his standing. On the Grant Tour in 1753 he spent a considerable time studying composition and the violin at Mannheim. On his return he wrote minuets for the Edinburgh debutantes and became the native British leader of the Mannheim style of musical composition.

The Earl of Kellie

Boswell considered Kellie a boor and repeated this opinion on several occasions. Certainly he is recorded as having a habit of cracking outrageous puns in a loud voice with a Fife accent in the best eating-places in Edinburgh. At concerts, when one of the players stumbled, the Earl would instantly prompt the performer in a loud voice.

Among Edinburgh performers who achieved wide recognition in the eighteenth century were Thomas Foster (1760-1825) and John Mackintosh (1767-1844) the bassoonist. In the nineteenth century, Helen Hopekirk (1856-1941) was a noted pianist, and the tenor John Templeton (1806-1886) sang well enough to be embraced by the composer Bellini after a performance of *La Sonnambula* in London.

Music in Edinburgh is heavily indebted to Jolly **General Reid.** Colonel of the 88th or Connaught Rangers, John Reid of Straloch in Perthshire, music lover, flautist, and composer of 'The Garb of Old Gaul', enjoyed his student days at the University so much that he left £52,000 in his will in 1807 to establish a School of Music. One of General Reid's most famous military exploits was the capture in 1746 of the sloop *Hazard* in Tongue Bay carrying around 170 Irish troops in the French service. In spite of the reluctance of his superior officers to engage a force twice as great as their own, General Reid persisted and at the risk of a court-martial persuaded some of his soldiers to attack the *Hazard* with him. They captured the

General Reid

enemy along with a sum of £12,000 badly needed by the Jacobite army.

The first Reid Professor, John Thomson, was appointed in 1808, and the first Reid concert took place in 1841. When Thomson died, the fact that he had trained in Leipzig and was a friend of Schubert and Mendelssohn (who had visited Edinburgh in 1829) made the University authorities anxious to appoint Mendelssohn as Professor, but the composer had to refuse. **Sir Henry Rowley Bishop,** composer of 'Home, Sweet, Home', was the next Professor. Other Professors followed, and **Donald Francis Tovey** (1914-1940) established the Reid Orchestra at a time when there was no Edinburgh-based professional orchestra. After the War, **Professor Sydney Newman** was instrumental in having St Cecilia's Hall in the Cowgate reconstructed and installing the Raymond Russell collection of early keyboard instruments.

In 1938 **Hans Gal** (b. 1890 in Austria) came to live in Scotland and began lecturing at the University of Edinburgh in 1945. Composer and musicologist, Gal had been a friend of Schoenberg, Alban Berg and the painter Oscar Kokoschka and a lecturer at the University of Vienna. He is the longest-serving member of the Edinburgh Festival Council. Two of his string quartets and an orchestral work have been performed at Edinburgh Festivals. Hans Gal comments: 'The Festival has changed the whole atmosphere of Edinburgh'.

John Tainsh, who died in 1967, was a fine Lieder singer with a very full *heldentenor* voice. He was large, broad-shouldered and handsome, with blue eyes, but crippled with disease of the hip which frequently left him in pain. He was a distinguished concert artist who sang in St Cuthbert's Church at the West End and often on BBC radio. He had once been noticed by Vaughan Williams and could have made a career in opera but for the physical disability which restricted his movement on stage.

The only professional opera singer with an outstanding international reputation ever to come from the City was **Joseph Hislop** (1884-1977). Hislop began his musical career at the age of ten when he joined the choir of St Mary's Cathedral. After

Joseph Hislop

leaving the Edinburgh Cathedral School, he entered the photo-process engraving trade, eventually going to London to study colour photography at a technical college. He received an offer of a visit to Sweden to introduce three-colour photography to a printing firm in Gothenburg in 1907. While in Gothenburg he joined a male voice choir, eventually becoming an occasional soloist. A visiting professional singer happened to hear Hislop sing and suggested he' audition for Dr Gillis Bratt, a famous singer and throat specialist. At his audition Hislop was amazed to find that the accompanist was the reigning Olympic Champion and World Record Holder for the javelin, Eric Lemming. Hislop passed the audition and began a period of three and a half years' study with Gillis Bratt which culminated in his joining the Opera School attached to the Royal Opera House in Stockholm.

In 1914 he made his debut as Faust in Gounod's opera and went to London to make a number of recordings for HMV under the Zonophone label. While in London he saw Caruso at Covent Garden and after the performance was able to get Caruso's autograph in an Italian restaurant. The great singer was interested to meet the young Scottish tenor making his reputation in Sweden. Five years later Hislop travelled to Milan to study with Tullio Voghera. He began to take daily lessons in Italian through the Berlitz method. In due course he auditioned at the San Carlo Opera in Naples and was given a contract for the winter season. During this time he had to turn all the roles he had learned in Swedish into Italian.

Hislop made his Covent Garden debut in 1920 as Rodolpho and on the opening night was conducted at short notice by Thomas Beecham. The following day he was introduced to Puccini, who had happened to be in the audience. Hislop records, 'I was completely bowled over by the very complimentary things he said about my performance, which of course delighted me'. On the 17th of May he sang Pinkerton in *Madame Butterfly* as a last-minute replacement, singing in Swedish. Nine days later he repeated the role, this time in Italian. In the following year he toured the USA and Canada with the Scotti Company. A memorable performance of *La Bohème* took place in 1923: Hislop sang Rodolpho, and Melba was Mimi, both singing in Italian while the rest of the cast sang in English. Hislop repeated the role in La Fenice Opera House, Venice in 1924 and was a guest at La Scala and Turin. In 1926 he sang in the Liceo, Barcelona following Buenos Aires. Hislop's performance opposite the great Russian bass Chaliapin in *Faust* in 1928 was recorded by HMV. He moved into the lighter operatic field by playing Goethe in Franz Lehar's *Frederica* at the Palace Theatre, London in 1930.

At the end of his stage career he returned to Stockholm, where he remained from 1936 to 1948, teaching at the Royal Academy of Music there. Among his pupils were Jussi Björling and Birgit Nilsson. Upon his return to the UK he taught at the Guildhall School of Music and was an adviser in vocal production at both Covent Garden and Sadler's Wells. His pupils at this time included Peter Glossop and Charles Craig. Hislop, who lived to the ripe old age of 93, ending his days in Fife, was a keen golfer who had partnered Sir Harry Lauder. He remained all his life a skilful painter, his favourite painting being a self-portrait in the role of Cavaradossi. Grenville Eves writes that the 'romantic ardour of his singing, with the vibrancy of the voice throughout the whole range, the velvety and even quality and the tremendous expansion and intensity of the top range, made Hislop's one of the really great voices'.

An outstanding modern composer from Edinburgh is **Thea Musgrave** (b. 1928). She studied for three years at Edinburgh University and spent a further four years in Paris under the tuition of Nadia Boulanger. Among her performed works are operas, *The Decision* and *The Voice of Ariadne*, which was given its first performance at the Aldeburgh Festival in 1974. She has also written a ballet for Scottish Theatre Ballet, *Beauty and the Beast* (1969), and her *Ballad of Sir Patrick Spens* was written in 1961 for Peter Pears and Julian Bream.

A contemporary composer associated with the City is **John McLeod**, formerly Director of music at Merchiston Castle School, whose works include *The Shostakovich Connection* (1974), the *Lieder der Jugend* (1979) which was awarded the Guinness Prize for British Composers, *Hebridean Prayers* (1981) which won the Radio Forth Award for the best new work on the Festival Fringe, the *Seasons of Dr Zhivago* (1982), a symphonic song-cycle, and the *Gokstad Ship*, which constructs a musical analogy to the structure of a Viking longship. **Gian Carlo Menotti** lives near Edinburgh and makes regular contributions to the Edinburgh Festival in the form of productions of a number of his operas. **Ronald Stevenson** is also closely associated with Edinburgh. Among conductors, the late **Marcus Dods** was an Edinburgh man and **Roderick Brydon** likewise. Brydon is now music director of the Lucerne City Theatre, having previously conducted the Scottish Chamber Orchestra.

The Scottish Chamber Orchestra was founded in 1974 in order to take the load off the Scottish National Orchestra and the Scottish Baroque Ensemble, both of whom had shared the functions of giving concerts and opera accompaniment. The Scottish Philharmonic Society which was formed in the same year was intended to act as an umbrella organisation for the SBE and the SCO, and these developments signalled what

Conrad Wilson was to call an 'upsurge of musical industry in
the east of Scotland'.

As part of its growth as an orchestra the SCO began to play
with distinguished soloists. In 1977 these include the cellist
Rostropovich, James Galway and Teresa Berganza. The orchestra also embarked on an ambitious tour of Eastern Europe, to
Budapest, Bucharest and Sofia. The first of three summer
appearances at the Aix-en-Provence Festival followed where
the SCO was orchestra in residence, playing Handel's *Alcina* in
the open air under Raymond Leppard, who was later to be the
SCO's principal guest conductor. The SCO has by now developed a tradition of an annual Highland residency. In 1983, for
example, three hundred people boarded the SCO train at
Inverness and were treated to a horn fanfare at the platform.
Inside, Harold Lester, the SCO keyboard player, entertained
the passengers with selections from Cole Porter and Scott
Joplin; a bassoon trio made music in the guard's van, and there
were barber-shop quartets and the violin music of Boccherini.
The same year saw the SCO's second visit to the St Magnus
Festival in Orkney. There they premiered two works by Peter
Maxwell Davies: *Into the Labyrinth* (a cantata for solo tenor) and
the *Sinfonietta Academica,* which had been commissioned by
Edinburgh University to celebrate its quatercentenary. In 1984
the SCO made a triumphant tour of the Far East, visiting
Taiwan and the Hong Kong Festival.

The Queen's Hall dates from 1823 when it opened as Hope
Park Chapel. Edward Irving preached a series of sermons
there at seven in the morning during 1829. At one period it
was in use as Newington Parish Church. Robert Hurd and
Partners were given the architectural contract to redevelop this
fine Georgian church into a concert hall. The horseshoe shape
of the interior was retained, as were most of the pews. In the
gallery the rake was altered and promenade areas were
created. With moveable seating and an extending stage five
different arrangements of the new auditorium were available
to cater for a variety of scales in performance. The Queen's
Hall was officially opened in the presence of Her Majesty the
Queen in 1979 and provides a rehearsal base for the **Scottish
Baroque Ensemble** (formed in 1968 under the leadership of

The Queen's Hall

Leonard Friedman and since 1974 with the Duke of Edinburgh as its Honorary Patron), the Scottish Chamber Orchestra and the Scottish Philharmonic Singers (founded in 1976).

Leonard Friedman
(Scottish Baroque Ensemble)

Founded in 1969 as an opera orchestra for Ledlanet House, the **Scottish Baroque Ensemble** was later recruited for Scottish Opera performances of all of Benjamin Britten's chamber operas and several first performances in the repertory. Normally there are thirteen players in the Ensemble (including harpsichord) which plays in the tradition of the Baroque period (without conductor). The SBE has been invited to play in two documentaries about Gian Carlo Menotti; it has commissioned Scottish composers (David Dorward, Edward Harper and Thomas Wilson) and played command performances at Holyrood House and Edinburgh Castle. Major tours have been undertaken to Canada, the USA and Germany. Other appearances in Edinburgh have included performances at the Edinburgh Festival, in the National Gallery of Scotland and in the Signet Library.

The Edinburgh Quartet was originally formed in 1953 by Edinburgh University when Sydney Newman was Reid Professor of Music. In 1959 Professor Newman invited Miles Baster,

The Edinburgh Quartet

a young violinist on a scholarship from the Royal Academy of Music which took him to New York to study under Louis Persinger, to come to Edinburgh to re-form the Quartet. Now Scotland's only national resident professional quartet, since 1960 it has performed 1,600 concerts to a third of a million people in thirty countries. At home the Quartet has performed the music of Kenneth Leighton, the present Reid Professor of Music.

Criminals and Detectives

Edinburgh has the dubious distinction of having used a forerunner of the guillotine to punish criminals. The **'Maiden'**, as it was known, was commissioned by the Provost, the Baillies

The Maiden

and the Town Council in 1564, and after a long lifetime of almost continuous use, executed a last offender in 1710. It can still be seen in the Royal Museum in Queen Street.

As another evidence of former and very different times, we may mention the luckless Thomas Aikenhead, the son of an Edinburgh apothecary, who as a student jested about the doctrine of the Trinity and in 1697 was hanged for blasphemy.

The founding date of the **Society of High Constables** of Edinburgh is generally accepted to have been 1611, when the magistrates were advised to elect constables, half from the merchants of the town and half from the craftsmen through all the quarters of the town (which was divided into four). Previously the functions which were now delegated to the constables had been performed by the Baillies supervising four quartermasters who administered a body of 'visitors'. The twelve officers and twenty-six constables who were appointed had a great variety of duties. They were to apprehend suspected persons such as vagabonds and nightwalkers and imprison them. They were to challenge anyone wearing a pistol or dagger and present them to the Provost and Baillies to be punished. The constables were to intervene at times of public disorder such as riots or street-fighting and were given the power to break down doors when noise and nuisance were being caused. They were to search for Jesuits, seminarians, priests or 'Trafficking Papists' and deal with sturdy beggars or gypsies as well as idle persons. They were empowered to deal with murders, theft or other capital crimes and also to clear the streets and passages of filth, middens and swine. They were to see that those liable for the King's service had adequate armour, and theirs was the duty of apprehending swearers and blasphemers in the streets, at the markets or at the wells.

With such superhuman tasks before them, it is little wonder that the constables were unsuccessful in cleansing the streets, where refuse lay 'like mountains' and roads had to be cut through it to the closes and booths. The constables seemed to be used for everything: they oversaw the sending of beggars and vagrants to the workhouse and correction house in the Calton district; they were used as tax-gatherers, as officers of the local census, for billeting soldiers and to patrol the streets at Hogmanay (New Year's Eve) to prevent the 'throwing of dead cats' and other riotous behaviour. They were ordered to quell snowball fights and Chartist demonstrations and to assist at fires in the High Street or in public buildings elsewhere in the City.

Today the City is divided into twenty-three wards with twelve High Constables in each at full strength, making a total of 276 members. Their duties include escorting the Lord Provost at ceremonies such as the Kirking of the Council and at the opening of the Edinburgh Festival or during the conferring of the Freedom of the City. In their black top hats, white gloves and morning suits, carrying varnished black wooden batons, the High Constables are a familiar and traditional sight.

Hugo Arnot, in his *History of Edinburgh*, gives a horrific picture of the squalor of the **Tolbooth** in 1778: 'In the heart of a great city, it is not accommodated with ventilators, with water-pipe, with privy. The filth collected in the jail is thrown into a hole within the house, at the foot of a stair, which, it is pretended, communicates with a drain; but, if so, it is so completely

choked, as to serve no other purpose but that of filling the jail
with disagreeable stench ... When we visited the jail, there
were confined in it about twenty-nine prisoners, partly debtors,
partly delinquents; four or five were women, and there were
five boys ... All parts of the jail were kept in a slovenly
condition; but the eastern quarter of it, (although we had
fortified ourselves against the stench), was intolerable. This
consisted of three apartments, each above the other. In what
length of time these rooms, and the stairs leading to them,
could have collected the quantity of filth which we saw in them,
we cannot determine. The undermost of these apartments was
empty. In the second, which is called *the iron room*, which is
destined for those who have received sentence of death, there
were three boys; one of them might have been about fourteen,
the others about twelve years of age. They had been confined
about three weeks for thievish practices. In the corner of the
room, we saw, shoved together, a quantity of dust, rags, and
straw, the refuse of a long succession of criminals. The straw
had been originally put into the room for them to be upon, but
had been suffered to remain till, worn by successive convicts, it
was chopped into bits two inches long. From this, we went to
the apartment above, where were two miserable boys, not
twelve years of age. But there we had no leisure for observation; for, no sooner was the door opened, than such an
incredible strench assailed us, from the stagnant and putrid air
of the room, as, notwithstanding our precautions, utterly to
overpower us.'

James Nasmyth, in his *Autobiography,* describes the fateful
moment in 1817 when the black Heart of Midlothian was
finally gouged out of the Tolbooth and exposed to the light of
day: 'At one of the strongest parts of the building a strong oak
chest, iron-plated, had been built in, held fast by a thick wall of
stone and mortar on each side. The iron chest measured about
nine feet square, and was closed by a strong iron door with
heavy bolts and locks. This was the *Heart of Midlothian,* the
condemned cell of the Tolbooth. The iron chest was so heavy
that the large body of workmen could not, with all their might,
pull it out. After stripping it of its masonry, they endeavoured
by strong levers to tumble it down into the street. At last, with a
'Yo! heave ho!' it fell down with a mighty crash. The iron chest

was so strong that it held together, and only the narrow iron door, with its locks, bolts, and bars, was burst open, and jerked off amongst the bystanders. It was quite a scene. A large crowd has assembled, and amongst them was Sir Walter Scott. Recognising my father, he stood by him, while both awaited the ponderous crash. Sir Walter was still The Great Unknown, but it was pretty well known who had given such an interest to the building by his fascinating novel, *The Heart of Midlothian*. Sir Walter afterwards got the door and the key for his house at Abbotsford. There was a rush of people towards the iron chest, to look into the dark interior of that veritable chamber of horrors. My father's artist friend went forward with the rest, to endeavour to pick up some remnant of the demolished structure. As soon as the clouds of dust had been dispersed, he observed, under the place where the iron box had stood, a number of skeletons of rats, as dry as mummies. He selected one of these, wrapped it in a newspaper, and put it in his pocket as a recollection of his first day in Edinburgh, and of the total destruction of the 'Heart of Midlothian'.'

In the late eighteenth and early nineteenth centuries the Tolbooth was replaced by the **Calton Jail,** which stood where St. Andrew's House stands now. An interesting insight into life in 1859 is given by William Brown, an Edinburgh merchant, who was sent to the Debtors' Prison for refusing to pay the widely unpopular Annuity Tax (for the upkeep of the clergy of the Established Church normally amounting to 6% of the rents of homes or shops). Brown writes that at the foot of a long narrow winding stair a massive gate had to be unlocked. 'I can never forget the word the under-governor or turn-key cried up the stair to announce my coming. He shouted the word with a voice like thunder . . . "D-E-B-T-O-R".' His allotted cell, No. 92, was 'a small, square room, 12 feet by 9 feet, the walls and roof of which were white as snow. The floor was stone. An iron bed, one chair, and a small table, comprised the furniture'. But there were some comforts, notably the kitchen, where other petty offenders were 'all happy, some debating, some cooking and some playing at draughts'. There was wholesome food available as signalled by 'the buzzing, hissing noise, arising from herring roasting, ham and steak frying etc. A regiment of teapots lined the upper rib of the grate, and a number of small tables, on which the debtors has arranged their breakfast-ware'.

Deacon Brodie's father was a wright and cabinetmaker in the Lawnmarket in Edinburgh, and a member of the Town Council. William, an only son, succeeded to the family business

Deacon Brodie

in 1780. The following year he was made an ordinary Deacon of the Councillors of the City. By this time he had acquired a taste for gambling, with a reputation for a gambler's tricks (such as loaded dice). He spent most evenings in a gambling club in Fleshmarket Close but was able to keep this side of his life more or less unknown and maintain the facade of a respectable citizen. He probably started on his career of crime around 1786. In 1787 a series of robberies took place in and around Edinburgh in which shops were broken into and goods disappeared as if by magic. There is a story that on one occasion an old lady had been too ill or tired to go to church. And she sat in her chair at home alone, a man with a black cloth over his face came into the room. He picked up the keys lying on the table, opened her bureau, took out a large sum of money from it, re-locked it, replaced the keys on the table, and, with a low bow, left the room.

Brodie and his cronies decided to break into the Excise Office. Brodie visited the office deliberately on a number of occasions to spy out the land, learn the layout of the premises, and make an impression of the key to the outer door. On 5th

March 1787 he and his accomplices made their break-in. The whole affair was a bit of a fiasco, as Brodie and his men found only £16. At 10 o'clock the same night, the theft was discovered. In due course one of Brodie's accomplices who was under sentence of deportation in England, seeing the advertisment of reward and pardon for information on the robbery, turned King's Evidence. Brodie escaped to Dunbar, then south again to Newcastle, London, Margate, Deal and Dover, sailing from there to Ostend. Unfortunately for him he had given three letters to a passenger to deliver to Edinburgh. The passenger recognised the name of Brodie's brother-in-law, opened the letters and reported Brodie to the British Consul in Ostend. Brodie was traced to Amsterdam and arrested in an alehouse on the evening of his departure for America. Brodie was tried in 1780, found guilty and taken for execution to the west end of the Luckenbooth near St Giles. He behaved coolly and nonchalantly on the gallows. His hair was dressed and powdered; twice the rope proved to be too short, and twice he calmly waited as it was lengthened. The third attempt was fatal. His double life is said to have inspired Stevenson's *Dr. Jekyll and Mr. Hyde.*

Robert Knox (1791-1862) was the son of a mathematics teacher at George Heriot's School. His early education took place at home and then at the Royal High School. In 1815, after graduating from Edinburgh University, he was in Brussels as an assistant Army surgeon, tending the wounded of Waterloo. Two years later he was at the Cape of Good Hope with the 72nd Highland Regiment during the Fifth Kaffir War. He undertook ethnological and zoological research, collecting Bantu skulls. Returning to Edinburgh, he became a Fellow of the Royal Society of Edinburgh and in 1825 a Fellow of the Royal College of Surgeons and a conservator of their Museum of Comparative Anatomy and Pathology. He bought Sir Charles Bell's anatomical collection from London and soon became the foremost anatomy lecturer in Edinburgh his classes drawing over 500 students.

However, an unfortunate association was to cloud his reputation. Knox believed that his students should be able to use fresh bodies for their studies. There was only a limited supply legally available for dissection, all of which went to the University's Professor of Anatomy, who had them preserved in spirits and used them over and over again. In 1827 an old man named Donal died owing £4 rent to his landlord, William Hare, an Irishman. Hare persuaded a lodger, William Burke, to take the old man's body to Surgeons' Square. One of Knox's students sent **Burke and Hare** to Knox. They were paid £7.10s and told to bring more bodies if they could. They proceeded to

Burke and Hare

pick live victims, plied them with drink and smothered them, doing so at least sixteen times. A year later shouts of 'Murder' prompted police investigation which led to the discovery of the body of a woman still lying unpacked from her box in Knox's anatomy room. Burke and Hare were tried for murder, and Burke was hanged in front of a large crowd. Hare turned King's Evidence and saved himself. The mob attacked Knox's house and burned him in effigy, and he was condemned on all sides for his cynical or indifferent no-questions-asked attitude. In course of time his fortunes and reputation declined, but he lives on in James Bridie's play *The Anatomist* (1931), a role which the Edinburgh-born actor Alastair Sim made very much his own.

James McLevy was born in Ballymacnab, County Armagh in Ireland, where he trained as a linen-weaver before coming to

James McLevy

Edinburgh to work as a builder's labourer. He was a night-watchman with the Edinburgh Police Force in 1830. Falling ill, he was taken to the Royal Infirmary where he made his first recorded arrest, that of a nurse who was secretly swigging from a bottle of wine at McLevy's bedside. After his recovery he became a member of the police force. He wrote a number of books about his life as a policeman which gave a very vivid picture of what criminal life in Edinburgh was like. During Deacon Brodie's time there had been fifty-two brothels between Castle Hill and the top of the Canongate, and in McLevy's day there were notorious spots such as the 'Holy Land' and the 'Happy Land', which McLevy describes as 'numerous dens, inhabited by thieves, robbers, thimbles, pickpockets, abandoned women, drunken destitutes and here and there chance-begotten brats, squalling with hunger, or lying dead for days after they should have been buried'. McLevy tells of the madame, Jean Brash: 'the house she occupied in James Square was a 'bank of exchange', regularly fitted up for business. In the corner of a door-panel of every bedroom, there was a small hole neatly closed up with a wooden button, so as to escape all observation. Then the lower panels were made to slide, so that while through the peep she could see when the light was extinguished, she could by the opened panel creep noislessly on all fours and take the watch off the side-table or rifle the pockets of the luckless wight's dress'. Conan Doyle, in his characterisation of Sherlock Holmes, owes something to McLevy, for while he was studying medicine at Edinburgh there appeared a popular but spurious collection of crime stores by 'James McGovan' (in reality W. C. Honeyman), all based on McLevy's writings. The analytical methods employed by McLevy (as recorded by Honeyman) are found in the procedures of Holmes.

The late **Chief Constable Willie Merrilees** was born in Leith. He was under height, short on education and had four fingers missing. In spite of these shortcomings he was admitted into the police force as a local lad, a rare occurrence as in those days the police was largely made up of farmers or Highlanders. He was appointed a constable in 1924 and soon acquired a reputation for 'shadowing' which he was well able to do as he was a master of disguise. Probably his most famous disguise was as a baby in a pram with a linen cap on his head: this was the only way he could approach a 'flasher' close enough to catch him in the act. He moved to the Vice Squad and was required to clean up the illicit stills (sheebeens) and brothels in the City. On the former assignment he once kept the merrymakers singing near the still till the police arrived in force. In the 1920s there was considerable prostitution taking place openly in the City streets. At the coffee-stalls at the Mound, 27 confirmed prostitutes were arrested, and children of 13 and 14 could be seen importuning on the streets.

Perhaps Merrilees' greatest adventure was during the Great Kosmo Club Battle in 1933. Originally known as the Bohemian Club behind St Mary's Cathedral and the Theatre Royal in the early 1920s, by 1928 it was named the Kosmo and was run as a dance-hall with a curtained-off area at one end. The Kosmo girls advertised themselves in the newspapers and were supplied with clothing and jewellery for which they had to sign, a debt which bound them to the proprietor. Some of the girls went to local offices and nursing homes to perform their services. Willie Merrilees even went so far as to disguise himself as an elderly street-walker so as to be able to loiter by the club door. When the raid took place, over a hundred people were found in the club, a number of whom felt considerable embarrassment to be apprehended there on account of their high standing in the community. In 1938 Merrilees dressed as a railway porter so as to catch Werner Walti, apparently a German spy of an amateurish variety. Walti had in his possession a German wireless transmitter, a Mauser automatic, a national registration card and a wireless code. Towards the end of his career Chief Constable Merrilees received the OBE and – the ultimate accolade – an appearance on 'This Is Your Life' on TV.

Dancing

In 1966 the Madama Ada School of Dancing celebrated its half-century of existence. It had been founded in 1916 by Mrs Ada Calder. Dance and, to a lesser extent, classical ballet, have for many years been fashionable in Edinburgh, as a preparation for dancing assemblies, balls or Saturday night 'hops'.

The Scottish Ballet School was the creation in 1927 of its long-time director the late Miss Marjory Middleton, who was made MBE in 1964. During the Second World War in 1944 she started the Edinburgh Ballet Club and the Edinburgh Ballet Theatre. Among her graduates are Kenneth Bannerman who danced with the Ballet Rambert, and Alex Bennet who was first soloist with the Royal Ballet and also danced with Sadler's Wells.

There was an ill-fated attempt to form an Edinburgh International Ballet Company after the 1958 Festival. The forty-strong company had a triumphant tour of Yugoslavia but on their return were forced to disband. In much the same way Elsie Roya, a former member of Pavlova's Corps de Ballet, had tried to start a ballet company in Edinburgh in 1930, but she died tragically.

If ballet in Edinburgh seems to be dogged with failure, the same cannot be said about popular dance. Edinburgh was full of dancing in the eighteenth and nineteenth centuries, and the twentieth century has been no exception. St Cecilia's Hall was in later times known as the Excelsior; and there were Assembly Rooms at Leith and in George Street. Another was in Buccleuch Square, while in Carubber's Close Signora Violante in the eighteenth century prepared her students for the weekly balls in the Assembly Rooms in what is now Old Assembly Close.

The famous Palais de Dance in Fountainbridge was opened in 1920. It was remembered as the resort of the West End set with their shining limousines, white ties and tails, fur wraps and long sheath dresses. Inside, the ballroom would be covered in streamers and balloons, with exciting lighting effects. From above the dancers' heads came the chorus played by Jean Morel on tenor sax perched on the centre of the roof support. Mecca took it over in 1938 and it was run by the Delfont Brothers. While still Prince of Wales, the Duke of Windsor with the Duke of Kent visited the Palais, and the Prince danced with red-haired Jose Kelly, one of the instructresses. In a 'box' or 'pan' at the foot of the main staircase were the instructors and instructresses who could be hired for a dance. Thousands of married couples first met at the Palais, and many of the best bands played there: Nat Gonella in the early '40s, Victor Sylvester in 1944 and Geraldo in 1952. In 1945 the Hollywood film star, Sabu the Elephant Boy, danced there, and Sarah Vaughan announced in 1953 that she had 'had a ball' at the Palais. There were Royal Nights and rugger international nights (when all kinds of high jinks were got up to).

In 1923 Fairley's Dunedin Assembly Rooms opened. It was said that women customers there were 'the toughest in town', and its owner had a huge Alsatian dog constantly with him. The Silver Slipper in Springvalley Gardens started in 1938. Inside was a huge cage with canaries, and in the ballroom the glass-topped tables had shoals of goldfish swimming under them. Cabaret in the Silver Slipper was often provided by artistes from the Theatre Royal, but the resident musician was Symon Stungo, whose speciality was 'Kitten on the Keys'. Stungo was still a student at Edinburgh University when he was hired to bang out the Charleston and the Black Bottom in the Wemyss Place Drill Hall. He was able to pack the joint: he toured in Variety and was invited to play at Fairley's Dunedin Palais in Picardy Place and well remembered the huge Alsatian. In 1931 he was working in the Havana in Princes Street. The Drill Hall had been the abode of Jack Dunbar and Charlie Goldfar and specialised in jazz around 1930. Two years later the Cavendish opened (formerly Player's Riding Academy).

All of Edinburgh's old dance halls have closed or undergone change: the Plaza in Morningside which had seen dancing since 1926 closed in 1975 and is now a supermarket. Stewart's Ballroom, latterly known as the Astoria, shut its doors for the last time in 1982.

A new passion for dance reigns supreme in dozens of disco bars: there were gold-plated tables and chairs in Annabel's at Fountainbridge in 1979; in 1984 Coasters at Tollcross had revolving silver balls for the over-forties to dance beneath and disco and roller-skating in what used to be the New Cavendish. In 1981 Tiffany's changed into Cinderellas Rockerfellas in St Stephen Street, and in Buster Browns disco in Market Street famous names like Status Quo or Billy Connolly have been seen. So the dance lives on.

Lindsay Kemp, the Edinburgh-born mime artist, unites all the forms of dance. He first toured in tawdry musicals, then choreographed a striptease, clowned in circuses and studied

Lindsay Kemp

the Noh Theatre of Japan and the Commedia dell'Arte and with Marcel Marceau. He is obsessed by Buster Keaton and has taught at the Guildhall School in London.

Divines

John Knox (c.1505-72) was born near Haddington in East Lothian and went on to study, it is believed, either at Glasgow or at St Andrews University. He was ordained a priest and held

John Knox

the position of papal notary in Haddington from 1540 to 1543. In the following year he worked as a tutor to the sons of the lairds of Ormiston and Longniddry in East Lothian who favoured the reformed religion. By this time Knox himself had substantially rejected Roman Catholicism, not least because of the martyrdom of the reformer Patrick Hamilton in 1528. When the noted reformer George Wishart returned to preach in Scotland and arrived in East Lothian in 1545, Knox became his companion, guarding him, while he preached, with a two-handed sword. When Wishart was in turn executed in 1546, Knox became even more firmly committed to reform, and because England had already gone down that road, he identified himself with anti-Papal England.

In 1546 Cardinal Beaton, Archbishop of St Andrews, was assassinated. His executioners took over St Andrews Castle and made it a Protestant stronghold. Knox arrived there in the following year with his pupils and began work as a Protestant minister. When the castle surrendered to the French some weeks later, Knox was made a galley-slave. Two years later he was released at Edward VI's request and began to take a very active part in the English Reformation. He was a minister at Berwick, at Newcastle-upon-Tyne and in London. He was appointed a Royal Chaplain and was offered the bishopric of Rochester, but declined it. When Archbishop Cranmer was drawing up his articles of religion, Knox was one of his consultants, as he was over the writing of the Second Prayer Book in 1552. During the reign of the Catholic Queen Mary of England, Knox was on the Continent: he was minister to the English exiles in Frankfurt, and in Geneva he ministered to the radical reformers who were opposed to the English settlement, and met Calvin, whose theology and church order he approved of greatly.

It was in 1559 that Knox was finally recalled from his self-imposed exile on the Continent. By 1560 the Estates (Scottish Parliament) had decided on religious reform. Knox and five assistants prepared the Confession of Faith which was approved by the Estates. It repudiated Papal jurisdiction and forbade the celebration of Mass. Next came Knox's Book of Discipline which outlined a non-episcopal church constitution and a national plan for universal education from parish school to university, as well as a systematic programme of poor relief, all of these to be financed by the revenue received by the Kirk. In the same year the General Assembly of the Church of Scotland first met, and four years later the Book of Common Order appeared which regulated the forms of public worship. John Knox was appointed minister of St Giles, an office he held until his death.

When Queen Mary returned to Scotland in 1561, she immediately had Mass celebrated. Knox had already made his views clear on women as rulers of nations in his *First Blast of the Trumpet against the Monstrous Regiment* [Government] *of Women*, a publication which Queen Elizabeth never forgave. However, Knox returned to England in 1566 where he wrote his *History of the Reformation in Scotland*. In 1572 he was back in Edinburgh, preached for the last time in St Giles and died shortly thereafter. The epitaph of Regent Morton on Knox was: 'Here lies one who neither flattered nor feared any flesh'. Knox, who liked to compare himself to the Old Testament prophets, Amos and Jeremiah, saw himself very much in their mould as bringing a call to repentance from country pastures to the decadent cities. He has left the stamp of his character upon the Scottish nation, its Kirk and its system of education, which bear the imprint of his moral integrity and sense of purpose.

In Greyfriars churchyard stands the Martyrs Monument, erected in 1683 to the Covenanters who gave their lives in the Capital and all over Scotland. The Covenanters were originally so called because they accepted the National Covenant, written in the Tailors' Hall in Edinburgh's Cowgate. The Covenant was first signed in Greyfriars Kirk in 1638 to demonstrate the widespread opposition to Charles I's anglicisation of worship and the introduction of bishops into the Scottish presbyterian system. When the General Assembly was convened in the peaceful small town of Glasgow, away from the mobs of Edinburgh, the members condemned the new prayer book and ruled that the King had no power to control the Kirk. The office of bishop was abolished. The Covenanters began to raise an army with the support of the most powerful man in Scotland, the Earl of Argyll. Among the Covenanter generals was Alexander Leslie who had spent most of his life abroad as a mercenary and had risen to be a Field-Marshall in the Swedish army. The Covenanters seized Edinburgh, Stirling and Dumbarton castles. The ladies of Edinburgh helped to carry earth and stones to fortify the defences of the port of Leith, and General Leslie and his army stood ready on Leith sands, but a truce was eventually signed with the King's army.

The King had his own battle in England with Parliament: both sides wanted the Covenanters to join them. The Covenanters eventually drew up a Solemn League and Covenant with the English Parliament in 1643. The latter promised to make the English church presbyterian. This promise did not materialise, but at a conference in the Palace of Westminster the Scottish Kirk accepted what is known as the Westminster Confession, which, after the Bible, has been the cornerstone of the Church of Scotland. The Covenanters dominated Scotland for eleven years, and the Kirk grew more powerful than ever. Religion became increasingly important, if in a narrow, exclusive sense: those who were not for the puritanical regime were considered to be beyond redemption.

With the accession of Charles II bishops were once again introduced into the Kirk in 1622. The Covenanters were forced to meet secretly in conventicles in private houses or in the hills, watching for the approach of the dragoons. At Rullion Green in 1666 the Covenanter army was defeated by General Tam Dalyell, and thirty were hanged in Edinburgh. By the 1680s – known as 'the Killing Times' – there were few Covenanters left. Those who were apprehended were taken to Edinburgh to stand trial before 'Bluidy Mackenzie' (Sir George Mackenzie, the Lord Advocate). Those who were not sent to the West Indies were hanged. Many were very courageous, singing psalms or preaching a sermon to the crowd. The Covenanters called this 'glorifying God in the Grassmarket', and the spot where they died is still marked with a circle of stones there and an inscription.

Entering a more rationale era we may mention in passing **James Blair** (1656-1743), an episcopalian minister thought to have been born in Edinburgh, who emigrated to Virginia in 1685 and in 1693 founded William and Mary College there. From 1740 to 1741 he was Governor of Virginia.

The Reverend **Alexander ('Jupiter') Carlyle** was born in Prestonpans in 1722. He studied in Glasgow and Leiden and was chosen as minister of Inveresk, where he remained for

Alexander Carlyle

fifty-seven years, from 1748 to his death in 1805. Carlyle was the friend of many men of letters such as David Hume, Tobias Smollett and Adam Smith. He copied out the manuscript of his brother minister John Home's play, *Douglas*, and was censured by the more extreme clergy for attending the third night of the drama, for 'keeping company with an actress' and for 'taking possession of a box in an unlicensed theatre'. Nevertheless, Carlyle became Moderator of the General Assembly in 1770 as leader of the 'Broad Church' party. In 1789 he was Dean of the Chapel Royal. His first and only large-scale literary work (he published political pamphlets in the years 1758 to 1764) was his *Autobiography*, which gives an invaluable picture of eighteenth-century Scottish life and of Edinburgh society in particular, such as the following: 'Adam Smith, though perhaps only second to David Hume in learning and ingenuity, was far inferior to him in conversational talents. His voice was harsh and enunciation thick, approaching to stammering. His conversation was like lecturing, especially when he grew warm. He was the most absent man that ever I saw, moving his lips and talking to himself, and smiling, in the midst of large companies. If you awaked him from his reverie and made him attend to the subject of conversation he immediately began a harangue, and never stopped till he told you all he knew about it, with the utmost philosphical ingenuity . . . At this time, when David Hume was living in Edinburgh, his economy was strict; yet he was able to give suppers to his friends in his small lodging in the Canongate. He took much to the company of the younger clergy, not from a wish to bring them over to his opinions, for he never attempted to overturn any man's principles, but they best understood his notions, and could furnish him with literary conversation. Robertson and John Home and Bannatine and I lived all in the country, and came only periodically to the town. Blair and Jardine both lived in it, and suppers being the only fashionable meal at that time, we dined where we best could, and by cadies assembled our friends to meet us in a tavern by nine o'clock; and a fine time it was when he could collect David Hume, Adam Smith, Adam Ferguson, Lord Elibank, and Drs. Blair and Jardine, on an hour's warning.'

John Home was born in Leith, the son of the town clerk, in 1722. He went to Edinburgh University, and at the time of the '45 Rebellion enlisted in the First or College Company which was led by Lord Provost George Drummond. Captured at the Battle of Falkirk, he was imprisoned in Doune Castle, making his escape by a rope made from bedsheets and breaking a leg in the process. Trained as a minister, he took up a charge in Athelstaneford in East Lothian in 1747. His contemporary,

John Home

'Jupiter' Carlyle, writes that Home was 'very handsome and had a fine person, about 5ft 10½ins, and an agreeable catching address. He had not much wit and still less humour, but he had so much sprightliness and vivacity, and such an expression of benevolence in his Manner, and such an unceasing flattery of those he liked (and he never kept company with any body else), the kind commendations of a lover, not the adultation of a sycophant, that he was truly irresistible, and his entry to a company was received, like letting in the Sun into a dark room'. Home had a notion to be a dramatic poet. He went to London in 1749 with his *Tragedy of Agis*, but the actor-manager Garrick thought it would not work on the stage. During this time in the capital Home made friends with Smollett, the novelist. From hearing an old ballad, Home worked up the theme of his next play and his most famous one, *Douglas*. Carlyle copied the manuscript several times, and in 1755 it was completed for the stage, much to the admiration of the philosopher David Hume, who thought it was 'a Perfect Tragedy'. Home set off for London, 'the Tragedy in one Pocket of his Great Coat, and his Clean Shirt and night cap in the other . . .', as Carlyle has it. Again Home's work was rejected by Garrick, so the author returned to Edinburgh and persuaded West Digges to put it on in the City. The play, which was based on the agony of a mother whose son is killed by her husband, was stoutly patriotic but aroused the strong condemnation of that part of the clergy who frowned on the theatre. Its first performance proved a triumph, and the famous cry 'Whaur's yer Wullie Shakespeare noo?' was shouted from the audience. The play had gone into twelve editions or more by 1800, and there were around twenty more in the nineteenth century. Home's own position as a minister became untenable, however, and he left the ministry to become private secretary to the Earl of Bute and later tutor to the Prince of Wales, who, on becoming George III, gave him an annual pension of £300. *Douglas* was performed in 1757 in London, and indeed Home became so friendly with Garrick that he was twice chosen as his second in two unfought duels. Garrick invited Home to his house for dinner and later received a lesson in golf from the playwright, who was proficient at the sport. The role of Lady Randolph, the tragic mother, was taken by Sarah Siddons and remained in her repertoire until she retired in 1819. Her brother, John Philip Kemble, had considerable success as Douglas, and Charles Kean made his debut in the role in 1827. Home wrote four other plays, but none had the success of *Douglas*. He wrote a *History of the Rebellion of 1745* which relates his personal experiences, and he spent the final years, before his death in 1808, in Edinburgh.

George Hay was born in Edinburgh in 1729, the son of a solicitor. His family were strong Jacobites and Episcopalians. Apprenticed to a surgeon at the age of sixteen, along with other Edinburgh doctors and medical students he was required to treat the wounded after the battle of Prestonpans, when Prince Charles Edward Stuart's army defeated the Government forces under General Cope. Hay went with the Jacobites into England, but took sick and was sent back to Scotland. After the battle of Culloden he was imprisoned in Edinburgh Castle and in London. In 1747 he was released and returned to Edinburgh. During his imprisonment in London he had met a Catholic, and after his release he took instruction in the Catholic faith and became a convert in 1748. He continued to study medicine, but was unable to graduate from the University because of the restrictions imposed on Roman Catholics by the Penal Laws. Hay went to the Scots College in Rome in 1751 to train for the priesthood, was ordained in 1759, and was soon back in Scotland, where he was sent to Preshome to assist Bishop Grant. He was given a pony and rode out into the countryside, using his medical skill on Catholics and Protestants alike. He often travelled to Edinburgh on business for the Bishop. At his home in Edinburgh he rose very early to pray, ate little but vegetables and drank milk or water. His clothes were poor but clean, and he slept on a mattress with two blankets and no sheets.

C

Bishop Hay

In 1767 he was posted permanently to Edinburgh to minister to the Catholics in the city, large numbers of whom were evicted Highlanders. He worked as agent for the Catholic Mission in Scotland, and in this capacity liaised between missionaries in Scotland and the seminaries abroad. In 1769 he was appointed a bishop and consecrated by Bishop Grant. Part of Bishop Hay's new work was to assist Catholics who had been evicted from South Uist to emigrate to Canada. He also helped to re-establish the Scots College in Madrid. Bishop Hay next travelled to Rome to organise the running of the Scots College there. His return journey was through snow, hail and rain, and he was forced to walk most of the way from Italy to Paris. Back in Scotland he moved his headquarters to Aberdeen and sometimes walked enormous distances: 'A tall figure, striding along and wrapped in a Highland plaid with a Highland boy behind carrying a knapsack'. At Miss Rankine's Boarding School in Aberdeen a different side of his character could be seen, for there 'the Bishop would sit at tea with all the young ladies about him, and gratify them with his pleasant conversation. He would then call for a little music, and asking some of the older pupils for their new song, would sing it at sight with perfect ease and accuracy'.

Hay had opened two chapels in Edinburgh, one in Black-friars Wynd and another in Leith Wynd. He played a leading part in the unsuccessful attempt in 1778 to have the Penal Laws repealed. This aroused the antagonism of those who were opposed to Catholicism, and the Bishop had the unpleasant experience of having to stand watching at the roadside while his house was looted. Bishop Hay eventually retired to the new seminary he had opened in Aquhorties near Inverurie for thirty boys. He had by now written three works on Christian doctrine and a two-volume treatise on miracles as well as a number of pamphlets. By 1800 there were 30,000 Catholics in Scotland ministered to by forty priests, with twelve chapels. Even as an old man, Bishop Hay made several journeys to Edinburgh on horseback. He was an expert horseman as well as a sturdy walker. He still loved music, despite his reputation for severity (which mellowed in old age) and on one of his expeditions to the City bought 'five shillings worth of the best fiddle strings'. He died in 1811, aged 83, dreaming perhaps of the adventures he loved to describe of his early days following the Jacobite army.

Thomas Chalmers was born in Anstruther in Fife in 1780, the son of a dyer, shipowner and general merchant, and at the age of twelve entered St Andrews University. Although he is

Dr Thomas Chalmers

said to have declared at the age of three that he intended to be a minister, and often gave sermons in his childhood, at University he at first appeared to be more interested in football and handball than his studies. All that changed in his third year when he became enthused about mathematics and in 1795 began serious studies for the ministry, although his heart was reckoned to be in mathematics and chemistry. He was licensed to preach at nineteen and delivered his first public sermon in Wigan in 1799, returning to Scotland to read chemistry, natural philosophy and moral philosophy at the University of Edinburgh. In 1803 he went to St Andrews University as assistant to one of the professors and taught mathematics. He was ordained minister at Kilmany and proceeded to open his own extramural classes in mathematics and chemistry at St Andrews. He was appointed to the Chair of Moral Philosophy at St Andrews in 1823 and to the Chair of Divinity at Edinburgh in 1828. In the following year he actively campaigned for the emancipation of Roman Catholics and helped to set up Catholic schools. Other academic honours soon followed: he was Fellow of the Royal Society of Edinburgh in 1834 and a Doctor of Civil Law at Oxford.

The vexed question of church patronage came to a head when Robert Young was presented as minister by his lay patron to the church at Auchterarder and was almost unanimously rejected by the congregation. Young appealed to the Court of Session, which ruled that a lay patron had the right to present regardless of the wishes of the congregation. This ruling, in the eyes of many, interfered with the right of the Kirk to govern its own affairs, and Chalmers, believing strongly in the principle of a church separate from the state, left the established Church of Scotland in 1843 with 470 other ministers (out of about 1200) in what has come to be known as the Disruption. Out of this brave gesture grew the Free Church, and it was to be 1929 before a majority of its members re-united with the Church of Scotland. Chalmers himself ministered to the poor in Edinburgh's West Port, believing that private Christian charity, and not state intervention, was the answer to poverty. He became the first Principal of the new Free Church College in 1845, and died two years later, remembered for his principles, his magnificent oratory, and for his indefatigable energy and powers of organisation in so swiftly and successfully founding the Free Church.

Dr Thomas Guthrie was a native of Brechin, born in 1803. He studied at Edinburgh University and was licensed to preach in 1825. He studied extra-murally with Dr Robert Knox (the

Dr Thomas Guthrie

Anatomist), taking classes in Surgery and Anatomy, before going to the University of Paris to continue his medical studies. In Paris he saw vice and degradation which left a permanent impression on him. He returned to Edinburgh and worked in a bank before going to Forfar as a parish minister. Guthrie was a firm opponent of the patronage system whereby a local laird had the right to impose a minister on a congregation against their wishes. Moving to Old Greyfriars in Edinburgh's Cowgate, he was immediately aware of the human suffering there. In 1840 he opened a new church, St John's, and at the time of the Disruption was one of the leaders of the new Free Church. His next church was Free St John's in the West Bow, and it was from there that he launched his appeal for a Ragged School System to cope with the hundreds of destitute children who roamed the streets of the City. He proposed to offer education, clothing and industrial training. The response of his congregation was disappointing so he appealed to the general public in 1847 in his *Plea for Ragged Schools*. This pamphlet was favourably reviewed by Hugh Miller and led to a meeting with the Lord Provost, Adam Black, and the drawing up of a constitution and code or rules for the new Society at a public meeting in the Music Hall in George Street. Two more *Pleas* followed, in 1849 and 1860. As early as 1847 three schools had been established with a total of 265 children. By 1851, 216 young people trained by the Schools were recorded as having found secure employment. The Governor of the Calton Jail in Edinburgh revealed that the number of persons under the age of fourteen in prison had fallen from 5% of the prison population in 1847 to less than 1% in 1851. Through the efforts of Dr Guthrie, after many vicissitudes, the Government passed a new Industrial School Act in 1866 which established the schools on a sound financial footing.

Dr Guthrie, who died in 1872, was a strong supporter of total abstinence and Sunday closing as well as the strict control of the sale of liquor, derived from his observations of the effect of alcohol on the labouring poor. He travelled abroad to Switzerland (he preached in Geneva), Brittany and Belgium. He supported the Waldensian Church and was made Moderator of the Free Church in 1862. Guthrie was a magnificent preacher, but he also loved fishing and riding and was an eager botanist. He took an active interest in the Home for Fallen Women, in the Edinburgh Royal Infirmary (where he was a manager), in the Blind Asylum and in The House of Refuge and Night Refuge.

By way of postscript, here is a typical example of the way Dr Guthrie interviewed a street arab (as the uncared-for urchins of Edinburgh were known): So, soon as you have satisfied him that you are not connected with the police, you ask him, 'Where is your father?'. Now, hear his story, and there are hundreds could tell a similar tale. 'Where is your father?'. 'He is dead Sir'. 'Where is your mother?' 'Dead too'. 'Where do you stay?' 'Sister and I, and my little brother, live with granny'. 'What is she?' 'She is a widow woman'. 'What does she do?' 'Sells sticks, Sir'. 'And can she keep you all?' 'No'. 'Then how do you live?' 'Go about and get bits of meat, sell matches, and sometimes get a trifle from the carriers for running an errand'. 'Do you go to school?' 'No, never was at school; attended sometimes a Sabbath-school, but have not been there for a long time.' 'Do you go to Church?' 'Never was in a Church'. 'Do you know who made you?' 'Yes, God made me'. 'Do you say your prayers?' 'Yes, mother taught me a prayer before she died; and I say it to granny afore I lie down'. 'Have you a bed?' 'Some straw Sir.'

Alexander Forbes, born in Edinburgh in 1817, was the son of a Scottish judge. He was educated at Edinburgh Academy and at the University of Glasgow. He began his working life with the East India Company, but poor health forced him to return to Britain, and he decided to study for Holy Orders at Oxford. His first curacy was in Oxford, but he returned to Scotland in 1846 as rector of the Episcopal church at Stonehaven. He returned to England to the Anglo-Catholic church of St Saviour's in Leeds, but in 1847 was recommended by Mr Gladstone and elected Bishop of Brechin. As a result of his work there he became known as the father-figure of Episcopacy in Dundee and throughout Scotland. Bishop Forbes introduced greater ritual and symbolism into Episcopal services along the lines favoured by the Oxford Movement, which stressed the closeness of the Episcopal church to the Roman Catholic. This change was not achieved without opposition, as there were many who felt the Episcopal church should be closer to traditional Protestant simplicity. Bishop Forbes died in 1875.

Dean Ramsay, of St John's Scottish Episcopal Church in Princes Street, was one of the few people to have a memorial erected to them by public subscription. The monument, which stands at the West End beside St John's, takes the form of a Celtic cross. His *Reminiscences of Scottish Life and Character* was a humorous tour de force and ran to some twenty-two editions. He founded the Church Society and contrived to raise funds to send needy pupils to Trinity College, Glenalmond in Perth (an institution which he helped to found). He was the friend of many of the greatest men of his time: Gladstone, the Archbishop of Canterbury (Dean Stanley), the Duke of Buccleuch and the Rev Thomas Chalmers. He was a respected philanthropist and was also a keen musician who excelled in playing the flute; he lectured on music (especially on Handel, whom he admired above all) and was reputed to have the best church choir in the City.

Dean Ramsay was an authority on bell-ringing, church architecture, and voice-training (he advocated the use of three pebbles in the mouth to improve elocution). Lastly he was a master of finance and was responsible for raising public interest and capital to erect a monument to Dr Thomas Chalmers. Dean Ramsay, who died in 1872, presided at St John's for forty-four years.

Lord George MacLeod of Fuinary was born in 1895. He was educated at Winchester and Oriel College, Oxford, and during the First World War served as a Captain in the Argyll and Sutherland Highlanders, winning the Military Cross and the Croix de Guerre. In 1921 he was a Post Graduate Fellow at Edinburgh University and in the following year a missionery to the lumber camps in British Columbia, Canada. From 1926 to 1930 he was a minister at St Cuthbert's Church, Edinburgh, attracting a great following by his magnetic oratory and the force of his personality. Dr Harry Whitley has recorded in his autobiography, *Laughter in Heaven* (1962), that it was a chance meeting with George MacLeod in Edinburgh at that time – he

Lord George Macleod

calls him the 'most controversial minister in the Church of Scotland' and 'a prince among preachers' – that changed his life and led him to become a minister.

Next Dr MacLeod worked as minister of Govan Parish Church in Glasgow from 1930 to 1938. It was during these years that he became convinced that the congregation as agent of mission in the parish had failed and that there was an urgent need for a new form of mission to meet the needs of industrialised Scotland. The Iona Community was set up in 1938. George MacLeod resigned from his church at Govan and left Glasgow for the island of Iona with twelve young men, half of whom were recently qualified ministers, and the other half craftsmen. With the hopelessness of Govan during the Depression still fresh in their minds, they began an act of faith: the rebuilding of the ruined Abbey of Iona. The purpose of the Iona Community was to create community among its members, to come in this way to an understanding of the Christian faith and to bring industrial·workers and ministers together.

During the Second World War the minister of the Canongate Kirk, Dr Ronald Selby Wright, served as a military chaplain. Acheson House, the manse of the Canongate Kirk, was staffed by George MacLeod and the Iona Community. Replying to one of Dr Selby Wright's letters from the Middle East, George MacLeod wrote: 'I am glad, my dear Ronnie, you are mouldy and lonely, so was Abraham when he went out from Ur of the Chaldees and Moses from Egypt and our Lord from Nazareth. The road to the Kingdom is paved with broken hearts. Christians are pioneers, not map-makers and we are fool enough to expect that electric lights and drawing-boards and central heating will accompany our journey'.

In 1949 the Church of Scotland agonised as to the place of the Iona Community in its fold. It was decided that the Community had no official place. George MacLeod was invited to return to Govan but the General Assembly voted against his return. Finally the controversy was resolved in 1954 when the Iona Community Board was made a Committee of the General Assembly. MacLeod himself was chosen as Moderator in 1957 and in the following year became Convener of the Home Board. The Iona Community provided further training for young ministers and was recognised in 1968 as the only body in Britain offering training after theological college.

Lord MacLeod has made Edinburgh his home. The Iona Community continues its work, now in the field of ecumenism, as a focus of Christian unity for all denominations, and a power-house for the Church of Scotland. It is typical of Lord MacLeod that, having been a gallant soldier, he has seen the futility of war, and is now firmly committed to pacifism: 'Out of the Lion came forth Sweetness'.

Margaret Sinclair was born in Edinburgh in 1900 in a basement flat of a dilapidated tenement, the third child of a dustman. Educated at St Anne's School in the Cowgate, she

Margaret Sinclair

took certificates in sewing, cooking and dressmaking at the Atholl Crescent School of Domestic Economy, working part-time as a messenger for a business firm to support the two younger children in the family. She then worked full-time as a French polisher in the Waverley Cabinet Works and became an active member of her trade union. In 1918 the Cabinet Works closed down and she was made redundant, but found employment instead in McVitie's biscuit factory. Joining the Order of

Poor Clares, she spent two years in a convent in Notting Hill, London before her death from tuberculosis in 1925. Over the years many cures and apparent miracles have been reported as resulting from prayer to Margaret. The mother of the television personality, Jimmy Savile, attributes his recovery from a fall at the age of two to prayers she said after seeing the photograph of Margaret Sinclair in Leeds Cathedral. Known as the 'Edinburgh Wonder Worker', she has a special place in the life of the Capital. Cardinal Gray has pointed out that 'Margaret Sinclair may well be one of the first to achieve the title of Saint from the factory floor'. She was declared Venerable by the Roman Catholic Church in 1978.

Dr Harry Whitley was born in Edinburgh in 1906 and was in his youngest days a member of the Catholic Apostolic Church. He was educated at Daniel Stewart's and Heriot's and early

Dr. Harry Whitley

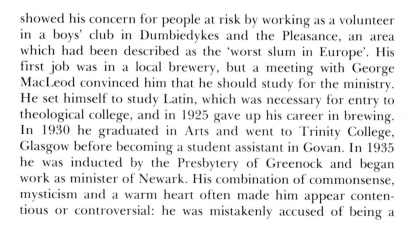

showed his concern for people at risk by working as a volunteer in a boys' club in Dumbiedykes and the Pleasance, an area which had been described as the 'worst slum in Europe'. His first job was in a local brewery, but a meeting with George MacLeod convinced him that he should study for the ministry. He set himself to study Latin, which was necessary for entry to theological college, and in 1925 gave up his career in brewing. In 1930 he graduated in Arts and went to Trinity College, Glasgow before becoming a student assistant in Govan. In 1935 he was inducted by the Presbytery of Greenock and began work as minister of Newark. His combination of commonsense, mysticism and a warm heart often made him appear contentious or controversial: he was mistakenly accused of being a

Communist, he acted as an air-raid warden at Kingston shipyard and was audacious enough to ask Sir James Lithgow, the shipbuilder, for financial assistance in making church improvements (assistance which was nevertheless given). As part of the Kirk's Huts and Canteens scheme, Dr Whitley went as a chaplain to France and was wounded in the battle for Falaise Gap. In Holland he was seriously ill just before the Rhine crossing and was operated on in the middle of the night in a German barracks (in Bayeux he had been one of the first guinea-pigs for testing penicillin, this time in a tented hospital). Back in Newark he was elected to the Town Council, holding the office of Convener of Steamies and Baths. Again he persuaded Sir James Lithgow to help in modernising the steamies and building a new swimming-pool. In 1950 in Partick he was again accused of being a Communist because he protested at the poverty and degradation he saw around him. Again the Lithgows provided finance to renovate the closes, largely through self-help schemes. In 1955 he was awarded a Doctorate of Divinity from Glasgow University. He continued to work for better conditions: he threatened to collect rats for the Lord Provost to prove how bad conditions were. Dysentery was rife from the lack of toilet facilities and the middens which were still a feature of many of the older housing areas. Dr Whitley was instrumental in having proper WC's installed.

The year 1954 was a turning-point in Dr Whitley's life, for it was then that he was appointed minister of the High Kirk of St Giles in Edinburgh, and so began an even more turbulent period in which the religious establishment of the Capital was subjected to a full frontal attack by the simplicity and directness of Harry Whitley. He made the pulpit of the High Kirk a place of relevant comment on contemporary issues, and a place of prophecy. He also introduced music at St Giles under the distinguished supervision of his organist, Herrick Bunney, who, with Dennis Townhill at St Mary's Episcopal Cathedral and Arthur Oldham (later chorusmaster of Scottish Opera and the Edinburgh Festival Chorus) at St Mary's Roman Catholic Cathedral, greatly improved the standard of church music in the City. One of the final controversies was the wrangling over Dr Whitley's appointment of the episcopalian American John Tirrell to St Giles, over which Canon (now Bishop) Montefiore took the minister of St Giles to task. Dr Whitley's own analysis of his achievements was that he turned St Giles into a lively parish church, a family church with children; a singing church where young people were free to come and go. He died in 1976.

Although born in Glasgow in 1908, **Ronald Selby Wright** tells us that 'I have never regarded myself as a Glasgow citizen since I came at the age of three to Edinburgh where I have had

Ronald Selby Wright

my home for the rest of my life . . .' His early education at Edinburgh Academy and the Edinburgh Institution (later Melville College) was followed by Edinburgh University and a training for the ministry at New College, at which time a special memory was the sight of the arrival of Earl Haig's body in Edinburgh.

He started the Canongate Boys' Club in 1927 and continued to support and develop it as a minister. When War broke out he was a chaplain with the Edinburgh Territorial Infantry Regiment and in 1940 took part in the Second Expeditionary Force's landing in France and then escaped back to England after Dunkirk. When he was chosen as the Radio Padre, he addressed an audience of up to ten million people and received up to 10,000 letters a day as he built up his audience. He became Senior Chaplain to the Edinburgh Garrison in 1943 and after visiting the Middle East was appointed Senior Chaplain, NE London. Subsequently he was a Senior Chaplain to a Division in Italy and travelled all over Europe, visiting Dachau and Hitler's Eagle's Nest before returning to Edinburgh and the Canongate. One of his innovations was the annual May Day service on Arthur's Seat. When Dr Selby Wright set about restoring the Canongate Kirk shortly after the War, he had the stonework cleaned and refurbished on the exterior, and inside he removed the large galleries which blocked the light, had the walls painted a light blue instead of dull brown, installed a new organ and acquired the pulpit of Thomas Chalmers. Lastly, he introduced a new restored Order of Service. The Canongate Kirk is the parish church of the monarch when in residence at Holyrood Palace. In 1961 Dr Selby Wright became Extra-Chaplain to the Queen and two years later, Chaplain, an office he held until 1978. In 1971 he was Moderator of the General Assembly, a capacity in which he travelled the world. Dr Selby Wright retired in 1977.

Cardinal Gordon Joseph Gray was born in Leith in 1910. He was educated at Holy Cross Academy, St John's Seminary, Wonersh, and the University of St Andrews. He was ordained

Cardinal Gray

in Edinburgh in 1935 and was given his first parish at Hawick, where he worked from 1941 to 1947. After four years as Rector of Blairs College, he was consecrated archbishop in 1951 and founded St Andrew's College, Drygrange in 1953. He was created cardinal priest of the title Santa Chiara a Vigna Clara in 1969. Cardinal Gray, who took an active part in the Second Vatican Council and in the elections of Popes John Paul I and II, was a member of the Pontifical Congregations for the Evangelisation of Peoples, Divine Worship and Social Communications. He has been a pastor of his flock for over thirty years and played a truly cardinal role in the development of

the Christian church in Scotland. He played host to Pope John
Paul II on his visit to Scotland in 1983. His sonorous bass voice
and obvious sincerity make him a preacher of power and
authority, while his sparetime interests range from gardening
to motor vehicle maintenance.

An Inverness man, **Father Anthony Ross,** O.P., was for
many years a familiar sight in and around George Square,
Edinburgh where the University's Roman Catholic Chaplaincy

Father Anthony Ross

is situated. With his wrestler's figure and Old Testament shock
of white hair, he was a truly charismatic presence for generations of students. For a time he also served as Chaplain at
Heriot-Watt and Stirling Universities, and as Rector of Edinburgh University, where he had read History. Keenly interested in the history of Scotland, he lectured widely and
wrote about it, was a Fellow of the Society of Antiquaries of
Scotland, and became the first editor of the *Innes Review.* He
also cared deeply about the after-care of prisoners, and was
Chairman of the Scottish Association for the Care and Resettle-
ment of Offenders, pioneering new ways of group living. He
was for several years Chairman of the Edinburgh branch of the
Telephone Samaritans, and a member of the National Council
of Cyrenians. In 1982 he became Provincial of the Dominican
Order, the Order of Preachers, in Britain. Fr Ross, writing in
Whither Scotland? edited by Duncan Glen (1971), analyses the
problems of urban decay in Edinburgh and the fragmentation
of its culture: 'The summer guides still spin yarns to the
tourists who gape at the high lands of the Royal Mile, telling
them with unconscious irony of how all classes mingled on the
common stairs of old Edinburgh. Meanwhile the divisive
planning goes on. City government and University combine

with property speculators from London and elsewhere to drive "John the Commonweal" into the new ghettos. The last thing the city "fathers" and the academic empire-builders want is that all classes should mingle. "Scatter and rule" might be their motto. "The people are the trouble." The people had an identity in the Grassmarket, the Pleasance, the Cowgate, the West Port, Blackfriars Street, and those other places whose names and buildings made them at least to some degree conscious of belonging to the city and its history. They lived round the castle, Holyrood, St Giles and the Parliament House, as they had always done, and still to some extent mingled with the lawyers, the members of the General Assembly of the Kirk and of the University. They were moved into dreary 'schemes' with no amenities except what voluntary bodies might provide; with no appreciation of the economic and psychological problems created by the change, and with scant help towards adjustment. Scotland is sick and unwilling to admit it. The Scottish establishment at least will not admit it. The tartan sentimentality, the charades at Holyroodhouse, the legends of Bruce and Wallace, Covenanters, Jacobites, John Knox and Mary Stuart, contribute nothing towards a solution. Small wonder that so many of the ablest people she produces emigrate rather than face the struggle of living here in the fog of romantic nostalgia for a world that never existed, and lies and half-truths about the world that does exist'.

Probably the controversial event in recent church history in Edinburgh was the appointment of **Professor James P. Mackey** as Thomas Chalmers Professor of Systematic Theology at New College in the University of Edinburgh. The

Professor James Mackey

controversy arose because Professor Mackey, as well as being Professor of Systematic and Philosophical Theology at the Jesuit University, San Francisco, was a laicised secular priest who had trained at Maynooth in Ireland and stated quite categorically: 'once a priest, always a priest'. Thirty-three commissioners presented an overture to the General Assembly protesting against the rumoured impending appointment of Professor Mackey. The General Assembly at first expressed 'grave disquiet' at the prospect. However, when the terms of the Universities (Scotland) Act 1932 had been investigated, it became clear that the Church of Scotland had no legal right to insist on the appointment of a Presbyterian to the Chair. Cardinal Gordon Gray, the Roman Catholic Archbishop, sympathised with the General Assembly over their evident embarrassment but gave it as his opinion that they had no cause for complaint. In 1979 Professor Mackey was appointed and called it a 'a very fine ecumenical gesture' on the part of the University. The Moderator, the Right Reverend Professor Robin Barbour, expressed his satisfaction at the appointment. In spite of the fact that the General Assembly had voted 412 to 254 in favour of a motion to reject the nomination of a priest or former priest to the post, the Church of Scotland Committee on Education announced themselves satisfied with the existing system of selection. Professor Mackey has demonstrated the breadth of his theological roots in stating that, with reference to God, Christ and the Trinity, 'I depend after Scripture mainly on Augustine, Aquinas, Calvin and Barth'.

The Edinburgh Jewish Community

It is important to note that, unlike England (where the Jews were banished in 1290 and only allowed back into the country by Oliver Cromwell in 1656), Scotland has never passed punitive legislation against its Jewish immigrants. Admittedly the Jewish community in Scotland did not develop until the end of the seventeenth century (the first Jewish resident is believed to have arrived in 1691). Earliest Jewish families came predominantly to Edinburgh, from Holland at first and then from Russia, Poland, Germany and the Baltic ports. In the early years of the nineteenth century they formed the first Kehillah (Congregation of Jews) in Edinburgh, celebrating the Feast of Tabernacles for the first time in the City in a building in the Pleasance.

Jews Close was in what is now the Sciennes district: it was in Braid Place that the Jewish cemetery was acquired for the Hebrew Congregation and the first Synagogue is recorded as having been in North Richmond Street in 1821. A few years later a Jewish school was opened and the first minister, the Rev. Moses Joel, appointed. The earliest Jewish families worked as jewellers, tailors, lead-pencil makers and manufacturers of sealing-wax. One, Philip Levy, a furrier active around 1814, was granted the title of Furrier to His Majesty in 1824.

One of the outstanding personalities in the history of the Edinburgh Jewish Community was Chief Rabbi **Dr Salis Daiches** who died in 1945 at the age of sixty-five years. He had gained his doctorate with a thesis on Edinburgh philosopher David Hume, and at the time of his appointment to the Graham Street Synagogue was one of the few in Britain to hold a full Rabbinic diploma which allowed him to perform all religious functions and legislate on Jewish law and ritual. Dr. Daiches, who held office in Edinburgh from 1919 to his death in 1945, had two sons both of whom distinguished themselves in their respective fields. Both inherited their father's oratorical gifts: Lionel Daiches, Edinburgh's premier advocate in the High Court of Justiciary, and Professor David Daiches, an outstanding teacher, writer and authority on many of the most vital aspects of Scottish life and culture, and a highly regarded literary critic.

Doctors

The history of medicine in Edinburgh is long and honourable. The emergence of professional men of medicine was a gradual one. We hear of an apothecary's shop in 1450 in one of the first of the High Street luckenbooths. In 1505 the Royal College of Surgeons was founded from the Corporation of Barber-Surgeons, receiving its charter from James IV in 1506 (it is now housed in Surgeons' Hall in Nicolson Street, built in 1833 after a design of W. H. Playfair). Medical education in Edinburgh owes a considerable debt to Continental medical schools, in particular that of the University of Leiden in Holland.

Robert Sibbald, Edinburgh's Professor of Physic (Medicine), matriculated at Leiden in 1660, studied at Paris and graduated MD at Angers. **Archibald Pitcairne** studied first law then medicine at Paris, graduated MD at Rheims, and in 1692 was appointed Professor of Physic at Leiden, where one of his pupils was Herman Boerhaave. **James Halket** matriculated at Leiden as a medical student in 1675 and was to be joint Professor of Physic at Edinburgh with Pitcairne and Sibbald.

Herman Boerhaave (1668-1738) began lecturing at Leiden in 1701, and for twenty-nine years held three professorships: Medicine and Botany, Clinical Medicine, and Chemistry. He wrote two standard textbooks and had an enormous influence on medicine in Britain. In Edinburgh fifty of his former students became Fellows, Honorary Fellows or Licenciates of the Royal College of Physicians, founded in 1681 (its premises now in Queen Street in a building designed in 1844 by Thomas Hamilton, the facade adorned with statues of Hippocrates, Aesculapius, and Hygeia).

The Royal Botanic Garden

Edinburgh's Royal Botanic Garden has its origins in the small plot of land on which Dr Robert Sibbald and Dr Andrew Balfour grew medicinal herbs and plants. In 1670 they planted a twelve-metre-square piece of ground near Holyrood Palace, this being the second oldest botanic garden in Britain (Oxford's having been founded in 1621). In 1667 the two doctors began a second Physic Garden beside Trinity Hospital (where the booking office of Waverley Station now stands). When **John Hope** (1725-1760) was appointed Regius Keeper of the Gardens in 1761, he united the Royal and the Town Gardens and

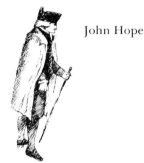

John Hope

transferred the whole collection of plants to a new site (near the present-day roundabout at the top of Leith Walk). Hope was the first to introduce the Linnaean system of botanical classification into Scotland.

One of Hope's students was **Archibald Menzies** (1754-1842). He was born in Aberfeldy in Perthshire and entered the Royal Botanic Garden intending to be a doctor of medicine. He sailed as surgeon-botanist on Captain George Vancouver's journey round the world in the *Discovery*, and whilst dining with the Spanish viceroy at St Jago in Chile, he noticed some unusual nuts which he put in his pocket and later planted in a glazed frame on board his ship. Five of the seeds took root on the voyage home: one flourished at Kew for almost a hundred years, and the other can still be seen as one of the Edinburgh Royal Botanic Garden's prize possessions, the Monkey Puzzle Tree.

The Garden was moved bit by bit from Leith Walk to its present site in Inverleith from 1820, using a transplanting machine invented by the Garden's William McNab. The operation finished three years later. One of the gardeners at this period was **John McLaren,** who was born in Stirling in 1846. He had acquired considerable experience as a gardener in a number of estates all over Scotland before coming to work in Edinburgh. In 1869 he sailed for California, where he continued to work as a gardener. In 1887 he was appointed Superintendent of Parks in San Francisco, having founded Golden Gate Park in 1870 at the age of twenty-four. McLaren wrote a book which had great influence on American gardens: *Gardens in California: Landscape and Flower* (1909). Before his death in 1943 he had gained the popular title of Grand Old Man of US horticulture.

In Edinburgh the growth of the Royal Botanic Garden led to an interest in botanical exploration: between 1904 and 1932 George Forrest made seven trips to Western China and brought back to Edinburgh 31,000 different species of flower. The Royal Botanic Garden also became a major centre for taxonomic research, cataloguing the plants of China and the Himalayas, such as rhododendrons and primulas.

Up to 1956 the posts of Regius Keeper of the Garden and that of Professor of Botany at the University had been held by the same person for almost 220 years. This arrangement was discontinued, and in due course the University Department of Botany began to transfer to King's Buildings. In 1984 the National Gallery of Modern Art, which had for a time been a unique feature of the Gardens, also moved to new premises at the former John Watson's School.

The Gregorys and the Monros

Edinburgh is famous for two extraordinary medical and scientific families. The first, **the Gregorys** had eight outstanding members: Dr John Gregory was Professor of the Practice of Physic at Edinburgh from 1766 to his death in 1773. His grandfather had been the first Professor of Mathematics at Edinburgh, a friend of Newton and the inventor of the reflecting telescope. His father was Professor of Medicine at King's College in Aberdeen. His son James held the Chair of Medicine at Edinburgh; his grandfather's brother David was a doctor and inventor whose son, also David, became Savilian

Professor of Astronomy at Oxford in 1962. A third David was Professor of Mathematics at St Andrews, and John's great-uncle, Charles, was also Professor of Mathematics at St Andrews. The family is probably best remembered by the patent medicine, Gregory's Mixture, made from magnesia, rhubarb and ginger, which has soothed generations.

The Monros had three luminaries: Alexander Primus, Secundus and Tertius, whose tenancy of the Chair of Anatomy at Edinburgh lasted from 1719 to 1846. Monro Primus was a brilliant anatomist who became Professor of Anatomy at the age of 21. It was he who established the reputation of the Edinburgh School of Medicine as a centre of international importance. It is reported that such was his pre-eminence that in the nineteenth century his grandson still dutifully read his grandfather's lecture notes *verbatim* to his long-suffering students, often with bizarre effect: 'When I was a student in Leiden in 1718 etc . . .'

James Lind, born in Edinburgh in 1716 and a graduate of the University of Edinburgh, joined the Navy as a surgeon's mate, serving on the Guinea coast, in the Mediterranean, in the West Indies and on the Channel fleets. During all his service he kept detailed records of the diseases he had to deal with. He was particularly concerned about the serious outbreaks of scurvy during Anson's circumnavigation of the globe in 1740-44. Three years later he conducted a controlled trial on board HMS *Salisbury* and was able to demonstrate conclusively the power of oranges and lemons to cure and prevent scurvy. His conclusions were published in his *Treatise on the Scurvy* (1753), one of the world's classic medical texts. Within two years of the general introduction of lemon juice in 1795, scurvy virtually disappeared from the Navy. Lind's hygienic measures also eliminated typhus, and his recommendation of a high-energy protein diet with a high-fibre content had a revolutionary effect on naval and military health and in due course on dietary practices in civilian life. Lind was also the first to identify the signs of hypothermia from exposure and immersion, and the first to warn of the fatal effect of administering alcohol in such cases. In addition it was Lind who advocated intermittent chest compression and mouth-to-mouth resuscitation for those rescued from the water. He died in 1794 at Gosport, having been head of a new 2,000-bed hospital at Haslar.

Andrew Duncan (1744-1828) was a St Andrews man who studied medicine at Edinburgh and then travelled to China as a Company surgeon with the East India ship *Asia*. In 1770 he settled in Edinburgh and started practice where he soon founded the Aesculapian Society for the promotion of business and good relations between physicians and surgeons. Part of the club's ritual was a toast recommending the club to the care and patronage of Apollo, Bacchus and Venus. In 1789 he became President of the Royal College of Physicians, and in the following year was given the Chair of Physiology at Edinburgh. He campaigned for the institution of a Chair in Medical Jurisprudence, to which his son was eventually appointed in 1807. It is believed that his plan for the establishment of a lunatic asylum in the City may have been inspired by the wretched death of the poet Robert Fergusson. In 1807 came the Royal Charter for an Asylum which he had been so instrumental in promoting. He is remembered by the Andrew Duncan Clinic at Morningside.

James Syme (1799-1870) was born in Edinburgh and attended the University as a medical student. He came to hold the Chair of Clinical Surgery and was known as the 'Napoleon of Surgery', the greatest surgeon of his day. Something of the

James Syme

atmosphere of medicine in his time can be found in the Edinburgh Hospital Reports of 1893 where one of Syme's house-surgeons describes his superior in 1853 as follows: 'His hospital life was on this wise – two clinical lectures a week, operations two days more (perhaps three), a ward visit when he wished to see any special cases; he spent generally about two hours in the hospital. Driving down in his big yellow chariot, with footman, hammercloth and C-springs, with two big, rather slow and stately white or grey horses, he used to expect his house surgeon to meet him at the door and move upstairs with him to his little room, where he at once took up his post with his back to the fire and his hands under the flaps of his swallow-tail coat. In this little room he generally held a small levée of assistants, old friends, practitioners wanting to arrange a consultation, old pupils home on leave; and before this select class he examined each new and interesting case that could walk in. The new cases had been collected, sifted and arranged by the dresser in a little room on the stair, irreverently known as 'the trap', and Mr Syme then and there made his diagnosis, which to us young ones seemed magical and intuitional, with certainly the minimum of examination or discussion. One was sent off with a promise of a letter to his doctor, another was fixed for tomorrow's lecture or next day's operation. Then, if it was lecture day, a tremendous rush of feet would be heard of the students racing to get to the nearest seats in the large operating theatre where the lecture was given. Chairs in the arena were kept for colleagues or distinguished strangers; first row for dressers on duty; operating table in centre; Mr Syme on a chair on left centre. In his later days it was a fine cushioned chair called the 'chair of clinical surgery'. (In 1854 it was a meek little wooden chair without arms.) House surgeon a little behind, but nearer the door; instrument clerk with his well-stocked table under the big window. He comes in, sits down with a little, a very little, bob of a bow, rubs his trousers legs with both hands open, and signs for the first case. The four dressers on duty, and in aprons, march in (if possible in step), carrying a rude wicker basket, in which, covered by a rough red blanket, the patient peers up at the great amphitheatre crammed with faces. A brief description, possibly the case had been described at a former lecture, and then the little, neat, round-shouldered, dapper man takes his knife and begins; and the merest tyro sees at once a master of his craft at work – no show, little elegance, but absolute certainty, ease and determination; rarely a word to an assistant – they should know their business if the unexpected happens; his plans may change in a moment, but probably only the house-surgeon finds it out; the patient is sent off, still anaesthetised, and then comes a brief commentary, short, sharp and decisive, worth taking verbatim if you can manage it; yet he has no notes, a very little veiled voice and no eloquence'.

Bathgate was the birthplace of **James Young Simpson,** but he began his studies at the University of Edinburgh at the tender age of fourteen in 1825. Fourteen years later he was

James Young Simpson

appointed Professor of Midwifery and in 1847 made the momentous discovery of the anaesthetic properties of chloroform, as James Miller, in his *Principles of Surgery* (1852), relates: 'Late one evening – it was the 4th of November, 1847 – on returning home after a weary day's labour, Dr Simpson, with his two friends and assistants, Drs Keith and Matthews Duncan, sat down to their somewhat hazardous work in Dr Simpson's dining-room. Having inhaled several substances, but without much effect, it occurred to Dr Simpson to try a ponderous material, which he had formerly set aside on a lumber-table, and which, on account of its great weight, he had hitherto regarded as of no likelihood whatever. That happened to be a small bottle of chloroform. It was searched for, and recovered from beneath a heap of waste paper. And, with each tumbler newly charged, the inhalers resumed their vocation. Immediately an unwonted hilarity seized the party; they became bright-eyed, very happy and very loquacious – expatiating on the delicious aroma of the new fluid. The conversation was of unusual intelligence and quite charmed the listeners – some ladies of the family and a naval officer, brother-in-law of Dr Simpson. But suddenly there was a talk of sounds being heard like those of a cotton-mill, louder and louder; a moment more, then all was quiet, and then – a crash. On awaking, Dr Simpson's first perception was mental – 'This is far stronger and better than ether', said he to himself. His second was to note that he was prostrate on the floor, and that among the friends about him there was both confusion and alarm. Hearing a noise, he turned round and saw Dr Duncan beneath a chair; his jaw dropped, his eyes staring, his head bent half under him; quite unconscious, and snoring in a most determined and alarming manner. More noise still, and much motion. And then his eyes overtook Dr Keith's feet and legs, making valorous efforts to overturn the supper-table, or more probably to annihilate everything that was on it . . .' Simpson inspired such confidence in his discovery that chloroform was administered to Queen Victoria in 1853 at the birth of Prince Leopold. Simpson founded the modern practice of gynaecology and even introduced sound as a method of diagnosis of uterine displacement and new methods for the dilation of the neck of the uterus. Having been made Physician to the Queen in Scotland in 1847, Simpson was created a baronet in 1866.

Henry D. Littlejohn (1826-1914) began his studies at Perth Academy, then transferred to the Royal High School in Edinburgh and finally to the University, where he graduated in

Sir Henry D. Littlejohn

1847. He lectured on medical jurisprudence from 1856 and established himself as a lecturer of great dramatic power, holding the interest of classes of over 250 students at a time. It was in the field of public health that he made his greatest contribution, from his appointment in 1862 as the first Medical Officer of Health in Edinburgh. The death-rate per thousand in many Edinburgh wards was high, due mainly to severe epidemics. In 1865 he produced a report on the sanitary condition of the city and urged the Town Council to obtain an Act from Parliament compelling the notification of every case of infectious disease. This was done in 1879, and Edinburgh became the first city in Britain to obtain such an Act. Typhus and smallpox virtually disappeared, and Littlejohn, through the demolition of insanitary parts of the city and the construction of new streets, eliminated these virulent diseases. In 1903 he helped to have a new City Hospital built, and his pioneering care for public health became a model of good practice.

Joseph Lister (1827-1921) was born in London and was a graduate of University College, London. He went to Edinburgh in 1853 to work as an assistant to Professor Syme, occasionally performing surgery in the Edinburgh Royal Infirmary. In the next year he was appointed a surgeon at the Royal Infirmary and a lecturer in surgery at the Royal College of Surgeons. His day was one of routine and hard work: 'I get up by alarm at 5.30 and light my fire . . . My coffee boils while I dress. I take it and a bit of bread, work for 3 or 4 hours and set off to my 10 o'clock lecture when my mind is brim full of it'. He was in the habit of visiting an Edinburgh slaughterhouse to conduct experiments in blood coagulation. He married Professor Syme's daughter in 1856 and then went to Glasgow as Regius Professor of Surgery. Nine years later he learned that Louis Pasteur had written a paper on fermentation and rotting, pointing out the role of dirt in breeding microbes. Some time after Lister heard that carbolic acid was being used in Carlisle for purifying sewage. Putting the two ideas together, he introduced carbolic spray for his serious operations, and it proved successful in reducing infection and fatalities. When Syme retired in 1869, Lister was chosen to take his place as Professor of Surgery. He built up an enormoius private practice in Edinburgh. When Queen Victoria had an abscess at Balmoral, she sent for Lister. In the interim he developed more effective dressings from muslin gauze he had found in an

Edinburgh drapery store. In due course Lister left Edinburgh for King's College Hospital, London where he took up the post of Professor of Surgery. By this time antisepsis was being used more and more widely. He was made a baronet in 1883 and retired ten years later. In 1898 he was presented with the Freedom of Edinburgh. He was the first doctor to be President of the Royal Society and the first to be given a peerage.

Sir Robert Philip (1857-1939) studied medicine in Edinburgh before going to Berlin to do postgraduate work under the famous Professor Koch, who had discovered the tubercule bacillus. In 1887 Philip founded the Victoria Dispensary for Consumption in Bank Street, Edinburgh, pioneering what came to be known as the Edinburgh System. He and his fellow-workers went out into the closes of Old Edinburgh, tackling the problem at source: the need was to go into the house from which each case sprang in order to trace the contacts. The established view had been that tuberculosis was hereditary but, he said, 'Mankind is responsible for tuberculosis. What an ignorant civilisation has introduced, an educated civilisation can remove'. He became President of the Royal College of Physicians and Professor of Tuberculosis at Edinburgh in 1917, and by the time of his death his anti-tuberculosis scheme had grown in Britain to 630 dispensaries with 35,000 beds. More than any other man Philip is credited with the conquest of what had been a killer disease.

Sir Arthur Conan Doyle (1859-1930) belonged to an Edinburgh family of Irish descent. He studied medicine at Edinburgh and distinguished himself in rugby, cricket (he played for the MCC), boxing, skiing and motor-racing. He is most

Sir Arthur Conan Doyle

famous for his novels based on the investigations of Sherlock Holmes, the detective who lived at 221b Baker Street with his assistant Dr Watson. Conan Doyle wrote four Sherlock Holmes novels and fifty-six stories, taking the characteristic method of investigation from Conan Doyle's experience of the well-known Edinburgh surgeon, Dr Joseph Bell, and perhaps also from the case-histories of the Edinburgh detective McLevy as re-worked by James McGovan in his popular novel *Brought to Bay*. Conan Doyle, who had been a field surgeon in the Boer War, was responsible for a number of technical innovations. He persuaded the Army to use tin helmets, and introduced inflatable lifejackets to the Navy. He was interested in the reform of the divorce and criminal law, and promoted women's rights and inter-racial marriage; he also advocated the construction of a Channel tunnel. In 1900 and 1906 he stood twice unsuccessfully for Parliament for Edinburgh and the Borders. He was a special adviser to the police in a number of criminal cases. In later life Conan Doyle became fascinated by the supernatural and lectured on the subject. In *The Silver Mirror* (1908) he describes a recurring vision of the murder of Mary Queen of Scots' secretary, the Italian musician, David Riccio: 'But I saw more to-night. The crouching man was as visible as the lady whose gown he clutched. He is a little swarthy fellow, with a black, pointed beard. He has a loose gown of damask trimmed with fur. The prevailing tints of his dress are red. What a fright the fellow is in, to be sure! He cowers and shivers and glares back over his shoulder. There is a small knife in his other hand, but he is far too tremulous and cowed to use it. Fierce faces, bearded and dark, shape themselves out of the mist. There is one terrible creature, a skeleton of a man, with hollow cheeks and eyes sunk in his head. He also has a knife in his hand. On the right of the woman stands a tall man, very young, with flaxen hair, his face sullen and dour. The beautiful woman looks up at him in appeal. So does the man on the ground. This youth seems to be the arbiter of their fate. The crouching man draws closer and hides himself in the woman's skirts. The tall youth bends and tries to drag her away from him. So much I saw last night before the mirror cleared. Shall I never know what it leads to and whence it comes? It is not a mere imagination, of that I am very sure. Somewhere, some time, this scene has been acted, and this old mirror has reflected it. But when – where?'

Ian Aird was born in Edinburgh in 1905 and received his education at George Watson's, where he had the distinction of being the only boy of his era to study Russian. In 1923 he entered the Edinburgh Medical School where he displayed an amazing photographic memory. Even as a house-surgeon he was nicknamed 'The Professor'. He visited the USA on a Rockefeller Scholarship, and also studied in Paris and Vienna. In 1939 he was put in charge of the Royal Edinburgh Hospital for Sick Children and then as a Lieutenant-Colonel with the Royal Army Medical Corps was twice mentioned in dispatches. In one famous incident he saved the life of a patient on whom he was carrying out an abdominal operation by leaning over him when a bomb dropped on the hospital. After the War he was a surgeon at the Emergency Medical Service Hospital in Gogarburn and in 1946 became Professor of Surgery at the University of London and Director of the Surgical Unit at the London Post-Graduate Medical School. Professor Aird's original contribution to surgery was his discovery of the relation of blood-groups to disease. He also led the team which developed the first British pump oxygenator and the first British team to transplant a kidney from a donor to a recipient who were not twins. He was well known for his work with conjugated twins. In 1953 he separated the first Siamese twins to be so operated on in the UK and repeated the operation in 1962. He also carried out research into hole-in-the-heart operations. Professor Aird was a unique combination of a sawbones and a pedagogue. When asked what had led him to take up medicine, he replied that 'In the playground of the old school you could look up to the windows of the operating room in the Infirmary and see, through a thick glaze, the shadowy white figures of the theatre staff shrouded in mystery and power, and a glimmer of the operating lamp'.

The contribution of women to the practice of medicine in Edinburgh has been of great significance; but it was not always so: at first women were barred from studying medicine. **James Miranda Stuart Barry** was an extraordinary example of the

Dr. James Miranda Barry

persistence of some women in seeking out a medical qualifica-
tion in spite of the official exclusion of women from schools of
medicine. Barry (1799-1865) began to study medicine at
Edinburgh at the age of ten. A contemporary description
records that she was very slightly built and had short reddish
hair; her nose was long and she had large eyes. Yet no one
suspected she was a woman. She served forty-six years in the
armed forces as a medical officer in Malta and the West Indies
where she had yellow fever. The doctor attending her
discovered the truth of her real sex but was sworn to secrecy.
In Canada she rose to become Inspector-General of Military
Hospitals. When she dies, the woman who was laying out her
body rushed out of the room in consternation, crying: 'What
do you mean by calling me to lay out a general, and the corpse
is a woman's and one who has borne a child'.

Sophia Jex-Blake adopted a more frontal attack on that
bastion of male privilege, as it was at the time, the medical
profession. In 1869, at the age of twenty-nine, she approached

Dr. Sophia Jex-Blake

the Faculty of Medicine at Edinburgh with a request to study
medicine, having already completed two years of a medical
course in the United States. When they got wind of her
application, the medical students staged a riot to keep women

from their classes at the Surgeons' Hall. In 1872 a judgement was given in favour of seven female applicants to the Medical Faculty which had refused to award graduate degrees to women. Unfortunately this judgement was reversed by the Court of Session, and it took a Parliamentary Bill in the following year to clear the way for the female sex in the medical profession. In the next few years Dr Jex-Blake graduated MD at Berne in Switzerland and founded the London School of Medicine for Women. She set up the first dispensary for women and children at 4 Manor Place in Edinburgh, where she worked for twenty-one years as a general practitioner. In 1886 she became Dean of the Women's Medical College in Surgeons' Square and helped to found the Edinburgh Hospital for Women and Children (the Bruntsfield). She was described as 'a stout and compelling figure' with 'big brown eyes' and was frequently to be seen around the City wearing a close-fitting bonnet and travelling in a brougham pulled by a small and scraggy horse.

Dr Elsie Inglis, the Edinburgh surgeon, died in 1917 at the age of 53, having sailed into Newcastle after service with the Scottish Women's Hospitals field unit on the Serbian Front.

Dr Elsie Inglis

During her first tour in Serbia she was operating on the wounded for fifty-eight hours out of sixty-three. She helped Serbian doctors combating typhus and typhoid fever; many doctors died. In her second spell of duty in Serbia she was captured by the Austro-Hungarian army and then repatriated. After the war the Serbs built a monument to Dr Inglis and her staff, and the Yugoslav administration awarded her their highest honour (never before awarded to a woman), the Order of the White Eagle, to which was added 'the swords' after her death. The Russians, whose troops she had also treated, gave her the St George Medal for bravery, and the French decorated her for valour.

She had trained at Edinburgh University, where she was one of the first women medical students, but had become so dissatisfied with the lack of proper tuition for women that she set up her own medical school for women in 1892. In 1902 she opened a hospice for mothers and children from the slum areas of Edinburgh which developed into the Elsie Inglis Memorial Hospital after her death in 1917. She also founded the Scottish Women's Suffragette Federation.

In more recent times **Dr Winifred Rushforth** was prominent as a pioneer psychoanalyst. She was born in 1885 in West Lothian at a time when Freud was working in Paris. After Edinburgh Ladies' College and the University she went to India as a medical missionary in 1909 for five years. On her return she began practice in Mid Calder and a year later returned to India, becoming president of the YMCA of all India, Burma and Ceylon. On her return to Britain in 1929 Dr Rushforth trained as a psychoanalyst at the Tavistock Clinic in London and began private practice as a psychotherapist in Edinburgh in 1932. In 1940 she founded the renowned Davidson Clinic devoted to group therapy and child psychology. In 1973 the Clinic closed but Dr Rushforth continued her work through the Sempervivum Trust, the Salisbury Centre and the Wellspring Clinic. Dr Rushforth, who died in 1983, gained the Rosicrucian Humanitarian Award in 1980 and was awarded the OBE.

Veterinary medicine has been practiced in Edinburgh for over one hundred and sixty years. At first the treatment of animals was carried out by cow-leaches and farriers. During the early part of the eighteenth century numerous animal plagues made veterinary medicine a pressing problem. Edinburgh was relatively slow to follow the lead of France and London in establishing schools of veterinary medicine, but in 1823 **William Dick,** with £50 from the Highland Society, began to give a course of lectures in veterinary science. Dick (1793-1866) was a farrier, and the son of a farrier, who had studied at the

London Veterinary College. He was appointed Lecturer in Veterinary Surgery based at his father's forge in what is now the Bus Station in St Andrew Square. Dick built up the premises and on his death made the Town Council his Trustees to carry on the development of the College.

D

The Festival

Although Lord Cockburn tells us that the first Edinburgh Music Festival took place as early as 1815 in the Parliament House, it was not until 1944, at the height of the Second World War, that a vision of an International Festival of Music, Drama and the Visual Arts took shape in a restaurant in Hanover Square, London, during the course of a conversation between Rudolf Bing and H. Harvey Wood, who as representative of the British Council was to have a decisive influence on the development of the Edinburgh Festival, of which Rudolf Bing was to become first Director.

The high ideals of reconciliation and regeneration which the Edinburgh International Festival embodied were seen in the deeply felt reunion in Edinburgh between Bruno Walter (who was Jewish) and his beloved Vienna Philharmonic Orchestra, a reunion which took place in their first public concert together since the war. That first Festival of 1947 was also host to an outstanding quartet: Arthur Schnabel (piano), Pierre Fournier (cello), Joseph Szigeti (violin), and William Primrose (viola). There was a magnificent performance in 1948 of Bach's *B Minor Mass* with Kathleen Ferrier (who had sung Mahler's *Song of the Earth* the previous year), Isobel Baillie and Owen Brannigan.

In 1950 the Tattoo became a part of the official Festival; Sir John Barbirolli made one of his eleven Festival appearances, as did Sir Thomas Beecham (who was to make three visits to the Festival), conducting Handel's *Music for the Royal Fireworks* on the Castle Esplanade. Two conductors made their debuts: Leonard Bernstein and Guido Cantelli (who was tragically to be killed in a plane crash). A gripping performance of Verdi's *Requiem* came in 1951 with the New York Philharmonic Orchestra conducted by Victor de Sabata with the Chorus of La Scala. In 1952 the Hamburg State Opera came with six German operas, while John Cranko's ballet, *Pineapple Poll*, and Stavinsky's *The Rake's Progress* were offered by Sadler's Wells

Ballet Company. The exhibition entitled *Homage to Diaghilev* in 1954 was followed in 1956 by Kenneth Macmillan's *Noctambles*, again danced by Sadler's Wells. In the same year Sir Arthur Galina Vishnevskaya, Peter Pears, Dietrich Fischer-Dieskau and the Edinburgh Festival Chorus with Giulini as conductor.

La Piccola Scala played Bellini's *La Sonnambula* in the King's Theatre in 1957 with Maria Callas in the role of Amina. Shortly afterwards she caused a storm by cancelling her engagements, failing to show up at a press conference and leaving Edinburgh complaining of exhaustion. That year also saw Ram Gopal with his Indian Ballet bring a new dimension to the Festival.

In 1960 the first Russian orchestra performed: the Leningrad Symphony. It was also the year of the birth of the Scottish Festival Chorus (the predecessor of the Edinburgh Festival Chorus). Joan Sutherland sang *Lucia di Lammermoor* with the Covent Garden Company in 1961 and the incredible *The Four Sons of Aymon* astonished audiences at Murrayfield ice rink in the 1962 production by the Ballet du Vingtième Siècle of Brussels. Martha Graham brought her dance company in 1963 and gave a memorable version of *Clytemnestra*. Julian Bream performed with his Dowland Consort, Larry Adler and Yehudi Menuhin appeared together, and Herrick Bunney (conductor of the Edinburgh Choral Union, Master of Music at St Giles and conductor of the University Singers) demonstrated his experience and artistry. Mahler's Eighth Symphony in the Usher Hall was a triumph. It was in 1967 that Scottish Opera, the brainchild of Sir Alexander Gibson, made its first appearance along with the newly formed Scottish Opera Chorus.

Sir Alexander Gibson

Under their dynamic chorusmaster, Arthur Oldham (once a pupil of Britten and then choirmaster at St Mary's Roman Catholic Cathedral) the Opera Chorus gave an account of Stravinsky's *Rake's Progress*.

The Alvin Ailey Company danced *Knoxville: Summer 1915* in the Church Hill Theatre in 1968, Scottish Opera performed Britten's *Peter Grimes,* and Yehudi Menuhin made a moving address to the audience before playing the Beethoven Violin Concerto (the Russians had just invaded Czechoslovakia). Britten's *Voices for Today* was also performed to celebrate the twentieth anniversary of the United Nations Organisation (with words by Sophocles, Blake, Lao Tzu, Shelley and the Russian Yevtushenko). It was Britten's *War Requiem,* however, which had the greatest poignancy, sung by the Russian soprano Galina Vishnevskaya, Peter Pears, Dietrich Fischer-Dieskau and the Edinburgh Festival Chorus with Guilini as conductor.

Tito Gobbi sang and directed one of his favourite operas, Puccini's *Gianni Schicci,* in 1969, and the great Scottish bass, David Ward, sang Wotan in Scottish Opera's 1971 production of Wagner's *Die Walküre.* In the next year Scottish Opera put on Berlioz' gigantic work, *The Trojans,* with Janet Baker as Dido, and the Ensemble National de Senegal gave thrills of a very different kind in their vigorous folk dances to the rhythm of the drums.

Verdi's *Requiem,* with Luciano Pavarotti, Raffaele Arie, Fiorenza Cossotto and Martina Arroyo and the Edinburgh Festival Chorus, was the highlight of the 1974 Festival, but there were other very good things such as Colin McLean's and Reginald-Barrett-Ayres' *Hugh Miller* (an opera), the Kathakali Dance Troupe, Cleo Laine and Johnny Dankworth, the King's Singers, and works by Edinburgh composer Thea Musgrave. Geraint Evans played Leporello in a production of Mozart's *Marriage of Figaro* by Peter Ustinov, and the Royal Stockholm Opera (the company for which Edinburgh's greatest tenor, Joseph Hislop, sang) also appeared.

Geraint Evans produced Mozart's *Marriage of Figaro* in 1975 and played Leporello to the Count of Dietrich Fischer-Dieskau and the Countess of Teresa Berganza. Robin Orr's *Weir of Hermiston,* an opera based on Robert Louis Stevenson's unfinished story, was a long-awaited contribution from a Scottish composer of opera (the libretto was by Bill Bryden). Wieland Wagner produced *Lulu* and *Salome* for the Deutsche Oper Berlin, giving two contrasting portraits of two fascinating women, and Galina Vishnevskaya and the Edinburgh Festival

Chorus gave a thrilling interpretation of Prokofiev's *Alexander Nevsky* Cantata. Among the conductors were Bernstein, Pierre Boulez, Giulini, Zubin Mehta and Claudio Abbado. The cellist Rostropovich played, and Rudolf Nureyev danced with the Royal Ballet. On the Fringe Neil Innes and Roger McGough appeared in *G.R.I.M.M.S.*, a musical spectacular.

A most powerful team of soloists sang Verdi's *Macbeth* at the 1976 Festival for Scottish Opera: Norman Bailey in the title role, David Ward as Banquo and Galina Vishnevskaya as Lady Macbeth. She was more fortunate than her predecessor in that role in the 1947 Festival, when Margherita Grandi was twice poised to launch into the sleep-walking scene when the violins wailed to a halt as the lights failed. *Parsifal* came with the Deutsche Oper Am Rhein, who also presented Schönberg's *Moses und Aron*. Jean-Pierre Ponnelle, the most talented of modern opera producers, was responsible for a sparkling version of Rossini's *L'Italiana in Algeri,* while the Monteverdi Choir gave Handel's *Jephtha.*

Beethoven's *Missa Solemnis* was given a majestic performance with the Edinburgh Festival Chorus under Giulini, and Radu Lupu delighted his audience with Beethoven's Piano Concerto No 1 in C Major. Elizabeth Schwarzkopf (whose career had begun in the same year as the first Edinburgh Festival) sang lieder in the Usher Hall, and James Galway entertained in the Freemasons' Hall.

Placido Domingo was in Edinburgh in the following year to sing in *Carmen* with Teresa Berganza and Mirella Freni, and there was the world premiere of Thea Musgrave's opera, *Mary Queen of Scots.* Scottish Ballet danced with their guests Natalia Makarova and Fernando Bujones. In marvellous unison Janet Baker, Thomas Allen and the Edinburgh Festival Chorus with the Scottish National Orchestra performed Britten's *Sinfonia da Requiem* and Arthur Oldham's (the chorusmaster of the EFC) *Psalms of War.* Giulini conducted Mozart's *Requiem*; Jessye Norman and Herman Prey sang, and James Galway returned to bewitch with his flute. Finally those distinguished artists with a long connection with Edinburgh, Louis Kentner and Yehudi Menuhin, played three Beethoven sonatas. Late-night there was a Paul Tortelier recital and the guitar of Paco Peña, as well as Mike Martin in R.L. Stevenson's *Penny Whistles.*

A new note struck in 1978 with *Pelléas et Mélisande* by Debussy, staged by Scottish Opera, and two Monteverdi operas beautifully produced by Zürich Opera. Jessye Norman and Stuart Burrows sang Berlioz' *Damnation of Faust* under Daniel Barenboim, Isaac Stern played Sibelius' Violin Concerto, and the Scottish National Orchestra gave a stirring account of Janacek's *Glagolithic Mass*. There was a Jazz Festival on the Fringe and a Rock Festival, but the most moving musical moment was *A Festival Garland,* a tribute to the departing Director of the Festival, Peter Diamand, given by Teresa Berganza, Dietrich Fischer-Dieskau, Jessye Norman, Isaac Stern, Daniel Barenboim and Sir Alexander Gibson with the Edinburgh Festival Chorus.

A new concert hall opened in 1979, the lovingly restored Queen's Hall. It opened with a concert under the direction of Edinburgh conductor Roderick Brydon, Artistic Director of the Scottish Chamber Orchestra. In another new venue, a tent in the Meadows, the National Ballet of Cuba and Sadlers Wells Royal Ballet danced, the latter especially memorably with *Elite Syncopations* (music by Scott Joplin, costumes by Spurling and choreography by Kenneth MacMillan). There was *Music from China* given by the Central Conservatory of Music, Peking, and Scottish Opera staged Rimsky-Korsakov's *The Golden Cockerel* and Tchaikovsky's *Eugene Onegin*.

From Orkney came Peter Maxwell Davies with his Fires of London in 1980. André Previn, Ravi Shankar with his sitar, and the Amadeus Quartet gave concerts. Three of the world's finest pianists played a rich variety of works: Claudio Arrau, Emile Gilels and Jorge Bolet. Elizabeth Schwarzkopf gave master-classes, and Oscar Peterson played jazz at a late-night show. On the Fringe there were folk groups such as Silly Wizard and Boys of the Lough (both with close links with Edinburgh) and Mike Maran with Robert Burns' *The Jolly Beggars*. In the closing concert (Berlioz' *Te Deum*) the organist Gillian Weir played the organ of St Mary's Palmerston Place, and was linked by TV monitors to the conductor, Claudio Abbado, in the Usher Hall.

Scottish Opera brought a well-loved work to the 1981 Festival in *The Beggar's Opera*, while Cologne Opera paid tribute to Thea Musgrave by bringing her *The Voice of Ariadne*. The

Julian Bream Lute Consort and the Consort of Musicke under Anthoney Rooley provided contrasting kinds of early music, while Yehudi Menuhin and Vladimir Ashkenazy gave powerful accounts of music from later periods. The King's Singers added a mixture of liturgical composition and swing.

The Dresden State Opera and La Piccola Scala, Milan delighted audiences in 1982, the first with Richard Strauss's *Ariadne auf Naxos* and *Il Seraglio*, and the second with a Handel and a Rossini opera. Welsh National Opera also brought *Tamburlaine* by Handel, and Scottish Opera performed *Manon Lescaut* by Puccini. In the magnificent setting of St Mary's Cathedral, Palmerston Place Britten's *Noye's Fludde* was given, sung by a choir of Edinburgh schoolchildren, with Bill McCue and Linda Ormiston from Scottish Opera. Claudio Abbado conducted Verdi's *Requiem* with José Carreras, Jessye Norman, Margaret Price and Ruggiero Raimondi. The Monteverdi Choir under John Eliot Gardner, with Patrizia Kwella as soloist, reminded audiences of the texture and line of early music; Jorge Bolet and Radu Lupu showed their artistry on the piano keyboard, as did Katia and Marielle Labeque playing together on two pianos. The New Music Group of Scotland under Edward Harper performed a variety of contemporary Scottish music. Julian Bream returned to Edinburgh, and Kyung Wha Chung played the violin. Finally, there were recitals from Elizabeth Söderström, Luigi Alva, and Hermann Prey, and the First Edinburgh International Harpsichord Competition which tied in well with the fine collection of early keyboard instruments housed in St Cecilia's Hall in the Cowgate. In the Assembly Rooms, which housed four theatres, fifty-three companies and seven hundred performers, the Flying Pickets performed to an enthusiastic following. They were one of the discoveries of the Festival, and their success led to even greater success in the pop music charts.

Among the many riches of the 1983 Festival were the Czech Philharmonic Orchestra, the City of Birmingham Symphony Orchestra and the Concertgebouw from Amsterdam. The Fireworks Concert was an overwhelming experience and a vast popular success. Scottish Opera brought their production of Britten's *Death in Venice* as their contribution to the Festival theme of *Vienna 1900*. Hamburg State Opera presented Zemlinsky, and the Opera Theatre of St Louis *Fennimore and Gerda* by Delius and *The Postman Always Rings Twice* by Colin Graham. The Man and Music programme had a variety of ethnic folk groups performing all over the City: a West Indian Steel Band; Folk Music from Rajasthan; Street Musicians from Mexico; the Praise Singers from the Ivory Coast and Folk Musicians from Morocco. Late-night there were the Gamelan Orchestra and Dancers from Bali. The great Wagnerian bass-baritone Hans Hotter gave master classes in the Reid School of Music, and John L. Paterson (who had recently been chosen as consultant designer for the new Museum of Theatre at Covent Garden) had arranged *From Sunrise to Sunset: The Ring Cycle,* at the Royal Botanic Garden to celebrate the centenary of Wàgner's death. The audience sat in a golden ring of seating with a mirrored pyramid at the centre, listening to the sweep of Wagner's great Ring Cycle. The Flying Pickets returned again to Edinburgh and Pookiesnackenburger, a group of buskers, came too as well as the Children's Music Theatre and Dick Gaughan for the Folk Festival.

Cleo Laine and Johnny Dankworth starred in 1984, also John Williams playing guitar. That favourite of Festival audiences, Jessye Norman, joined Pierre Boulez and the BBC Symphony Orchestra to sing *Trois Ballades de François Villon.* The composer, Hans Werner Henze, conducted the Scottish Chamber Orchestra, while Yo Yo Ma played Dvorjak's Cello Concerto with the Boston Symphony Orchestra under Seiji Ozawa. Fischer-Diskau returned to sing with the Royal Philharmonic Orchestra as well as giving a number of recitals. In the Queen's Hall the Modern Jazz Quartet gave polished and witty performances, and Ronnie Scott was a late deputy for the indisposed Zoot Sims. Humphrey Lyttleton brought his Jazz Band to the Jazz Festival, while Alexei Sayle and Marika Rivera gave contrasting but riveting performances in their one-man shows. Composer Gian Carlo Menotti, with a home near Edinburgh nowadays, supervised the production of two of his operas, *The Medium* and *The Telephone,* and Scottish Opera performed their enchanting period piece, *Orion.* The Paris Opera Ballet performed a delightful *Commedia dell'Arte,* and the Komische Oper, Berlin gave *Swan Lake.* In complete contrast were the Royal Thai Orchestra and Dancers. A welcome return to Edinburgh was made by Edinburgh dancer, Alex Bennet (formerly of the Ballet Rambert and the Royal Ballet) with his Scottish American Ballet, which he founded in 1969 at Chattanooga in Tennessee, where Bennet now lives.

Drama in the first Edinburgh International Festival came in the shape of the Old Vic on the one hand, and Jean-Louis Barrault on the other. Fringe theatre began in that year (1947) with the Marxist Company's production of Gorky's *The Lower Depths*, while John Grierson, now Director of Mass Communication at UNESCO in Paris, opened the first International Film Festival ever held in the United Kingdom (although it did not receive official recognition till 1949). *Ane Satire of the Thrie Estaits* was the glory of the 1948 Festival. Its author, Sir David Lindsay, had been in charge of plays and masques at the court of James V; his play was an attack on the corruption of society, full of coarse humour and biting wit as well as spectacle. In Robert Kemp's adaptation (and Sir Tyrone Guthrie's production) the play was an overwhelming success, and its setting, the Assembly Hall (home of the General Assembly of the Church of Scotland, often said to be the Parliament of Scotland), gave the production added universality and force.

In the following year Allan Ramsay's *The Gentle Shepherd* was given as a late-night entertainment in the Royal High School; Irene Worth and Alec Guinness appeared in T. S. Eliot's *The Cocktail Party*, while, on the Fringe, Joan Littlewood's Theatre Workshop generated life, humour and social comment. John Gielgud and Flora Robson came in 1951 in Peter Brook's version of Shakespeares *A Winter's Tale;* and the Fringe saw the birth of the Edinburgh People's Festival guided and encouraged by Norman and Janey Buchan and Jack Kane. Unhappily the EPF was to last only two more years.

Richard Burton played Hamlet to Claire Bloom's Ophelia on the Assembly Hall stage in 1953, an elemental contrast between masculine and feminine. The Fringe grew by leaps and bounds: a number of groups came to Edinburgh, living and working together to create considerable onstage rapport. Risks were being taken: Douglas Young's *The Puddocks* (Aristophanes' *The Frogs*, in Scots) was produced in the neglected Braidburn Outdoor Theatre.

It was the turn of the Comédie Française in 1954. They performed an enchanting *Le Bourgeois Gentilhomme* by Molière, with music by Lully sung by a Festival Chorus directed by Richard Telfer (former doyen of Edinburgh cinema organists, teacher of music, and impresario), with dancers trained by Marjory Middleton of the Scottish Ballet School.

Robert Burns stepped onto the scene in 1955 in the person of Tom Fleming, who played him in Robert Kemp's *The Other Dear Charmer*, with Lennox Milne as Miss Nimmo. Moira Shearer and Robert Helpmann performed an enchanting *Midsummer Night's Dream* at the Empire Theatre (with Stanley Holloway as Bottom), and *Macbeth* was staged at the Assembly Hall. On the Fringe, Ned Sherrin appeared as a writer of late-night revue.

Onto the Assembly Hall stage in 1956 strode Christopher Plummer as *Henry V* in a riotously colourful production full of movement and declamation. He was part of Tyrone Guthrie's Stratford Ontario Festival Company which Guthrie worked with in Canada on an apron stage similar in many respects to the apron stage of the Edinburgh Assembly Hall. Sir Donald Wolfit had considerable success on the Fringe with *The Strong are Lonely*, in which he starred.

The Gateway Company from Edinburgh staged *The Flouers o'Edinburgh* by Robert McLellan in 1957, with Lennox Milne, Tom Fleming, Walter Carr, Bryden Murdoch and Duncan Macrae. Barbara Jefford, Judi Dench and Joss Ackland were the leading actors in the Old Vic's production of *Twelfth Night* in 1958 on the Assembly Hall apron, where, two years later, Iain Cuthbertson generated the kind of enthusiasm normally reserved for the football terraces, in Sydney Goodsir Smith's blank-verse epic, *The Wallace*. In similarly heroic vein was Roger Planchon's *Les Trois Mousquetaires*, which introduced sleight of hand and infectious cameraderie into Dumas' swash-buckling tale. And 1960 marked the appearance of *Beyond the Fringe*, the beginning of a period of energetic satire, with Jonathan Miller, Alan Bennett, Dudley Moore and Peter Cooke. Tom Courtenay, by contrast, as Konstantin, in Chekhov's *The Seagull*, gave a moving and restrained perform-ance.

Duncan Macrae had a personal triumph in *Let Wives Tak Tent*

Iain Cuthbertson as William Wallace

(a Scots version of Molière's *L'Ecole des Femmes*) in 1961, while, in the Oxford Review, John Wells, William Rushton and Richard Ingrams created theatrical subversion. In the following year it was the turn of Tim Brooke-Taylor and John Cleese in the Cambridge Footlights Revue, while Trevor Nunn directed Ibsen's *Brand*. In the official Festival there was *The Doctor and the Devils* (a play by Dylan Thomas on the Scottish 'Resurrectionists' – or grave-robbers), with Leonard Maguire as Dr Knox, while at the Gateway a youthful John Cairney acted the part of Boswell in *Young Auchinleck* with considerable aplomb.

That multi-levelled catacomb in Victoria Street, the jazz and folk club known as The Place, also began in 1962 as a venue for Fringe music-making. That year you could have seen artists such as Chris Barber or Memphis Slim blow their hearts out or tinkle the ivories. John Calder organised an International Writers' Conference, partly in honour of Hugh McDiarmid, whose seventieth birthday it was. Councillors and headlines screamed over the 1963 International Drama Conference (also organised by John Calder). It was chaired by Kenneth Tynan, and writers attending included Arthur Adamov, Arnold Wesker, Max Frisch and Edward Albee. The trouble came about when a naked girl was transported in a wheelbarrow across the balcony of the McEwan Hall in full view of the Conference. This was a fairly stagey version of what was to be no more than a passing phenomenon in public life: the 'happening'. Worse was to come some years later with the prospect of James Joyce's

Ulysses being shown in Edinburgh cinemas. Possibly no more, though, than the outcry that had greeted Home's *Douglas* many years before.

The Traverse Theatre had established itself as an integral part of the Festival Fringe. From its beginnings, with the 1960 production by the Sceptics of Hume's *First Dialogue Concerning Natural Religion* at the Paperback Bookshop in Charles Street, it had progressed under the tutelage of Jim Haynes (the Bookshop's proprietor, an ex-US airman and Edinburgh University graduate) to *David Hume on God and Evil* (1961) over claret

Jim Haynes

followed by audience discussion, then to Fionn MacColla's *The Curetes* (1962) in the former brothel known as Kelly's Paradise, which Haynes had converted into a sixty-seat theatre made up of two facing tiers separated by an acting area which *traversed* them. The next year saw the premiere of Stanley Eveling's *The Balachites*, while all along Richard Demarco brought his own dynamism to the committee of management.

Joan Littlewood arrived in Edinburgh in 1964 with her production of Shakespeare's *Henry IV*. She floated the idea of using the Caley Station site as a People's Palace (this in the context of the continuing saga over Edinburgh's phantom Opera House). Russell Hunter, later to be a regular resident in Edinburgh, appeared as Costard in the Bristol Old Vic's *Love's Labour's Lost*, and Marlene Dietrich sang her siren songs late-night at the Lyceum. On the Fringe there were now some thirty-two groups performing over a much wider area of the City. There were the Cambridge Footlights, with Richard Eyre, Eric Idle and Graeme Garden, while their Oxford counterparts sported Terry Jones and Michael Palin (in all, three members of the Monty Python team and one Goodie).

Theatre Workshop was born in 1965, designed to provide activity in arts and drama for children. By 1970 Reg Bolton had taken over from Ros Clark and Katherine Robin, and in 1977 the Workshop had its own permanent home in Stockbridge, where it organised an all-the-year-round programme of in-house activities and outreach. Reg Bolton's own speciality was the art of the clown, and the skills associated with clowns (walking on stilts, juggling) were now handed on to generations of young people in Edinburgh.

Jim Haynes resigned from the Traverse in 1966, and Richard Demarco left as Traverse Gallery Director. On the official Festival the Piraikon Theatre from Athens brought Sophocles' *Electra* and Euripides' *Medea*. Duncan Macrae made his last Festival appearance in Douglas Young's adaptation of Aristophanes's *The Birds* (directed by Tom Fleming), and a new playwright emerged at the Cranston Street Hall: Tom Stoppard with his *Rosencrantz and Guildenstern Are Dead*.

For all its upheavals, the Traverse continued to be in the vanguard of theatrical experiment. Between 1964 and 1966, for example, the Traverse had thirty-eight World or British premieres out of fifty-one plays. Calum Mill took over from Jim Haynes in 1964. Frank Dunlop brought *The Tricks of Scapin* to the Assembly Hall in 1967; La Mama Troupe from New York put on *Tom Paine* at the Traverse, and in Cambridge University Theatre Company's production of *Love's Labour's Lost* another rising star war born: Julie Covington, who also sang in late-night revue.

Leonard Rossiter played Hitler in Arturo Ui in 1968, the Abbey Theatre gave *The Playboy of the Western World*, and Clive James refined his invective at the Traverse, where in 1969 it was the turn of the Scottish mime Lindsay Kemp with the Music of the Incredible String Band. On the Assembly Hall apron Ian McKellen, a former member of the Cambridge University Marlowe Society, revealed the range of his abilities by acting the leading roles in Shakespeare's *Richard II* and Marlowe's *Edward II*.

The Teatro Libero of Rome exploded onto the 1970 Festival with a larger-than-life version of Ariosto's *Orlando Furioso* in which mechanical monsters and declaiming horsemen milled around the floor of the Haymarket ice-rink. Timothy West with the Prospect Theatre Company impersonated Dr Johnson, while Calum Mill portrayed the nineteenth-century Edinburgh actor, Charles Mackay, and John McGrath's play *Random Happenings in the Hebrides* was performed.

McGrath returned in 1971 with his newly formed 7:84 Theatre Company (the title referring to the fact that in Scotland seven percent of the population own eighty-four percent of the land). The Pool Lunch Hour Theatre Club began, and McGrath and Billy Connolly put on *The Great Northern Welly Boot Show* in the Waverley Market.

Edward Fox played Antipholous of Edinburgh in Frank Dunlop's production of *A Comedy of Errors,* while Tom Fleming, Lennox Milne and Richard Todd paid a bicentenary tribute to Sir Walter Scott in the form of the entertainment *A Singular Grace.* Timothy West returned to play *King Lear. A Comedy of Errors* came back in 1972 to the Haymarket ice-rink; along with *Bible One* (a double bill of the Genesis Creation Story from the Wakefield Mystery Cycle and *Joseph and his Amazing Technicolour Dreamcoat*). The Hosho Noh Company from Tokyo added a new dimension, while the Glasgow Citizens created carnage at the Assembly Hall in Marlowe's *Tamburlaine the Great.* In a class of his own was Russell Hunter who had given a celebration of Lord Cockburn in *Cocky* in the 1970 Festival Fringe. He followed this with *Jock* (1972) and *Knox* (1974), both one-man shows and both by W. Gordon Smith, exploring the world of the Scottish Soldier and the Scottish Reformer respectively. The Actors Company had been born in the 1972 Festival with their motto 'All for one, one for all' and their spirit of co-operative creation. In 1973 they staged Chekhov's *The Wood Demon* and *Knots,* based on the book of the same name by the Scottish-trained psychiatrist, R. D. Laing.

Drama in the Festival of 1974 was notable for the *Oedipus* of the Abbey Theatre, Dublin and a colourful phantasmagoria *The Fantastical Feats of Finn MacCool,* with designs by painter/ playwright John Byrne. Two other aspects of Edinburgh's literary history were examined in *Carlyle and Jane,* in which Edith McArthur and Tom Fleming explored the story of the Carlyles, and *Robert Fergusson* (a celebration of the Edinburgh poet) with Clifford Hughes and James Cairncross.

The Edinburgh theme was continued in 1975 with *Mr*

Topham's Diary in which the writings of a well-known visitor to the City were brought to life by the versatile Timothy West. *Scottish Love Poems* were read by Ludovic Kennedy and his wife Moira Shearer (in a selection by Antonia Fraser), and Lennox Milne, James Cairncross and John Westbrook entertained with *King James VI and I.*

Edinburgh Academical Paul Jones starred in *Pilgrim,* given by the Prospect Theatre Company in the Assembly Hall (based on Bunyan's *Pilgrim's Progress*), while the perennially pawky Russell Hunter added colour to *The North British Working Man's Guide to the Arts.* Ray Bradbury's *Martian Chronicles* brought mystery and surrealism in the hands of the University of Southern California.

More contrasts came in 1976: Princess Grace of Monaco, with Richard Kiley and Richard Pasco, presented *An American Heritage,* while Ian McKellen in *Words, Words, Words* showed that communication can exist in the strangest places (such as a telephone directory). Russell Hunter again delighted as Meercraft in Edinburgh visitor Ben Jonson's *The Devil is an Asse,* and the National Puppet Theatre of Japan showed a new aspect of theatre to Western audiences, *Bunraku.* Other rare and original fare came from Quentin Crisp in his *A Cure for Freedom;* and Carlo and Alberto Colombaion showed the traditional artistry of *The Clowns.* Donald Campbell's play, *The Jesuit,* and Leonard Maguire, in his *The Wasting of Dunbar,* again demonstrated that Scottish history and literature are a rich source of inspiration.

Yet another Edinburgh Academical, the newscaster and author, Gordon Honeycombe, adapted Milton's *Paradise Lost* for the 1977 Festival, with Timothy West as Milton and Alec McCowen as Satan. The Eve was Barbara Jefford whom Edinburgh had seen as Viola in the Old Vic's 1958 Festival production of *Twelfth Night.* Rex Harrison read some of George Bernard Shaw's theatre criticism (Shaw had been to Edinburgh with a company early in his career), and another star of the silver screen, the Greek actress and politician, Melina Mercouri, appeared as *Medea* in the State Theatre of Northern Greece's production of Euripides's play. It was the year of the Prospect Theatre Company, however, with two versions of the Anthony and Cleopatra story – Shakespeare's and Dryden's – *War Music* (adapted from the *Iliad* of Homer by Chris Logue), and *Hamlet* with Derek Jacobi. On the Fringe The Iron Clad Agreement from the USA gave six celebrations of the lives of American inventors, Robert Halpern offered The Festival of Hypnosis, and the Craigmillar Society brought the vitality of folk theatre to their *The Craigmillar Recipe.*

Andrew Cruickshank, who had had the exciting task of presiding over the Festival Fringe, presided in 1978 over his Critical Mornings. There was an acknowledgement of an

Andrew Cruickshank in 'Ane Satire of the Thrie Estaits'

Irishman's critical role in Scottish history and culture in the Adamnan Players's *Columba,* and the fruitful partnership of W. Gordon Smith and Russell Hunter elaborated some of the complexities of the literary critic and poet Coleridge in their piece *Xanadu.* The official Festival had rich dramatic fare: Shakespeare's *Tempest* and *Midsummer Night's Dream* from Edinburgh Festival Productions, and his *Twelfth Night* and Chekhov's *Three Sisters* from the Royal Shakespeare Company. A strong home team of Tom Fleming (who read the poems) and Jean Redpath (who sang the songs) provided a celebration of Robert Burns.

Billy Connolly leapt into the Festival in 1979 with his play on prison life, *The Red Runner,* produced at the Moray House Gymnasium by the Traverse Theatre. The primal energy of the Rustaveli Theatre from Soviet Georgia brought an elemental account of Shakespeare's *Richard III,* which overcame language barriers to resurrect the attack of a style of acting which is often criticised as merely melodramatic. The Film Festival brought Jonathan Miller's version of *La Traviata,* and focused on the achievement of Luis Buñuel and Francis

Coppola. There was the medieval art of flag throwing from the Contade di Cori in Parliament Square, the Meadows and Craigmillar Castle. The poets Sorley McLean, Ian Crichton-Smith and Norman McCaig read in St Cecilia's Hall, and the Festival Club made a concession to the times by introducing a disco.

The highlight of the 1980 Festival was surely the virile adaptation of the medieval Mystery plays, *The Passion*, adapted by former Lyceum director, Bill Bryden, for the National Theatre. The Royal Shakespeare Company gave the versatile Alfred Marks the opportunity of playing Falstaff in both parts of *Henry IV*. Ian McKellen and Janet Suzman presented *D. H. Lawrence: The Tarnished Phoenix* (soon to be made into a film), and Alistair Cooke presented *An Hour of American Humour* at the Queen's Hall. At the 1980 Writers' Conference, among the speakers were Frank Muir, Kingsley Amis, John Wells, Gore Vidal, George Steiner and Christopher Logue. Dualchas-Heritage evoked the culture of the Gaelic community, while the 7:84 Company brought *Blood Red Roses,* and there were other fine things from Panes Plough, Wildcat Theatre, and Pamela Stephenson.

The 1981 Festival Cavalcade featured two thousand performers, with six hundred musicians, and was seen by one hundred thousand people. This was indeed a Festival on the

Festival Cavalcade 1982

grand scale, with Abel Gance's 1927 film *Napoleon* on show at the Playhouse Theatre from 10.30 am to 17.30 pm, accompanied by a forty-seven piece orchestra playing a score written by Carl Davis. Alec McCowen sustained the apparently impossible feat of reciting *St Mark's Gospel* from memory; Paul Scofield came to read poetry, and David Kossoff did a one-man show. The Conference at the Television Festival (started in 1976) was on the theme 'Television and the Arts', with two Scots, Jeremy Isaacs, Managing Director of Channel 4, and Magnus Magnusson (an adopted Scot), and an Irishman who has made Edinburgh his home: Owen Dudley Edwards. Rowan Atkinson, one of the many discoveries of previous Festivals, announced he would be unable to attend. The American Repertory Theatre, which was formed to give innovative versions of the classics, brought four farces by Molière, and *Lulu* by Wedekind. Peter Ustinov played the Stage Manager in his adaptation of *The Marriage* by Mussorgsky (which he also produced). The Colla Family Marionettes gave *Prometheus and Cinderella* with a cast of around three hundred. It was a year of extraordinary events: the Sankai Juku company from Japan, leading exponents of a new dance form *Butoh*, acted and mimed with white bodies and shaven heads. In Parliament Square they performed *Sholiba* (a stage between an abattoir and the butcher's shop) by descending for half an hour suspended upside down on ropes fixed to the roof of the headquarters of Lothian Regional Council. The Sbandieratori from Gubbio in Italy also performed in Parliament Square, Princes Street Gardens, the Meadows, Leith Links and Craigmillar Castle, throwing banners and shooting medieval cross-bows with deadly accuracy. Finally there was the stirring *Blood Wedding* and *Flamenco Suite* from the Antonio Gades Ballet, a gory·reading of *Beowulf* by Julian Glover, and a fine interpretation of James Boswell by David McKail in *Bozzy*. The Film Festival rose to new heights with showings of *Blade Runner*, *E.T.*, *Fitzcarraldo* by Werner Herzog, Peter Greenaway's *The Draughtsman's Contract*, and *Scotch Reels*, a celebration of Scottish kitsch, with such films as *Whisky Galore*, *The Prime of Miss Jean Brodie* and *Brigadoon*. Also shown was H. J. Syberberg's production of Wagner's *Parsifal*.

Glasgow Citizens brought the huge *Last Days of Mankind* by Karl Kraus to the 1983 Festival, showing the disintegration of European culture between 1914 and 1918; they also acted *Rosenkavalier* by Hugo von Hofmannstal. The Haifa Municipal Theatre contributed to the Vienna 1900 theme with *The Soul of a Jew*. Nigel Stock produced a fascinating theatrical experience, playing Dr Watson in *221B*, and Claire Bloom illustrated Shakespeare's heroines in *These Are Women*. The theme of sexual equality and female emancipation was picked up by 7:84 in their two rude comedies by Aristophanes, adapted by John McGrath. Joan Plowright and Frank Finlay played in Chekhov's *The Cherry Orchard*, directed by Lindsay Anderson: again on the theme of decadence and decay. The Poppie Nonagena Company from New York explored the life of a black woman in *South Africa*. At the 1983 Film Festival were: *Merry Christmas, Mr Lawrence*, with David Bowie and ex-Lyceum actor, Tom Conti; a Nagisa Oshima retrospective; and a Student Animation section.

Films in 1984 included Bill Forsyth's new *Comfort and Joy* and the film version of ex-Edinburgh teacher Bernard MacLaverty's novel *Cal*. Max Wall gave a powerful account of *Malone Dies*, Marius Goring offered *Coleridge and the Ancient Mariner*, and the Berliner Ensemble gave *Brecht Songs and Poems, Scenes from Faust* and *Galileo Galilei*. Tom Fleming (himself once a memorable Galileo at the Lyceum) directed a rumbustious production of the *Thrie Estaits* at the Assembly Hall, which caught the imagination of all by its power, passion, and humour. Peter O'Toole was on hand presenting Christopher Fry's *A Sleep of Prisoners*, while the versatile voice-over specialist, Miriam Margoyles, gave a pungent account of *Gertrude Stein*, and the Theatre of New York held a Samuel Beckett Season at the Churchill Theatre.

Art exhibitions did not become an official part of the Festival until 1950 with the Rembrandt Exhibition at the National Gallery of Scotland. The Degas Exhibition in 1952 was followed by Renoir and, in 1954, Cézanne at the Royal Scottish Academy. Parallel to this was *Homage to Diaghilev* at the Edinburgh College of Art, the first of Richard Buckle's imaginative re-creations. There were one thousand exhibits including the Tower from Utrillo's backdrop for *Barabau*, and eight model theatres with ballet scenes; there was décor by Picasso, and there were posters by Cocteau (who was later to design a Festival poster). Magnificent costumes from a variety of ballets completed the display. Gauguin followed in 1955, and Braque in 1956, and the 1960 exhibition was devoted to

Kandinsky, Marc and the Blue Rider Group. In 1961 Richard Buckle arranged a unique Epstein Exhibition in Waverley Market, and designed his third Edinburgh exhibition in 1964, the quatercentenary of Shakespeare (again in Waverley Market). After exhibitions devoted to Corot (1965) and Rouault (1966), Derain in 1967 was accompanied by an imaginatively designed *Two Hundred Summers in a City,* in which John L. Paterson (later to be Principal of the Edinburgh College of Art) explored the special features of Edinburgh's New Town. In 1968 three hundred and fifty items were displayed relating to Charles Rennie Mackintosh, the outstanding architect and designer of the Art Nouveau period.

The 1970s saw an Early Celtic Art Exhibition in the Royal Scottish Museum, Alan Davie (in the Royal Scottish Academy), and a display of photographs and effects in memory of Sir Tyrone Guthrie, who had had such a seminal influence on Festival drama with his production of Sir David Lindsay's *Thrie Estaits.*

King James VI and I, so intimately linked with the history of Edinburgh, was the focus of a special exhibition at the Royal Scottish Museum in 1975, Elizabethan miniatures by Nicholas Hilliard were on view at the Scottish Arts Council's late-lamented Gallery in Charlotte Square, and the Scottish National Portrait Gallery presented *Painting in Scotland, 1570-1650.*

The following year was one of the great contrasts in the visual arts: the Fine Art Society focused on Bakst, the resonantly colourful theatrical designer; the Scottish Arts Council showed the spare but striking work of Dan Flavin in *Installations in Fluorescent Light;* Barbara Hepworth's work was in the picturesque setting of the Royal Botanic Garden; the Royal Scottish Museum reminded visitors of Scotland's contribution in two fields: the army, in the form of the Overlord Tapestry, and medicine in 'Edinburgh and Medicine'; and the Scottish National Portrait Gallery chose an evocative subject in its 'Childhood in 17th Century Scotland'.

Joan Eardley's works in the 1977 Festival were a welcome contribution from an artist essentially Scottish in mood and texture. The Fruitmarket Gallery showed Norman McLaren, while the Gallery of Modern Art and the Royal Scottish Academy were devoted to American art. The Armand Hammer Collection was the centrepiece of 1978's Edinburgh Festival, and 1979 saw John L. Paterson's superb *Parade* exhibition in the Edinburgh College of Art showing three centuries of dancers and dance from eighteenth-century Tuscan theatres to the stretch synthetics of Alwin Nicolais. Visitors entered the exhibition in total darkness and were then overwhelmed by music and necklaces of tiny lights, and changing spotlights which lit up different parts of the hall. The Talbot Rice Art Centre was given over to the work of Edinburgh's greatest contemporary artist, Eduardo Paolozzi.

The North-West Coast Indians of Canada and Alaska came in *The Legacy* at the City Art Centre and there was an Indian artist, Richard Hunt, in residence, carving a totem pole. Daumier was the Royal Scottish Academy's 1981 exhibition; the Museum of Modern Art, New York contributed an exhibition, and Murray Grigor took time out from filming to stage an enjoyable *Scotch Myths*, which traced the progress of one kind of distorted view of Scotland.

The glory of the 1982 exhibitions was the Codex Hammer of Leonardo da Vinci displayed at the Royal Scottish Academy, but there were also photographs by the surrealist Man Ray; *Miro's People* in the Gallery of Modern Art; *John Michael Wright: King's Painter* at the Scottish National Portrait Gallery; *Angels, Nobles and Unicorns* across the road in the new gallery of the National Museum at York Buildings; and *Scottish Art Now*, which showed some of the brighter sparks of modern Scottish art at the National Museum. This set the theme for the official Festival and was developed in a series of lectures and celebrations, such as *Coffee and Dreams* at St Cecilia's Hall. There was a fascinating display of paintings for the Mouton Rothschild wine labels, and the first Book Festival was staged in the sylvan setting of Charlotte Square. Edinburgh Book Week followed in 1984. *The Indispensable Fan* was a marvellously prepared exhibition at the City Art Centre, while Eduardo Paolozzi and Andrea Palladio were at the Royal Scottish Academy. John Cage exhibited prints and drawings, and the Royal Scottish Museum presented a mixture of Americana in *Treasures from the Smithsonian Institution*, ranging from humble artefacts and folk art to a moon buggy.

Folk Music

Scotland is one of the richest sources of native folk song in the English-speaking world. Edinburgh, as its capital, has long echoed to the folk-lament and the political ballad. It was the Folk Revival in the early 1950s, of which the People's Festival at the Oddfellows Hall in 1951 was a symptom, that brought folk music once again to prominence and recognition by the general public as an important part of the Scottish and the Edinburgh heritage as well as a living art form.

Hamish Henderson, the Second World poet, folklorist and founder-member of the School of Scottish Studies at Edinburgh University, was involved closely with the Revival from before the 1950s. By the end of that decade the earliest folk clubs in the City had been formed, the first probably being the Edinburgh University Folk Song Society. The focus for folk music in the City has for long been **Sandy Bell's** pub in Forrest Road. Here nearly every famous name who visited the Capital has played or sung: the Dubliners, Pete Seeger, Martin Carthy.

Sandy Bell's

Most opening times Bell's is full of folk talk and singing, and a wide cross-section of society patronises its premises.

One of the oldest professional folk groups with an international reputation is **the Corries,** who have sung the battle-songs and the love-poems of Scotland for more than twenty years. Ronnie Brown and Roy Williamson are responsible (among many other ballads) for 'Flower of Scotland', sung at international football and rugby games and to be heard on most street corners and in every public house. What are now the two remaining members of the original Corrie Folk Trio met while at Art School in Edinburgh and continued their partnership when they took up teaching. Their aggressive style and humour link them to the Irish Clancy Brothers and have led to the production of more than ten albums which sell worldwide.

The Incredible String Band ploughed a different musical furrow, concentating on more complex harmonies and instrumentation and developing a fruitful marriage between ancient Celtic themes and modern electronic instruments. Robin Williamson and Mike Heron founded ISB in 1965 and, until they split up in 1974, produced 22 albums: 16 LPs, 8 of which were chart hits in 1968-71. In that period ISB had more LP chart entries than any other British group apart from Cream, the Rolling Stones and the Beatles. Williamson, who played 35 different instruments on these recordings, now works solo on literary projects, and on music for film and theatre, appearing in the theatre and writing verse.

Of all Edinburgh's solo performers, the most passionate and the most direct and abrasive is **Dick Gaughan.** As his surname reveals, Gaughan, born in Leith, comes of Irish stock from County Mayo, and finds much of his inspiration in Irish folksong tradition. He is libertarian and egalitarian and sings with enormous conviction about the exploitation and oppression of the Scottish working class. Gaughan, who toured Russia with the 7:84 Theatre Company, has had two albums nominated as Melody Maker Album of the Year, one being 'Handful of Earth'. His guitar style is flexible. He mixes traditional ballads with contemporary songs of protest. He works from gut reaction with conviction and tremendous energy to point to the injustices of post-industrial Scotland.

The McCalmans, led by the disturbing edge of Ian McCalman's baritone, have for long played a prominent part in

Edinburgh's folk scene. The contribution of the McCalmans, who recently changed their line-up through the departure of Hamish Bayne and the arrival of Nick Keir, has been less aggressive than that of either the Corries or Dick Gaughan, less melodic than the Incredible String Band, but heavier on humour and vocal harmony.

Other bands based in Edinburgh include the **Boys of the Lough** (who in 1972 were the first traditional band to work on a fully professional basis) and **Silly Wizard,** whose Phil Cunningham, accordion player and composer, was born in the City. It should not be forgotten that the outstanding exponent of the Scottish folk-song, **Jean Redpath,** spent a period of her life at Edinburgh University and returns to the City regularly.

Mike Maran left Edinburgh University with a degree in politics and modern history after a secondary education at Scotus College. In 1977 he presented *Penny Whistles,* based on Robert Louis Stevenson's *Child's Garden of Verse* after returning from London (which has been his base since 1970). Among his many activities on the folk music scene, Maran has been the warm-up act for some of Britain's biggest rock bands, such as ELO and Uriah Heep. In 1983 he performed a concert entitled 'Songs of Robert Louis Stevenson' at the Book Fair in Charlotte Square, a venture which brought him to the attention of a television producer and led to his engagement to do six songs on the Sunday morning TV-am series 'Rub-a-Dub Tub'.

Francis Collinson (1898-1985) was the son of the first organist of St Mary's Cathedral, Palmerston Place. He studied under his father and, when at Edinburgh University, also with Sir Donald Tovey. Having acquired a taste for musical revues while still an undergraduate, he became musical director for C.B. Cochran in the 1930s and also for a time worked as Noel Coward's accompanist. In 1941 he was put in charge of the music for the new BBC programme, *Country Magazine.* In this post he had to travel all over Britain to collect, arrange and broadcast traditional folk-songs. His book, *Orchestration for the Theatre* (1941), was based on his early musical career, and in 1950 he was awarded an Italia Prize for his incidental music for radio, including *Rumpelstiltskin.* He was appointed Musical

Research Fellow of the School of Scottish Studies of the University of Edinburgh in 1951; in this role he concentrated his attention on the folksongs and traditional music of Scotland. In the three volumes of *Hebridean Folksongs* (1969, 1977, 1981), of which he was co-author, he contributed over two hundred musical transcriptions; his other major works are *The Traditional and National Music of Scotland* (1966) and *The Bagpipe: The History of a Musical Instrument* (1975). It was these achievements which made him Scotland's leading ethnomusicologist.

Ghosts and Witches

The night before the Battle of Flodden in 1513, while the cannon were being trundled out of the Castle and down the Royal Mile, around midnight, the spectres of heralds were said to have been seen at the Mercat Cross proclaiming the list of the ten thousand men who were to die in the battle, intoning their names to the terrified population.

An unusual case of premonition took place in Edinburgh a century later: this time it related to an affair of the heart. The young wife of the brutal Viscount Primrose, Lady Eleanor Campbell, had not had an easy marriage. One morning, as she was dressing, she saw in the mirror before her that her husband was creeping towards her with a knife in his hand as if to put an end to her life. She immediately made for the bedroom window and jumped into the street below from her first floor chamber. She survived the fall and left her husband for her relations. Her husband went abroad and for many months Lady Eleanor heard nothing. Then one day a fortune-teller came to Edinburgh. Lady Eleanor was persuaded to visit the fortune-teller and asked for news of her husband's where-abouts. She was taken to a mirror, and when she looked into it she saw her husband dressed as a bridegroom about to marry a bride in a church. Suddenly she saw her brother arrive and attack Lord Primrose. When she returned home Lady Eleanor wrote down exactly what she had seen, dated and sealed the account before a witness and had the paper locked away. It was only when her brother returned from travel on the Continent that she discovered that he had gone to Amsterdam and there heard of a noble Scotsman who was about to marry the daughter of a family her brother had met. When Lady Eleanor's brother had gone to the church, he found to his astonishment that the bridegroom was in fact his brother-in-law. Everything had gone as the vision in the mirror suggested and the ceremony stopped before the bigamous marriage could take place. When Lady Eleanor examined the document she

116

had signed describing her vision in the clairvoyant's mirror, she found it was dated the very day on which her brother had broken up Lord Primrose's second wedding. The facts of this case are worth taking seriously, as both Robert Chambers the writer and publisher and Sir Walter Scott noted the tale.

When the new Royal Exchange was built for the merchants of Edinburgh (the present City Chambers), it was constructed over some of the old closes. One of these, Mary King's Close, can still be seen by guided parties, under the present level of the Royal Mile, a reminder of what Old Edinburgh once was like. In the late eighteenth century a Mr and Mrs Coltheart lived in the Close. One Sunday afternoon, when her husband was not feeling well and had gone to bed, Mrs Coltheart sat reading her Bible. She glanced up for a moment and to her horror saw a ghastly head floating in the room, looking at her with sightless eyes. Her husband did not believe her, but it was not long before he also saw the head, and then a child and an arm, all suspended in the air. In spite of the Colthearts' prayers, the phantoms did not go away but increased in number until the room was full of them. Then suddenly there was a deep groan and everything vanished as quickly as it had come.

After Charles II's coronation at Scone in 1651, Cromwell's army marched on Edinburgh and a special detachment was garrisoned in the Castle. In the middle of the night a lonely sentry heard the sound of a beaten drum, the thud of marching feet and an old Scots march. He challenged but got no answer, so he fired his musket. His commanding officer did not believe his story, and the sentry was replaced. After a time spent on guard duty late into the night the second sentry heard an old Scots march, then an English one, then a French. He fired and there was a deathly silence.

When General Robertson rented an old building known as the Wrights Houses (near what are now the Meadows) in 1792, his coloured servant Black Tom complained of seeing a midnight ghost in the shape of a headless lady carrying a child in her arms. Around the turn of the next century, the Merchant Company bought the property and demolished it. When the old stone floor was being pulled up the workmen found the headless skeleton of a woman with the skeleton of an infant beside her. It seems that this was the French wife of James Clerk who had been given the house by his father in 1664. When James went abroad to fight in the army, he left his wife and young baby in the care of a brother who had murdered his sister-in-law and his niece when he heard that his brother had been killed in battle.

When the moon is bright in Corstorphine the figure of a woman dressed in white can sometimes be seen, wearing a white hood and carrying a sword dripping with blood. The White Lady is the ghost of Christian Nimmo, wife of an Edinburgh merchant, Andrew Nimmo. Her lover, James, Lord Forrester, was already married to the daughter of General Patrick Ruthven (1573-1651). Lord Forrester was fond of his ale and was often drunk. In one of his drunken moods he criticised Christian publicly. She sent her maid to tell him to meet in their usual place, the old sycamore tree near the dovecot in Corstorphine. Forrester came, drunk as ever, and spoke roughly to her. He told her to her face that he refused to marry her, as he had often refused before. In a desperate fury Christian pulled out Forrester's sword and ran him through the body. He died instantly. She left the body in a pool of blood and hid in Corstorphine Castle. She was discovered and sentenced to death, having confessed to the murder. She tried to avoid her punishment by petitioning the Privy Council (unsuccessfully), claiming that she was pregnant by Lord Forrester, and by escaping dressed in men's clothes. She was caught in the Fala Hills and locked up in the Tolbooth. On November 12th 1679 she appeared on the scaffold dressed in the mourning clothes of the time: pure white. She laid her head on the block and was beheaded.

In 1689 Lord Balcarres was in prison in Edinburgh Castle for his Jacobite views. He was lying in his four-poster bed with the curtains pulled when he had an unexpected visitor. The curtains were opened and he saw his great friend Graham of Claverhouse, Bonnie Dundee. There was no sound; Claverhouse merely looked at him without a word. He moved and then disappeared. Some time later Lord Balcarres received news of the Battle of Killiekrankie at which his friend had been killed.

Early in the eighteenth century the Old Craighouse held a

terrible secret and was haunted by the figure of the Green Lady. Sir Thomas Elphinstone had decided to marry a girl forty years younger than himself. Miss Betty Pettendale was herself in love with a dashing young officer whom she knew only as Captain Jack Courage, a nickname he had acquired by his exploits with Marlborough in the French Wars. They had declared their love for each other, but he had been unable to marry her until his father died and left him the ancestral home. In the meantime he was recalled with his regiment to Ireland. Betty became Lady Elphinstone, mainly due to the ambition of her parents. Four months later the old man was awaiting the return of his son from military service with the rank of Colonel. Lord Elphinstone arranged a lavish reception to introduce his wife into society. He appeared to the company with his young bride and introduced her to his son. At once Betty knew him. It was her sweetheart who was now revealed as the young Colonel Elphinstone. Colonel Elphinstone decided to go away for ever. At their last meeting he said goodbye to Betty and gave her one last kiss. At that moment his father came into the room, and stabbed his wife to death. Later that night he himself died over her dead body, consumed with remorse. Husband and wife were buried together. Then the appearances began, to one person, than another. The Green Lady put fear into the hearts of many in the house until an Eastern mystic was brought in to solve the mystery. He succeeded in raising the forms of Lord and Lady Elphinstone. The Green Lady asked that her body should be moved away from her husband's so that she could be near Colonel Elphinstone's when he came to be buried. This was done, and the Green Lady appeared no more.

Around the middle of the eighteenth century an Edinburgh minister was called out one night, and taken by sedan to his destination. The sedanmen were not ordinary chairmen; by their accents they were clearly aristocratic. During the midnight journey the sedan was curtained over to prevent the minister seeing where he went. He was set down and ushered up steps into a small room where a young woman lay unconscious. Then came the cry of a newborn child in a nearby room. The minister was told to start praying and shortly afterwards was taken away again by the sedan. As he left, a purse of gold coins was slipped into his hands and he heard a shot in the building above. The following morning he heard that a house in the Canongate, the town house of a noble family, had been destroyed by fire and the daughter of the family killed. Some years later, about 1750, the whole block, where the accident took place, caught fire. In the middle of the flames there suddenly appeared a young woman dressed in expensive clothes. She was heard to cry: 'Once burned; twice burned; the third time I'll scare you all'.

Almost two hundred years later, in 1920, an Edinburgh lady remembered the present sent to her from Egypt by a friend and opened the drawer where she had placed it. The present was a snake-like necklace of green stone, taken from an ancient Egyptian tomb. The lady did not think much of it and put it in a wastepaper basket, ready to throw out. Later that night as she bent down to pick something up, she felt a hand on her shoulder and heard a rustling sound. Her brother, a doctor, decided to try to get to the bottom of the mysterious happenings. He was shaken by thuds and tapping near his bed during the night. The following night his bed was shaken from side to side and he felt the presence of something bending over him. Other friends had similar experiences, and one lady who wore it during the night around her neck saw flashes of fire. Eventually the lady's brother threw it into Loch Leven on a fishing trip, and there it remains.

In 1932 the Edinburgh Psychic College was founded by Mrs Ethel Miller in Heriot Row. It replaced an earlier Scottish Psychical Society. The work of the College has been in part to keep a record of psychic events in the City.

Dr John Beloff of the Psychology Department of Edinburgh University, a past President of the Society for Psychical Research, was called in to investigate an event in a Royal Circus hotel in 1973. He spent many hours with a tape recorder and a thermometer trying to discover what had so distressed three of the hotel's porters. They claimed to have seen a ghost flitting through the corridors, a woman dressed in a long white dress with flowing black hair. They all refused to work at night except in pairs and even complained to their union. Dr Beloff's research was inconclusive.

A two-hundred-year-old central office block was the scene of peculiar apparitions in 1977. Staff saw a grey mist with two blinding white eyes and believed it was the ghost of a stable-hand who had hanged himself in the basement.

Four years later it was the turn of the Playhouse Theatre. Greenside, where the theatre is built, has a history of murders throughout past centuries. Locked doors in the backstage corridors were heard to creak open and slam shut. There were eerie footsteps in passages at night. The police were called in to speak to the caretaker, a man of forty-five wearing working clothes (except that there was no caretaker on the staff). One stagehand had gone onto the stage to plug in a lead and had seen the caretaker figure standing by the cinema screen curtains.

The present Curator of the Wax Museum in the High Street has the largest private library in the UK on the occult. Mr Charles Cameron has studied stage magic and psychology, he is a ghost-hunter, having had experience of the supernatural in Egypt, the Sudan and Palestine during the Second World War. Armed with his cameras, infra-red film and trip-wires of fine catgut, he investigates mysterious Edinburgh manifestations such as the Grey Lady of Ann Street or the phantom pianist of Charlotte Square.

In 1986 American psychologist **Dr Robert Morris** arrived in Edinburgh to take up the newly created Professorship of Parapsychology, funded from a £500,000 bequest from the late

Professor Robert Morris, with bust of Arthur Koestler

Arthur Koestler, the writer, who had had a lifelong interest in the paranormal. It was a controversial move on the part of the University to create such a chair but, said Britain's first professor of the paranormal, he brought no preconceived ideas and he would engage in the objective study of psychical phenomena, whether apparent or real.

There are those who believe that witchcraft is the old pagan religions gone underground after the coming of Christianity; there are others who see it as the product of the Counter-Reformation at a time when heretics had been tortured and burned and the people of Europe had acquired a taste for execution. Whatever the root cause, it is a historical fact that great numbers of persons were put to death for being witches. Between 1479 and 1722 more than 300 women were burnt on Castle Hill in Edinburgh and more than 17,000 were tortured and executed for witchcraft in Scotland. King James VI himself was a believer in witchcraft and contributed· to popular hysteria, publishing a treatise called *Daemonologie* in 1597. Sweeping powers to deal with those suspected of being witches were acquired by the Town Council of Edinburgh in 1661, and one of those caught in their net was **Major Thomas Weir.**

Weir was born in Carluke in 1599 and saw active service with Montrose's Covenanters in Ireland before being appointed a Captain in the Edinburgh City Guard. He was 'a tall black man, and ordinarily looked down to the ground', Chambers tells us; he hardly ever smiled, he wore a dark cloak and lived in a tall dark house in the West Bow. He had memorised many passages from scripture which he frequently quoted; he was possessed of great dignity and had a gift for extempore prayer. He was above all a leading member of a puritanical offshoot of the Presbyterians known as the 'Bowhead Saints'. In 1670 Weir suddenly confessed that he had committed incest with his sister Jane (now aged fifty years) from when she was sixteen. He accused himself of bestiality with mares and cows and of witchcraft. 'Angelical Thomas', as he was popularly known, stirred up a hornet's nest of hysteria and persecution. Stories were told about his walking-stick: it was carved with heads like satyrs and was reputed to carry messages for him, answer the door and act as a link-boy (torch-bearer) at night. Weir, who is now generally thought to have suffered from mental illness, was executed at Gallow Lee in the Grassmarket.

Legends still remained, for Chambers, writing in the early 1800s, reports: 'His apparition was frequently seen at night, flitting, like a black and silent shadow, about the street. His house, though known to be deserted by every human, was sometimes observed at midnight to be full of lights, and heard to emit strange sounds as of dancing, howling, and what is strangest of all, spinning. Some people occasionally saw the Major issue from the low close at midnight, mounted on a black horse without a head, and gallop off in a whirlwind of flame. Nay, sometimes the whole inhabitants of the Bow would be roused from their sleep at any early hour in the morning by the sound of a coach and six, first rattling up from the Lawn-market, and then turning down the Bow, stopping at the head of the terrible close for a few minutes, and then rattling and thundering back again – being neither more nor less than Satan come in one of his best equipages to take home the Major and his sister, after they had spent a night's leave of absence in their terrestrial dwelling . . .'

E

Inventors and Scientists

John Napier was born in 1550 at Merchiston Castle (now Napier College), in Edinburgh, where his father, who was Master of the Scottish Mint, was Laird. The year of his birth marked the beginning of the Reformation in Scotland, and the

John Napier of Merchiston

young Napier was early a Protestant champion. His educational formation began at St Salvator's College at the University of St Andrews, and he is thought to have travelled abroad, probably to the University of Paris, as well as visiting Italy and Germany. An interst in theology acquired at university was broadened by research into literature and science upon his return to Scotland in 1571, eight years after matriculating at St Andrews. By 1588 Napier had become a Commissioner to the General Assembly, representing the Presbytery of Edinburgh. In 1593 his *A Plaine Discovery of the Whole Revelation of St John*, an attack on the Church of Rome, was published. From that time Napier was occupied with the invention of secret instruments of war in preparation for an expected Spanish invasion. Like Leonardo da Vinci a hundred years before, Napier designed a tank: a round metal chariot so constructed that its occupants could move it rapidly while firing out through small holes in it. He also invented a mirror intended to burn enemy ships at a distance; artillery for destroying everything round an arc of a circle; and a hydraulic screw for clearing water from coal mines. He was a successful landowner and farmer, making innovations in land use and artificial fertilisers.

Polymath that he was, Napier took a keen interest in

124

alchemy, astrology, astronomy, magic and mathematics: subjects closely related in his time, as they had been for the Greek philosopher-physicists of the Ancient World. Napier entered into a written agreement with Robert Logan, undertaking to recover treasure which had been hidden in the latter's keep at Fastcastle, and although this endeavour may have been attempted on perfectly sound scientific principles, Napier's achievements in the field of mathematics were to be such that men could be forgiven for thinking there might be a touch of wizardry in him. He took nearly twenty years to construct the table of logarithms for which he is best remembered. *Rabdologiae* (1617) was an account of ingenious methods of calculating, using 'rods', or 'bones'. Also described were methods of using little plates of metal in a box. Napier can therefore be considered as one of the early fathers of computer science. He introduced the comma or full stop to separate the decimal from the integral part and improved the notation for writing numbers. He was a contemporary of Galileo and Kepler, and his work was known to the Danish astronomer Tycho Brahe. Napier died in 1617 and is buried in St Cuthbert's churchyard.

The Royal Society of Edinburgh

Despite the union of the Parliaments in 1707, which removed a considerable proportion of Edinburgh's status as a legislative power-base for the Scottish nation, the eighteenth-century Enlightenment brought a new upsurge of intellectual and literary vigour to Scotland's Capital.

At the heart of this literary and scientific renaissance was the Edinburgh medical school: by 1731 a 'Society for the Improvement of Medical Knowledge' had been founded by Edinburgh's professors, its first Secretary being Alexander Monro Primus, the anatomist. The transactions of the Society were published in six volumes over a number of years.

Six medical students founded an undergraduate 'Society for the Improvement in Medical Knowledge' in 1734. This was formally instituted in 1737 and finally and uniquely incorporated by Royal Charter in 1776. The Royal Medical Society today is still one of the most active of the student bodies.

The year 1737 is also significant for it was then that the mathematician, Colin McLaurin (who had been Secretary of an older Society for Improving Arts and Sciences) broadened the scope of the Medical Society to include general science and literature. The new Philosophical Society of Edinburgh, as it was called, had McLaurin and Plummer (the Professor of Chemistry) as its secretaries. McLaurin unfortunately met an early death through his activities against the Jacobites. The new Society suspended activity until the end of the Jacobite Rebellion when Alexander Monro Secundus and David Hume took over the secretaryship.

Many of the members of the Philosophical Society were professors at the University of Edinburgh. In 1782 William Robertson, Principal of the University, recommended the establishment of a new Society to serve both science and literature, basing his scheme on the academies of the Continent.

The first Charter of the Royal Society of Edinburgh was granted by George III in 1783 and the first formal meeting of its members was held in the University (then the College) Library with **Principal William Robertson** as chairman. Robertson, a true man of the Enlightenment, combined many

Principal William Robertson

interests. A clergyman, he also enjoyed a European reputation as a historian, and was admired by Gibbon and Voltaire.

The Royal Society was to a large extent a National Academy of Scotland: indeed, the Letters Patent attached to the Society's Armorial bearings so describe it. John Robison, Professor of Natural Philosophy, was the first Secretary. He had served with Wolfe at Quebec, been Professor of Mathematics at the Naval College at Kronstadt (now in the USSR) and had followed Joseph Black as Professor at the University of Glasgow. The

Fellows of the Society were divided into two classes; Literary and Physical. Sir Walter Scott was the only literary President ever appointed. Fifty years later, Robert Louis Stevenson read a scientific paper to the Society. The literary side, however, soon ceased to function as a separate entity.

In the Physical Class a great deal of important work was done. James Hutton contributed a paper to the first volume of the Society's transactions. Hutton's conclusions were tested and proved correct by the second President, Sir James Hall, who has been named the father of experimental geology. Thomas Hope announced his discovery of the element Strontium in the Transactions; Thomas Graham added his seminal 'Memoir on the Law of Diffusion of Gases', and Sir David Brewster with his world-famous papers on optics added considerably to the Society's reputation. James Clerk Maxwell submitted a paper on 'The Propeties of certain Oval Curves' in 1846, when he was still a fifteen-year old schoolboy at the Edinburgh Academy (his contribution was actually read to the Fellows by one of Maxwell's masters, as the author was considered too young to present the paper himself). The half-century which followed saw great activity on the part of the Royal Society under the aegis of Sir William Thomson (later Lord Kelvin), and Peter Guthrie Tait.

Among the more distinguished Honorary Fellows of the Society were Benjamin Franklin and the poet Goethe (elected during the presidency of Sir Walter Scott), not for his literary achievements but for his scientific researches.

Today the Royal Society of Edinburgh exists to enlarge Edinburgh's international reputation in the fields of science and learning. Papers contributed to the Society are issued regularly, particularly in mathematics, and the physical and biological sciences, with occasional papers in the arts. Recently the premises of the Society at 22/24 George Street have been upgraded to include a fully-equipped lecture theatre, smaller meeting-rooms and other facilities which will meet the demands of an increase in the activities of the Royal Society of Edinburgh.

Let us return to some notable individuals. **James Hutton,** 'the father of modern geology', was born in Edinburgh in 1726, son

James Hutton

of a merchant, and educated at the High School. In 1743 he was apprenticed to a Writer to the Signet to follow a legal career. However, instead of copying legal papers as he was required, he often amused himself and his fellow apprentices by conducting chemical experiments. This passion for chemistry led to his studying medicine at Edinburgh, Paris, and Leiden, where he graduated MD in 1749. In the following year he returned to Edinburgh and, having been left a small property in Berwickshire by his father, his thoughts turned to agriculture. With a friend, James Davie, he set up a small business to make salt from coal-soot. He went to Norfolk to study rural economy and during his time there made many journeys on foot through England. He began to study mineralogy and geology, his mind fired by his observation of the English landscape, and he travelled through Flanders. Returning to his farm in Berwickshire, he put the new techniques of husbandry which he had acquired into practice. He carried out experiments on his land using two horses to pull the plough and dispensing with a driver, a practice which local farm labourers thought very questionable. He continued with his sal ammoniac business. From 1768 he lived in Edinburgh until his death in 1797.

In 1785 Hutton read the first outline of his *Theory of the Earth* to the Royal Society of Edinburgh. This work was to lay the foundations of modern geology by putting foward a plutonic theory of the origin of earth. Hutton pointed to heat as the principal agent in elevating land masses in opposition to the then popular neptunean theory which saw the sea as the main force in shaping the earth.

Hutton, who never married and lived with his three sisters, dined early, almost always at home, ate sparingly and drank no wine. This sober picture is softened by the observation that

'When he joined the evening party a bright glow of cheerfulness spread over every face'.

James Watt was born in Greenock in 1736 and spent much of his working life either in Glasgow or in England. However, he did have strong connections with Edinburgh, notably in his capacity as a mathematical instrument maker, supplying scientific equipment to his friend and colleague, the Professor of Chemistry at Edinburgh, Joseph Black. During this fruitful relationship, lasting from 1768 until Black's death in 1799, Watt and his family visited Dr Black and made the acquaintance of many of the most influential men of the Capital. Not only did Watt design and supply items such as copper stills or measuring instruments to Joseph Black, he also sent him shoe varnish, a music organ, goggles, a monochord and an Aeolian harp, and he designed and made guitars, flutes and violins.

Lord Cockburn tells us in his notes on the Friday Club that 'The stranger we saw oftenest, and with the greatest pleasure, was old James Watt'. Watt, as well as visiting the Friday Club and meeting men such as Francis Jeffrey, was himself a member of the Cape Club. In 1805 he met Leonard Hunter at the Friday Club and another member, Lord Brougham, who was to compose the epitaph to Watt on his monument in Westminster Abbey. Sir Walter Scott had met Watt in 1814 and included a eulogy of him in his *The Monastery*.

Watt, who was elected a Fellow of the Royal Society of Edinburgh a year after its foundation in 1783, died in 1819, but it was not until 1852 that the Edinburgh School of Arts (founded by Leonard Horner as the first Mechanics' Institute in Britain) became the Watt Institution as the City of Edinburgh's memorial to James Watt. As early as 1821 subscriptions had been collected from men such as Henry Cockburn, Francis Jeffrey, Sir Henry Raeburn and Sir Walter Scott to create a lasting memorial to their friend and colleague, James Watt, harnessor of steam and polymath. The statue of Watt in Chambers Street, Edinburgh was erected in 1854.

Since that time the Institution has become the Heriot-Watt College (in amalgamation with the Heriot educational trust in 1885), and formed the basis in 1908 of the Edinburgh College of Art. In 1966 the Heriot-Watt became a university, and eight years later began the transfer to a new site at Riccarton. The Heriot-Watt University today offers courses of study in many branches of commerce and industry, not least – since the coming of North Sea oil – in petroleum engineering and marine technology.

James Tytler was the first man to ascend in a balloon from British soil, in 1784. Tytler was born in Brechin, Angus, and paid for his medical studies at Edinburgh University by joining a whaling trip to Greenland. He set up as a surgeon, got no patients, then opened a chemist's shop and got no customers. So, taking to drink, he established himself in the debtors' sanctuary at Holyrood where he erected a printing press, and composed and edited popular songs and three-quarters of the second *Encyclopaedia Britannica*.

For Tytler's balloon attempt a 300 lb. stove was suspended in a carriage under a cylindrical balloon. When sufficient hot air had risen into the envelope to a pressure of about half a ton of lift, the chains supporting the stove broke and the carriage was damaged. Replacing the carriage with a wickerwork basket, Tytler eventually cast off into the blue from his moorings beside the Queen's Park and floated about half a mile as far as Restalrig. Characteristically, after his fourth and final flight had lasted twenty minutes, he landed in a dungheap.

The first controlled flight using hydrogen instead of hot air came in 1785 with the arrival in Scotland of **Vincenzo Lunardi**, a charming and handsome young Italian of twenty-six, fresh from aeronautical triumphs on the Continent and in London. He immediately attracted hordes of adoring Edinburgh lassies whose grace, fresh complexions and sparkling eyes he re-marked upon at length. He was a competent writer of elegant verses, and the city's womenfolk and scenic beauty moved him to flights of poetic fancy. He checked in at Walker's Hotel in Princes Street where he met poor disreputable Tytler and drank lemonade with him, but he never saw him again. Tytler emigrated to the USA where eventually he died.

At first Lunardi intended to take off from George Square. Finally he received permission to use Heriot's Hospital Green. His magnificent red and yellow balloon was on show at Parliament House. As the day for his flight approached, the vital inflating equipment still had not arrived from London. Frantically he looked around for someone to make a replacement and at last found a plumber who made the great lead cisterns and the tin pipes he needed. The process of inflation involved pouring iron shavings into the cisterns. Carboys of nitric acid were them emptied over them, and the gas bubbled furiously up through tin pipes, through a cold water refrigerator, into the mouth of the balloon. A brisk south-west breeze was blowing, and six boats were sent out to the middle of the Firth of Forth in case Lunardi fell in. At 11 a.m. on 5th October a flag was flown from the Castle, a gun boomed, and hydrogen began to bubble out of the cisterns. Lunardi was dressed for the occasion: he wore a scarlet artillery uniform with blue facings and gold buttonholes that glittered in the sun, epaulettes, deep cuffs of frothing lace and a dress-sword in a gold-plated scabbard; on his head was a peruke and a tricorne hat. He also had a cork lifejacket.

The balloon rose rapidly after a delay of ninety minutes while Lunardi composed a poetic description of the scene. With its red and gold stripes it sailed north like a flying pumpkin, and soon the aviator was able to see Glasgow and Paisley from 2,000 feet and three small boats in the Forth below 'by the dashing of their oars making the water look like silver around them'. He made a descent towards Inchkeith to a height of 500 feet to reconnoitre, put on his cork jacket and threw out a sandbag to make the balloon rise again. At six minutes past he began to feel the cold and drank a glass of cordial after a light lunch. By now he could make out Arbroath and Montrose in the distance as he crossed the Fife coast. He began to drop towards Ceres. The reapers in the fields below were terrified. The Rev. Hugo Arnot saw from his barns what he at first thought was a hawk hovering at a great height: it turned into a globe, and he realised what it must be, having read a notice of Lunardi's intentions some time before. As he neared the ground Lunardi spoke through a silver trumpet to the farmhands as they ran in all directions among panic-stricken hens, ducks, sheep and cattle. Lunardi was eventually received in great state, and he and his flying-machine were carried in triumph to Cupar town hall where he was wined and dined and made a freeman of the town. He was taken to St Andrews,

where he was made a member of the Royal and Ancient Golf
Club and played the first hole in twenty strokes, being quite
unfamiliar with the game. When he returned to Edinburgh he
was made a member of the Royal Company of Archers, was
taken to a Canongate drinking club where he was initiated into
the society, and finally to the City Chambers where the
Corporation made hima burgess of the city. His admirers had
meanwhile collected £4,000 for him.

Flights followed to Kelso and Glasgow, and he is reputed to
have travelled 130 miles, breaking the world speed as well as
long-distance record for balloon flight. In December of 1785
he returned to Edinburgh to attempt a double launching. A
pilotless machine was to be attached over his own balloon as a
second-stage vehicle by 500 feet of rope. The new balloon was
made by the orphan girls of the Merchant Hospital. Unfortunately mist and drizzle prevented the launch until the first
sunny day when, dressed in the green uniform of the Company
of Archers, he set off down the east coast. He tried to land at
Gullane but fell short, landing about a mile out at sea near
Fidra. Half-drowned, he was picked up by a fishing boat. The
next year he flew again, rising into the air but staying quite
stationary for almost an hour due to the lack of wind, after
which he made a controlled descent at Duddingston Mill near
Edinburgh. He left Scotland within the week, never to return,
dying some years later, neglected, in Lisbon.

Son of the Edinburgh artist, Alexander Nasmyth, **James
Nasmyth** was born in the City in 1808. His father, besides
being a talented painter, was a proficient engineer: he designed

James Nasmyth

mechanically powered boats with the engineer Patrick Miller
and in 1788 carried Robert Burns in one of his pleasure craft.
Young James attended the Royal High School from the ages of
nine to twelve, during which period he spent much of his

leisure time working at his father's lathe making tops (peeries) and cannon for his fellow students. He set up a small lathe in his bedroom with a small brass foundry and became expert in the casting of alloys. Between the ages of thirteen and eighteen he studied at the Edinburgh School of Arts (the precursor of the present Heriot-Watt University) and had the good fortune to meet James Watt himself, then an old man of 82. Nasmyth made a large number of models, mainly steam engines, which he sold, and with the profits he was able to pay for attendance at certain classes at Edinburgh University. He made a point of visiting as many local engineering works as he could in order to sketch engines and other machinery.

At the age of nineteen he designed and built a working model of a steam road carriage which he exhibited before the Royal Scottish Society of Arts. It worked so well that he subscribed £60 for building a full-scale version of his car, which he ran up and down the Queensferry Road carrying eight passengers for some four or five miles. He can therefore be regarded as a pioneer of the modern motor car.

Independently of George Stephenson he invented the steam-blast on which the locomotive came to be based. Moving to London, Nasmyth became an assistant to Mr Maudsley, one of the first mechanical engineers. There he made a successful dinner-oven, the proceeds from the sale of which enabled him to live fairly comfortably. In 1834, after Maudsley's death, Nasmyth went north to Manchester at the age of twenty-six and set up in business on his own account. Soon the order-book at his Bridgewater Factory was full.

When in 1840 a paddle-shaft thirty-six inches in diameter was needed for Brunel's *Great Britain*, and no forge could be found big enough to make it, Nasmyth designed the steam-hammer in twenty minutes. But the ship's engines were changed from paddle to screw propulsion, and Nasmyth's steam-hammer was not built. While visiting the renowned Creusot works in France, Nasmyth was surprised to see an enormous crank forged with a steam-hammer. He was informed that this was indeed his design which had finally been given shape. He was invited by the French Government to tour France and place his experience at the disposal of the great arsenals. Then he went to Italy and Northern Europe and was received by the Czar of Russia.

The steam-hammer piledriver was his next invention in 1854. A whole catalogue of inventions were produced by Nasmyth, including a planing machine, a nut-shaping machine, and a hydraulic punching machine. After he retired in 1856, he made his own telescopes and carried out a number of interesting astronomical observations before his death in 1890.

Charles Darwin's grandfather, Erasmus, had been a student at Edinburgh University in 1754, studying medicine and 'sacrificing to both Bacchus and Venus'. Charles' brother, Erasmus, was also a student of medicine but left after a year. Charles Darwin himself arrived in 1825 at the age of sixteen to study medicine. He found the lectures of Dr Andrew Duncan at eight in the morning 'something fearful to remember'. As for Dr Alexander Monro, 'he made his lectures on human anatomy as dull as he was himself and the subject disgusted me'. Darwin could not stand to watch operations being performed, and ran out of the room during his second operation. He went on long walks with two friends, collecting zoological specimens from the tidal pools of the east coast and dissecting his discoveries. He joined the Newhaven fleet fishing for oysters and then read a paper to the Plinian Society of Edinburgh on the so-called ova of Flustra (sea-mat) which 'had the power of independent movement by means of cilia, and were in fact larvae'. In his second year Darwin decided he did not want to become a doctor and left Edinburgh, where, a century before, Lord Monboddo had given it as his opinion that there was a relationship between men and monkeys and that human beings were all born with tails (which the midwives cut off at birth).

James Clerk Maxwell, the son of a lawyer, was born in Edinburgh in 1831. His father, who was a keen amateur geologist in his own youth, encouraged him to collect rock specimens, wild flowers, insects, and the small animals which abounded in Galloway where Maxwell was brought up. At school, in the Edinburgh Academy, Maxwell was considered to be small for his age; he had a stutter and this, with his Galloway accent, earned him the nickname of 'Dafty'. After Maxwell entered the fifth year at the age of thirteen, his life changed. His childish habits of collecting specimens and analysing their

 James Clerk Maxwell

differences now matured into original research. At the age of fifteen, in 1846, his first paper was presented to the Royal Society of Edinburgh. He had attended meetings of the Royal Society from the age of fourteen. The following year he left the Academy for Edinburgh University where he studied Natural Philosophy, Mathematics, Logic and Metaphysics.

In 1850 Maxwell went to Cambridge and after graduating became a Fellow of Trinity. He produced two major scientific works at this time: he established the basis of modern colorimetry (measurement of colour) and paved the way for a theory of electromagnetism with a study of Faraday's Lines of Force. He moved to Aberdeen as Professor of Natural Philosophy but was dismissed for being such a poor lecturer. In 1860 he became Professor of Physics and Astronomy at King's College, London, perhaps partly because of his study of the stability of Saturn's rings and a paper on gyroscopic motion. Maxwell's career reached its climax when he was appointed to the Chair of Experimental Physics at Cambridge, as director of the Cavendish Laboratory. He had produced important work on a dynamical theory of gases, on physical lines of force and on a dynamical theory of the electromagnetic field. The 'Maxwell equations' which he formulated predicted the existence of waves travelling with the speed of light consisting of undulating magnetic and electric fields. Maxwell therefore identified light as an electromagnetic phenomenon. Without Maxwell's pioneering work radio, radar and television could not have occurred. He died in 1879.

Alexander Graham Bell was born at 16 South Charlotte Street, Edinburgh in 1847 and attended the Royal High School from 1858 to 1862, after which he left for London, where he studied physiology and anatomy and was introduced to Sir

Alexander Graham Bell

Charles Wheatstone, a scientist working in the fields of electricity, telegraphy, cryptography, the physiology of vision, and the science of sound. Upon Alexander Graham's return to Edinburgh, his father, a Professor of Elocution, challenged him and his brother to build a speaking machine. This they did from a lamb's larynx, two sheets of rubber, a gutta-percha facsimile of human jaws, teeth, and the pharynx and nasal cavities moulded from a real skull. They added soft rubber lips and rubber cheeks, a soft palate made from rubber stuffed with cotton and made a tongue from wooden sections which could be raised or lowered. When this contraption was complete they blew into a metal tube to imitate the action of the lungs. After some practice the speaking head was able to say 'Mama' in such convincing fashion that one of the neighbours who heard it on the stair of No. 13 South Charlotte Street, wondered 'what can be the matter with the baby?'

The groundwork for Bell's subsequent invention of the telephone was laid in the interests and achievements of his immediate family and in his own research. He had become an amateur telegrapher and had considered how to design an electric piano worked by an electro-magnet. He was assembling the range of skills and experience which would enable him to develop the telephone. At the same time he extended the range of application of his father's system of Visible Speech. In Edinburgh and in Lothian linguists had dictated passages from a number of languages to Melville Bell; he transcribed them into Visible Speech, and when his sons came into the room they were able to read the passages back very accurately. In 1870 Bell's father, worried about his son's health (after the recent death of his other brother from tuberculosis) and anticipating new fields to conquer, persuaded him to accompany him to Canada, and it was Alexander Graham's subsequent work, while Professor of Vocal Physiology at Boston University, which led to the invention of the telephone, which he patented in 1876.

On 20th October 1984, Lord Thomson of Monifieth unveiled a plaque at 9 Albyn Place, Edinburgh, the birthplace of **Alan Campbell Swinton**. Lord Thomson performed the ceremony as chairman of the Independent Broadcasting Authority and vice-president of the Royal Television Society. Swinton was born in 1863, a distant relative of Sir Walter Scott, and was the first person to suggest the idea of electronic television through the use of cathode ray tubes. This was the principle on which modern television works, and not on the electro-mechanical apparatus which John Logie Baird used in a private demonstration in 1926. Although Baird was the first to send moving pictures through space, the BBC rejected Baird's method in favour of cathode ray tubes when they were in the process of planning a national television service. Swinton in 1908 had been ahead of his time in that although his concept was the one that was finally chosen, he proposed it before it was technically feasible. He called his idea 'distant electric vision' and predicted that his invention would have far-reaching effects on society. He died in 1930.

Dr Stephen Salter was born in Johannesburg in 1938. He was educated at Cambridge and then took up an apprenticeship at what was then known as Saunders-Roe Ltd. He worked as a fitter, toolmaker and instrument engineer on the SR177, the Skeeter helicopter, the Hovercraft SRN1 and the Black Knight rocket. In 1962 he became a research assistant to Richard Gregory's Special Devices Group in the Department of Experimental Psychology at Cambridge. There he worked on the solid image microscope and on a seeing-corrector for astronomical telescopes.

Salter came to Edinburgh with Professor Gregory in 1967 to the School of Artificial Intelligence and built metal and electronic hardware for the robot group and a touch-sensitive screen for computer-aided instruction. In 1974 he moved to the Department of Mechanical Engineering, where he is currently working on a research project into the extraction of power from sea waves. The Salter 'duck' design has had worldwide publicity and is a leader in the field of alternative energy sources.

Jazz

The most eminent jazz musician to come out of Edinburgh was **Sandy Brown** (1929-75). Born in India, he was a clarinettist who came to the forefront in the 1950s. His style was one of idiosyncratic phraseology. A self-taught musician, he played with a hard-brush timbre and hair-raising rhythms. He worked with Humphrey Lyttleton and Chris Barber and was co-leader of the Al Fairweather-Sandy Brown Jazz Band. Among his mainstream recordings the most memorable is probably 'Doctor McJazz'. He was equally at home with trad, gospel music and ethnic African music and was a respected acoustical architect.

Alex Welsh (1929-1982) led superb bands for 28 years. He began his musical education with a silver band in Edinburgh, playing cornet. In the late 1940s he was with the Sandy Brown Band and later with the Archie Semple Capital Stompers. He had a flair for improvising jazz line-ups and excelled in the Dixieland style of jazz.

Charlie McNair has been blowing trumpet for twenty-five years in the capital and can be heard regularly in Preservation Hall leading the Charlie McNair Jazzband.

Charlie McNair

Jack Duff, a former pupil of the Royal High School, plays tenor sax and clarinet in the Jersey Jazz Club and on cruise boats on the West Coast of the USA. Johnny Keating, ex-trombonist and former chief arranger for Ted Heath, is best

known for his composition of the theme music for television's *Z
Cars*, but it is **Mike Hart** with his Scottish Jazz Advocates
(formerly the Scottish Syncopators) who has done the most to
put Edinburgh jazz on the map with his institution in 1979 of
the Edinburgh Jazz Festival, modelled on the Dixieland Jubilee

Mike Hart

in Sacramento, California. Hart, as Festival Director, plays his
banjo and presides over other regulars in the City, such as
George Chisholm (on trombone), the Louisiana Ragtime Band,
the Alex Shaw Trio and vocalist Jackie Macfarlane. The
Scottish Jazz Advocates played their last gig in 1984, with Mike
Hart forming a new eight-piece line-up to be known as the
Scottish Society Syncopators.

Most exciting prospect on the Edinburgh jazz scene is young
saxophonist Tommy Smith who studied at the world's top jazz
college, Berklee College in Boston, and has already made his
first records.

Stan Greig is part of the Royal High School jazz fraternity
which includes Sandy Brown and Al Fairweather. He played
piano and then drums with Sandy Brown in 1947 and later
with Ken Colyer. In 1955 he joined Humphrey Lyttleton.
Another spell with Sandy Brown in 1947 and later
then in 1960 Greig became a member of Acker Bilk's Para-
mount Jazz Band. He toured with Memphis Slim before
forming his own London Jazz Big Band. Later he toured with
George Melly.

Gordon Cruickshank runs BBC Radio Scotland's only regular jazz programme: *Take the Jazz Train*. He is also one of Scotland's best tenor sax players. Early in his career he played baritone sax in a rock band. At that time he played with a Rhythm and Blues band called the Memphis Roadshow and with a loosely formed group called Assassination Weapon. Cruickshank was self-taught but was fortunate to have lived in the flat below Alex Shaw, who tended to play loud jazz around three in the morning.

Jay Craig is Edinburgh's international baritone saxophonist. Born in 1958, Jay Craig's music teacher was Philip Greene, whom Craig persuaded to form the Edinburgh Academy Dance Band. Jay's big ambition had always been to be a professional musician with a big American dance band. It was a Duke Ellington concert at the Usher Hall which was the turning-point in his life: he heard Harry Carney play the baritone sax and was hooked on jazz. He played with the National Youth Jazz Orchestra at the age of seventeen and the American Youth Band of Delaware. After music studies at Napier College he trained as a teacher at Moray House and later taught at Boroughmuir and Leith Academy. Four nights a week he played with a Glasgow jazz band. He went full-time professional and worked with Radio Clyde, STV and the BBC Radio Orchestra. Joe Temperley, who played baritone sax in America, came home to Cowdenbeath and suggested Jay should try for a scholarship to Berklee College, Boston. After eighteen months at Berklee, Jay Craig was signed up with the Buddy Rich Orchestra, playing for artists like Tony Bennet, Frank Sinatra, Rosemary Clooney and Vic Damone. In 1984 the Orchestra gave a concert in the Usher Hall as part of a Buddy Rich European tour.

Lawyers

The law in Scotland has its roots in Roman, feudal and Germanic law. Most of Scotland's legal affairs were conducted by churchmen in medieval times. Many of these legal figures had been educated at Continental universities, formerly in France (Orléans, Poitiers, Bourges or Paris) and in the seventeenth and eighteenth centuries, until the traditional continental connections (in law as in other spheres), faded, in Holland, especially at Leiden.

Law was also administered by laymen in the sheriff courts or by *ad hoc* committees drawn from the King's Council. In 1532 the Lords of Council and Session who had been responsible for carrying out royal justice were re-organised on a more permanent basis as a College of Justice – the Court of Session. Up to the time of the Reformation the Lord President and half of the Court of fourteen other Senators were churchmen. Also included in the College were the Advocates (generally from landed or aristocratic families) and the Writers to the Signet (solicitors). Parliament House, in Edinburgh where the College of Justice now resides, became in the eighteenth century particularly the centre of the political, social and intellectual life of Scotland. Thus Edinburgh held, by reason of its prime position in the legal life of the nation, a unique importance.

Of central importance to the practice of Scots Law was the work of **Viscount Stair** (1619-95). His *Institutions of the Law of Scotland*, published in 1681, codified Scots Law into a coherent system. His daughter Janet's luckless marriage in 1669, incidentally, is said to have inspired Scott's *Bride of Lammermoor*. **Sir George Mackenzie** ('Bluidy' Mackenzie to the Covenanters), boasted that he had never lost a case for the King and is remembered for the ruthlessness with which he prosecuted the Covenanters. His *Discourse upon the Laws and Customs of Scotland in Matters Criminal* (1674) became a standard legal work, and he is also remembered for his gift of 1,500 books to the Advocates' Library which he founded in 1680, and out of which grew the

141

Viscount Stair

National Library of Scotland in 1925. The clarity of his legal judgements as Lord Advocate also helped to reduce the number of prosecutions for witchcraft which credulity and superstition had conjured up. For generations, Edinburgh schoolboys played the game of running up to Mackenzie's cavernous mausoleum in Greyfriars churchyard and shouting through the rusted grille of the door:

> Lift the sneck and draw the bar:
> Bluidie Mackingie, came out if ye daur!

Other notable judges were **Henry Home, Lord Kames** (1696-1782), who was held to be the ideal cultivated Scottish lawyer, an agricultural improver, moral philosopher, literary critic and historian; and James Burnett, Lord Monboddo (1714-99) who, although considered a bit of an eccentric, may also claim to have anticipated Darwin in believing that men were related to apes. Dr Johnson took the trouble to visit him to hear more of what were regarded as bizarre theories.

Duncan Forbes (1685-1747) was, through his character and position, the lynchpin of the kingdom at a critical point in the development of the Scottish nation. Born three miles from Inverness, he was educated at Inverness Grammar School, then Edinburgh, after which he went to Leiden to continue his studies, learning oriental languages and theology (he was said to have read the Bible in Hebrew eight times), returning to Edinburgh to specialise in the municipal laws of Scotland. He was admitted a Member of the Faculty of Advocates in 1709 and in the same year was appointed Sheriff of Midlothian, becoming Sheriff Depute of Edinburgh in 1714.

As Depute to the Lord Advocate in 1716, Duncan Forbes was

Lord President Duncan Forbes, by Roubiliac, in Parliament House

active for the Government but opposed the trials of Scottish Jacobites in England as he believed they would not get an unprejudiced hearing in Carlisle. Forbes considered that the transfer of Jacobite prisoners south of the Border was illegal and did not want to prosecute his fellow-countrymen in front of foreigners. By now he was one of the most influential men in Scotland. He was the Scottish counsel for the Argyll family and acted as a liaison officer between the authorities in Scotland and the ministers in London. His brother John was on good terms with Sir Robert Walpole, and regular intelligence was thus able to pass from Duncan to Walpole through John. Duncan was a voluminous correspondent.

The aftermath of the abortive Jacobite Rebellion of 1715 brought a great deal of work to the courts: estates were confiscated and Commissioners appointed to administer the new Crown lands. There was the vexed matter of the intervention of the House of Lords in cases of forfeiture which had been decided by the Scottish Court of Session: this appeared to be in contravention of the terms of the Treaty of Union which had guaranteed the independence and integrity of the laws of Scotland in all time coming. Although Forbes was in favour of the Disarming Act of 1716, he opposed its ramifications. The Act made it unlawful for anyone in the Highlands to have or to wear broadsword or target, poignard, dirk or side-pistol on the King's Highway or coming and going from church, market, fair or hunting. It abolished the feudal service which clansmen were required to give to their chiefs and made provision for schools to be established (this was scarcely done at all).

In 1722 Duncan Forbes became MP for Inverness district of burghs, a position he held to 1737. His great rival, Robert Dundas, entered the House of Commons at the same time. Both had entered politics in 1709 on opposite sides; and when Lord President Forbes died, he was succeeded by Dundas.

When Forbes became Lord Advocate in 1725, he was the unofficial Regent of Scotland, known as 'King Duncan'. In the same year he had, as a Burgess and Guild Brother of Glasgow, to undertake the unpleasant task of coping with the Shawfield Riots there in reaction to the introduction of a tax on malt. Forbes was closely involved with Scotland's banks which were described as Forbes 'own bairns'. He was involved in the incorporation of the Royal Bank in 1727 and in the following year was at work on the charter of the Mining Company in Scotland. As a close friend of Lord Provost George Drummond, he also had a hand in the establishing of Edinburgh's first Infirmary.

The Treaty of Union had promised two thousand pounds per annum for seven years for the establishment of new industries in Scotland. Forbes, one of whose uppermost concerns was the development of the Scottish economy, was one of the trustees of these monies which were ploughed into the linen industry and the spinning of coarse tarred wool. In Edinburgh French Protestant weavers from Picardy were brought over (hence Picardy Place in Edinburgh), and in 1746 the British Linen Company was founded, later to become a bank. Forbes himself started a spinning school on his estate of Culloden.

The Porteous Riots of 1736 in Edinburgh again exercised Forbes' powers. The response of the Government in 1737 to such civil disorder was to pass a Bill which would for life disable the Lord Provost from taking office and imprison him; the City Guard was to be abolished and the Netherbow Port dismantled. This Bill passed the Lords, but Forbes and his friends fought it in the Commons, and it was finally reduced to disabling the Lord Provost and fining Edinburgh Corporation. This was Forbes' last speech in the Commons. He became Lord President of the Court of Session in the same year and quickly set about reorganising the chaotic system of hearing cases in the Court of Session, ensuring that every case was heard in due order and making it unlawful for any case to wait more than four years before coming to court.

Following the Jacobite Rebellion of '45, the Disarming Act of 1746 had forbidden the wearing of the tartan or of Highland dress. Although Forbes approved of the Act in principle, he could not accept the ban on tartan and on the dress which he knew from experience was also a practical one for the Highland way of life. Nor could he accept that the clans which had been loyal to the Government would also have to suffer this penalty. A servant of Government, nevertheless he was not its tool, and always looked out for Scotland's interests. In the aftermath of the Rebellion he pleaded clemency towards the Highlanders, earning from the callous Duke of Cumberland the description of 'that old woman who talked to me about humanity'.

As well as being a man of law and of politics, Duncan Forbes was the first Captain of the Gentlemen Golfers of Edinburgh and is mentioned in Thomas Mathison's poem *The Goff* (1743). He was the friend of the poet Allan Ramsay and is said to have belonged to the same Literary Club frequented by Swift and Pope in London. James Thomson, the poet, was a friend of Forbes's son, and writes in his *Seasons:*

> Thee, Forbes, to whom every worth attends,
> As truth sincere, as weeping friendship kind –
> Thee, truly generous, and in silence great,
> The country feels thro' her reviving arts,
> Planned by thy wisdom, by thy soul informed.

In earlier years Forbes and his brother had been known as 'the greatest boozers in the north'. The story goes that on his mother's death Forbes and the funeral party drank so hard that on going to the burial ground they left the body behind. However, he was also well known as the author of theological works, and after his death there were few to quarrel with the description of him as 'one of the greatest men that ever Scotland bred, as a judge, a patriot, and a Christian'. His statue by Roubiliac stands in Parliament House.

Robert MacQueen, **Lord Braxfield,** was a formidable figure, and became the model for Stevenson's *Weir of Hermiston.*

Braxfield (1722-99) was a friend of Scott and presided over the Deacon Brodie trial. He was Lord of Session in 1776 and Justice Clerk in 1788. Braxfield was famous – or infamous – for his treatment of Thomas Muir, a Glasgow advocate. Muir had corresponded with the French revolutionaries, and went to France when war started with that country in 1793. On his return he was tried for encouraging the reading of Paine's *Rights of Man*, for attending meetings of the Friends of the People in James Court and supporting 'votes for all' in place of the grossly unfair electoral system of the time. Lord Braxfield handpicked the jury and openly displayed his prejudice, sentencing the accused to transportation to Botany Bay in Australia. To another accused who chose to conduct his own defence, Braxfield remarked that he was 'a clever enough chiel', but that he would be 'nane the waur (worse) o' a hangin''. Despite Lord Braxfield's coarse and uncouth behaviour, his unfeeling jests, and his rough treatment of his wife, he was admired for the courage with which he chose to walk home from court unescorted.

'When one finds oneself in possession of an interest founded partly on private friendship, partly on family connections, partly on the gratitude of friends whom he has had it in his power to oblige, and partly, I flatter myself, on grounds of a still more public nature, he is not fond of allowing it to be frittered away.' So wrote **Henry Dundas, first Viscount Melville** (1742-1811), to Robert Baird in 1795. Dundas was born and educated in Edinburgh. When he was twenty-four, after a mere three years as a lawyer, he was appointed Solicitor General for Scotland. Within eight years he became MP for Midlothian and lived mainly in London. At the time of the new Government formed by the Younger Pitt in 1783, Dundas was rewarded with a number of important positions: Treasurer of the Navy, President of the India Board, and, after 1891, Home Secretary. Lord Cockburn says of him: 'Henry Dundas, an Edinburgh man, and well calculated by talent and manner to make despotism popular, was the absolute dictator of Scotland'. He was also known as 'Harry the Ninth, uncrowned King of Scotland'.

The secret of Dundas's power was the control he gained over voting and the selection of candidates: he prepared the list of representative peers. When Dundas was at the height of his power there were only 2624 county voters and 1289 burgh voters. Edinburgh was one of three large constituencies, with thirty-three voters for one member. For Edinburgh, Dundas was returned without opposition in 1790, but became unpopular with the rise of radicalism in the 1790s. In 1806 Dundas was impeached in Westminster Hall for embezzling public funds while Treasurer of the Navy, but was acquitted. He is commemorated by the Melville Monument, a lofty column in the middle of St Andrew Square, designed by William Burn.

A native of Edinburgh (1773-1850), **Francis Jeffrey** went to the High School at the age of eight. He is recorded as having caught sight of Robert Burns, the poet, in an Edinburgh street and as having been struck by the poet's flashing eyes. He went to the Glasgow College at the age of 14 and already had developed methodical literary habits by taking full notes of the lectures he heard and expanding and commenting on them. At Glasgow he joined the Elocution Club and exercised his skill as a public speaker.

After graduating from Glasgow in 1789, Jeffrey attended two classes at Edinburgh University and then went to Oxford. By this time he had added to his brief meeting with Burns the singular distinction of having carried James Boswell, the biographer of Dr Johnson, up to his bed when 'Bozzy' was incapacitated by drink. Jeffrey found Oxford to be full of 'pedants, coxcombs and strangers'. After a year there he returned to Edinburgh with an anglicised accent. Cockburn reports that he had a 'high-keyed accent and a sharp pronunciation', and Jeffrey's friend Lord Holland adds that though he 'had lost the broad Scotch at Oxford, he had only gained the narrow English'.

In spite of pursuing further studies in Scots Law at Edinburgh University, Jeffrey declared himself disgusted with Edinburgh, 'For I am almost alone in the midst of its swarms, and am disturbed by its filth, and debauchery, and restraint, without having access to much of the virtue or genius it may contain'. At this time Jeffrey was still accumulating skills and experience; he had not yet found his role in life apart from his profession as a lawyer. He was admitted to the Bar in 1794 and took his place in the Outer House, which Cockburn identifies as one of the chief seedbeds of Scottish culture: 'For almost two centuries this place has been the resort and the nursery of a greater variety of talent than any other place in the northern portion of our island'.

On 10th October 1802 a number of friends gathered in Jeffrey's flat in Buccleuch Place, and out of their common interest in literature, politics and learning the Whig *Edinburgh Review* was born. Cockburn writes that 'The learning of the new Journal, its talent, its spirit, its writing, its independence, were all new . . .', and in nineteenth-century Britain 'The effect was electrical'. Jeffrey was editor of the new publication, and by 1808 had also contributed 79 articles. Author of the review of Wordsworth's *Excursion* beginning with the famous words 'This will never do', he in turn was attacked by the poet Byron in *English Bards and Scotch Reviewers*.

He restored and enlarged the old keep of Craigcrook in Edinburgh, and summer Saturdays there were always a festival, with friends on the bowling-green, in the garden or on the hill behind. In the evening came the banquets when conversation and laughter flowed. He visited the Continent in 1815, seeing Holland, Flanders and Paris. He was much struck by Waterloo: 'The people are ploughing and reaping, and old men following their old occupations, in their old fields, as if 60,000 youths had not fallen to manure them within these six months'. On the field of battle itself he picked up a bit of cloth and a piece of a bridle.

When the jury system was introduced into Scotland in 1816, Jeffrey made it his business to attend almost every Court to ensure that the new arrangements were given every chance of success by being properly implemented. He became Lord Advocate in 1830 and had some responsibility for the Reform Act of 1832. Conscious of the contrast between his ceremonial dress and his actual function, he wrote: 'You will find me glorious in a . . . silk gown, and long cravat, – sending men to the gallows, and persecuting smugglers for penalties, – and every day in a wig, and most days with buckles on my shoes'. In London he often met the poet William Wordsworth, who held no malice against him in spite of his criticisms of the Lake Poets. In 1840 he was chosen to write the monumental inscription for the foundation stone of the Scott Monument in Princes Street.

Henry Cockburn – 'Cocky' – (1779-1854) attended the High School of Edinburgh (which he disliked) for six years and in 1793 began his studies at the College of Edinburgh to fit him for the legal profession. In 1810 he helped start the Commer-

Francis Jeffrey and Henry Cockburn

cial Bank. Along with Francis Jeffrey and another companion, he toured the Continent, being especially struck by the beauty and decay of Venice. In the same year (1823), with Jeffrey, he helped found the Edinburgh Academy. Five years later he successfully defended the 'wife' of Burke, Helen MacDougal, in the Burke and Hare case. By 1830 Cockburn had become Solicitor General, but he retired in 1834, continuing to write for the *Edinburgh Review* with his long-time friend Jeffrey. In 1837 Cockburn was appointed a Lord of Justiciary, but his greatest political contribution was in the drafting of the First Reform Bill for Scotland as one of the leaders of the Scottish Whigs.

The *Edinburgh Review* of 1857 described him as 'rather below the middle height, firm, wiry and muscular, inured to active exercise of all kinds, a good swimmer, an accomplished skater, and an intense lover of the fresh breezes of heaven . . . He was the model of a high-bred Scotch gentleman . . . He spoke with a Doric breadth of accent . . . In temperament . . . he was naturally of an easy and careless hilarity . . . Cockburn was one of the most popular men north of the Tweed'.

Lord Cockburn is the high priest of Edinburgh, being so central to its traditions not only through his colourful writing in works such as *Memorials of His Time*, but through having been instrumental in preserving and celebrating what is best in the City, and therefore aptly chosen as the namesake of the Cockburn Association, which came into being in 1875 to foster appreciation of, and to preserve, the best of Edinburgh's buildings and environment. To Lord Cockburn himself we are indebted for his having protested against the defeated proposals to build on the south side of Princes Street, and thus saved the matchless view over the Gardens to the Castle and the Old Town skyline. Cockburn Street is also named after him. He was a friend of the distinguished early pioneers of photography, David Octavius Hill and Robert Adamson, and among his descendants were his great-grandson, the autobiographer and journalist, Claud Cockburn, and his great-great-grandson, the novelist Evelyn Waugh.

The **Lord Lyon King of Arms,** first found as a public title in 1318, can lay claim to be a descendant of the supreme judge of heraldries for the Celtic monarchy, the Royal Sennachie. The office of Lord Lyon is therefore the oldest in the Royal Household of Scotland. In the Scottish Coronation ceremony it was the Lord Lyon who acted as Inaugurator, and when the science of armoury came into use, he had the control and administration of armorial bearings. The Lord Lyon is a Judge of the Realm when he sits in the Lyon Court, the Scottish Court of Chivalry. In proclamations he is the official mouthpiece of the Sovereign, and his voice legally is heard throughout Scotland when he stands at the Mercat Cross of Edinburgh, gorgeously arrayed, a medieval peacock.

His functions in the twentieth century are as hard-headed as his official garb is brightly coloured and golden. New coats of arms for families, schools, district councils and industrial concerns are granted on petition and entered in a public register. The Lord Lyon gives judgement in cases of succession; he determines precedents, is the controller of State Ceremonial in Scotland, and is an authority on tartans. Such tasks provide the daily routine of the Lord Lyon. Twice a year the Head Court meets, and it is on such occasions that the Lyon Court can be seen in its full glory: in May and in November at Register House. The offices comprise six Heralds (Islay, Marchmont, Albany, Ross, Rothesay and Snowdon – only three are filled at any one time); six Pursuivants (Carrick, Unicorn, Dingwall, Bute, Kintyre and Ormond – again only three at any one time); and a Lyon Macer and Herald Painters who maintain the traditional arts of heraldic script and illumination.

Famous Lords Lyon King of Arms have included: Sir William Cuming who took the challenge to Henry VIII which led to the disastrous battle of Flodden; Sir David Lindsay of the Mount, author of the *Thrie Estaits* and compiler of a famous Armorial Register; Sir Robert Forman, Lyon to Queen Mary of Scots; Sir James Balfour who conducted the coronations of Charles I and II; Sir Charles Erskine who in 1672 established the public register of All Arms and Bearings; and Alexander Brodie who as Lord Lyon rode with the Duke of Cumberland during the whole of the 1745-46 Jacobite Rebellion, at a time when the Ross Herald, a Jacobite, proclaimed James VIII and acted as Herald to Prince Charles. **Sir Thomas Innes of Learney** held the office from 1945 to 1969, as secretary to the Order of the Thistle. He was the author of a number of works on heraldry, genealogy and ceremonial, and an eminent peerage and heraldic counsel.

Sir Thomas Innes of Learney

Literature

It is with **Allan Ramsay** (1686-1758) that Edinburgh begins to enter its golden age of literature. A native of Lanarkshire, Ramsay (father of the portrait painter of the same name) started his working life as an apprentice wigmaker in Edinburgh. In 1712 he opened a wig shop in the Grassmarket, but his interests and business acumen soon led in other directions. In 1712 also he founded the Easy Club and six years later published his first collection of poems. His *Tea Table Miscellany*, a collection of Scots songs and ballads, followed in 1724, and two years later he set up a bookshop at the end of the Luckenbooths beside St Giles. He had also started up the first lending library in Britain (1724) and finished a verse play, *The Gentle Shepherd*. In 1736 he founded the first regular theatre in Edinburgh and managed it until it was closed by the Licensing Act of 1737. Later in his life he moved into an octagonal villa on the north side of Castle Hill (now Ramsay Garden) from where he could indulge all his multifarious activities, including playing golf at Bruntsfield Links and drinking in good company. He was the complete professional writer, with his finger not only in production and distribution but also in public relations and finance, as that earlier patron of literature, 'Jinglin' Geordie' (George Heriot), has been up to his death in 1610. He helped revive an awareness of Scottish national culture which, on the one hand, had been impaired by the political and religious distractions of the seventeenth century and, on the other, by admiration in certain circles for English models.

The Gaelic poet **Duncan ban Macintyre** (1724-1812), originally a forester, after fighting on the Hanoverian side of the '45 Rebellion served in the Edinburgh Town Guard and wrote many poems in praise of the Campbells, and in favour of the revival of the kilt and bagpipe. He is unexcelled in his descriptions of nature, especially deer, his most famous poem being 'The Praise of Ben Doran'. He died and is buried in Edinburgh.

Meanwhile, to another sort of Gaelic: the poet **James Macpherson** (1736-96), born in Inverness-shire, the son of a small farmer, was educated at Aberdeen, then at Edinburgh University, with the intention of becoming a minister. But some literary talent, and some knowledge of Gaelic poetry still in oral circulation, eventually led to his publishing what he called a 'translation' of the works of a Gaelic poet called Ossian, said to have lived in the 3rd century A.D. Whatever was original was heavily doctored by himself, but it took the European and American fancy of the day – Goethe, Blake, Wordsworth, Scott and Byron were influenced (Napoleon was an admirer too); Dr Johnson remained sceptical. *The Works of Ossian* (1765) suited the taste of the day for something sublime and heroic which was outside the Greek and Roman tradition: Ossian was a Northern Homer, and also satisfied a growing nationalist movement in various quarters. *Ossian* is seldom read now, except by students of cultural movements, but perhaps it had some practical effect in portraying Highlanders in a favourable light: they had been considered until then – by Lowland Scots as much as anyone else – to be dangerous, thieving savages.

Suddenly Scottish writers were famous abroad. **Henry Mackenzie** (1745-1831), novelist and essayist, was educated at the High School in Edinburgh and was a lawyer by profession. He came to fame with his novel *The Man of Feeling* (1771), an exercise in sentimentality which has dated badly but had a great vogue in its day: Burns wore out two copies of it and said he prized it next to the Bible. Mackenzie also edited two journals, *The Mirror* (1779-80) and *The Lounger* (1785-7), modelled on *The Spectator,* and wrote most of the contributions himself, showing in his humorous observation a sharper appreciation of human nature than in *The Man of Feeling,* and influencing Scott and John Galt. He was also the first significant critic to praise Burns – in *The Lounger.* His reputation was international, but he stayed in Edinburgh, unlike the poet **James Thomson** (1700-48), son of a Border minister who, while studying Divinity at Edinburgh University, published in Edinburgh magazines, but sought his fortune in London where he came to international notice with *The Seasons* (1730). He also wrote 'Rule Britannia'.

Turning homeward again: **Robert Fergusson** (1750-74) was born in Cap and Feather Close (now disappeared under the North Bridge). He left St Andrews University without a degree

Robert Fergusson

and took up employment as a clerk in the Commissionary Office in Edinburgh. In 1772 he was made a member of the Cape Club and wrote two of his best poems, 'Caller Oysters' and 'Auld Reekie'. His poetic career lasted for three years until 1774, when he injured himself falling down a flight of steps and was incarcerated in the Edinburgh Bedlam as a madman. He was much admired as a writer by both Burns and Stevenson and influenced Burns by his colourful use of the Scots tongue and the virility of his language. See, for instance, his portrayal of Edinburgh street life in 'Auld Reekie'.

Sir Walter Scott (1771-1832) was born at the top of College Wynd, the son of a solicitor. At the age of 18 months he contracted polio, which left him with a permanent limp in his

Sir Walter Scott

right leg. He was educated at the Royal High School and Edinburgh University, and practised as an advocate in Edinburgh from 1792 to 1806. From 1806 until 1830 he held office as a Clerk to the Court of Session. He was Sheriff of Selkirkshire from 1799 until his death. Created a baronet in 1820, he acted as master of ceremonies during George IV's state visit to Scotland in 1822 – an occasion which may be said to have launched the popular tartan/Highland image of Scotland that has held sway ever since.

His first important literary work was *The Minstrelsy of the Scottish Border* (1802-3), in which he collated, adapted and arranged traditional ballads. He contributed to the *Edinburgh Review* and helped launch the rival, Tory *Quarterly* (1809). He wrote a series of Romantic narrative poems including *The Lay of the Last Minstrel* (1805), *Marmion* (1808) and *The Lady of the Lake* (1810), which were great successes, not least commercially. However, outshone by Byron, he turned to writing historical novels, at first anonymously ('the Great Unknown'), the best being those set in the Scotland of the seventeenth century, in which he portrays, with a strong sense of nostalgia, the 'heroic' values of an older civilisation but their increasing irrelevance in the coming world of commerce and order: there is both gain and loss.

Having himself been a commercial success as a writer, he displayed a 'romantic' side to himself in wanting to live as a landed magnate, which led to his buying Abbotsford in his ancestral Borders in 1811. This was a heavy drain on his resources, and when his publishers the Ballantynes, with whom he was involved, had a financial crisis, he was a debtor, but paid off his debts by incessant writing until his death – itself a 'heroic' act. Less widely read now, in the nineteenth century his reputation and literary influence were immense, extending from Cooper in America, through France and Germany, to Pushkin in Russia, and he may be said to have created an international interest in Scotland greater than ever before.

Susan Ferrier (1782-1854) was born in Lady Stair's Close in Edinburgh. Her father was a Writer to the Signet, and through the circle of his friends and clients (one of his friends was Robert Burns) she met many prominent and influential men and women in the family house in Morningside. One of her

F

father's clients was the 5th Duke of Argyll, and Susan spent a number of fruitful visits at Inveraray Castle where she was able to gather some of the raw material for her novels. At the Castle there were amateur theatricals, large house parties and other entertainments, all of which she recorded in her journal for later use. Another friend of her father's was Walter Scott, whom her father helped at the time of the novelist's financial troubles.

She describes her time at the Castle as 'writing to my sisters three, sewing my seam, improving my mind, making tea, playing whist and numberless other duties'. The result of this subservient role as a passive observer (common to most women of the age) wa the writing of three novels: *Marriage* (1818); *The Inheritance* (1824) and *Destiny* (1831), which provide an affectionate but ironic insight into the character and manners of the society of her time and situation.

Hugh Miller (1802-56) was a Cromarty man. He spent his childhood soaking up the environment in Cromarty, rock-collecting and beachcombing, entranced by the mineralogy of

Hugh Miller

the country around him, learning the culture of the Gaels, and finally being apprenticed to his uncle as a stonemason in 1820, fascinated by the colour and texture of rocks. He sailed to Edinburgh in 1824 to try and sell off a derelict property his family owned in Leith. He detested much of what he found in the City: the rowdiness, drunkeness and urban squalor contrasted with the stable values of Cromarty and its closeness to nature. He writes of a tavern in the Canongate: 'a low roofed room into which the light of day never penetrated, and in which the gas was burning dimly in a slow, close, sluggish atmosphere rendered still more stifling by tobacco smoke and a strong smell of ardent spirits. There was a trap-door which lay open, and a wild combination of sounds, the yelping of a dog, and a few gruff voices cheering him on, rose from the apartment below. It was customary at this time for dram-shops to keep badgers housed in long narrow boxes, and for working men to keep dogs; and its was part of the ordinary sport of such places to set the dogs to unhouse the badgers'.

Miller worked on the construction of Niddrie House and searched the Queen's Park for geological specimens. His experience in Edinburgh made him suspicious of radicals, chartists and the idea of universal franchise, for the specimens of humanity he came across in the labourers around him made him doubt the wisdom of social reform. He returned to Cromarty in 1825.

Nine years later he was again in the Capital, this time as an accountant with the Commercial Bank. Miller introduced himself to Adam Black the publisher, at that time Lord Provost, and was warmly welcomed. He worked not in Edinburgh but in Linlithgow, in West Lothian, and there was another opportunity to become acquainted with new geological structures and formations.

He returned briefly to Edinburgh in 1835, then went back to Cromarty. Two years later he contributed to *Chambers Journal*, and in 1839 made his way back to Edinburgh to edit the *Witness*, an evangelical paper. In three years its circulation had overtaken every other Scottish newspaper, with the exception of the *Scotsman*.

When the Disruption split the Church, Miller was at hand, reporting the proceedings and supporting the breakaway Free Church, whose leader, Dr Chalmers, backed Miller's editorship when critical voices were raised against him. By the late 1840s Miller had become one of the literary stars of Edinburgh; he posed for his friend David Octavius Hill, the photographer, as a stonemason.

He published *The Old Red Sandstone*, a collection of seven essays from the *Witness*, in 1841. It ran through many editions and established Miller as an authoritative populariser of science. He also wrote a fine autobiography, *My Schools and Schoolmasters* (1854). His geological researches convinced him that what he saw in the rocks was evidence, not of evolutionary progression, but of independent and separate creation, an interpretation that satisfied few. He put himself forward as a candidate for the Chair of Natural History at Edinburgh University but was passed over. He became increasingly neurotic, still suffering from the pneumoconiosis he had acquired as a stonemason, and began to have a persecution complex of sorts, installing a man-trap in his garden. He carried a six-bullet revolver and slept with a *sgian-dhu* and a broadsword beside him. On Christmas Eve, 1856, Miller, who had been suffering from nightmares and visions and strain from overwork, awoke and shot himself through the chest. In a note he left for his wife he wrote: 'My brain burns'.

His funeral service was conducted by Dr Thomas Guthrie in the presence of the Lord Provost and two Members of Parliament. It was as if half of Edinburgh had turned out as the cortège moved down Princes Street; all the shops on the route up the North Bridge to the Grange Cemetery were closed. He was buried not far from Dr Thomas Chalmers.

That Gaelic oral tradition has survived in Scotland is largely the result of the work of **John Francis Campbell** (1821-1885). Born in Edinburgh, Campbell spent much of his childhood in Islay which his family owned. Campbell was a cousin of the Duke of Argyll, and his formative years were spent under the charge of John Campbell, a piper, and later in the care of the future schoolmaster Hector MacLean. Campbell also received some years of education at Eton before going to the University of Edinburgh where he studied geology and photography and then qualified in law.

He was appointed private secretary to the Duke of Argyll who at that time held the office of Lord Privy Seal. Later he became secretary to a number of Royal Commissions, a post in which he was closely involved with the leading men of his day, one of whom, Sir George Webb Dasent. filled Campbell with a desire to record the folktales of his Gaelic-speaking homeland. Drawing from a number of collectors, Campbell gathered together some eight hundred tales, publishing only a small proportion in his *The Popular Tales of the West Highlands* from 1860 to 1862. As the leading authority on Gaelic folktales in Scotland, Campbell's name was suggested for the new Chair of

Celtic at Edinburgh University. However, he refused, preferring instead the freedom of action he enjoyed on his own, unfettered by organisational constraints.

Campbell wrote of his collecting activities: 'Men who cannot read a single letter or understand a word of any language but Gaelic, ragged old paupers men might pass as drivelling idiots, begin and sing long ballads which I know to be more than three hundred years old'. His many manuscripts are to be found in the National Library of Scotland in Edinburgh.

William McGonagall, self-styled Poet and Tragedian (1830-1902), was born in Edinburgh of an Irish father who worked as a cotton weaver and as a pedlar selling hardware. William

William McGonagall

eventually began work as a weaver in Dundee before starting out on a career as an amateur tragic actor in a theatrical booth to an amused audience of his workmates. In 1872 he gave three performances a night as Macbeth until he was hoarse-voiced. In the Theatre Royal in Dundee he even refused to die when Macduff stabbed him: 'he maintained his feet and flourished his weapon about the ears of his adversary in such a way that there was for some time an apparent probability of a real tragedy'. McGonagall himself had a different view of the proceedings: 'the applause was deafening, and continued during the entire evening, especially so in the combat scene'. He studied Shakespeare, Burns and Tennyson and in 1877 gave up the loom to peddle his poems in streets, shops, offices, clubs, societies and the penny gaffs. He was a figure of fun and a curiosity to amuse the drinking fraternity, and was encouraged rather cruelly by Edinburgh University students to take himself seriously. He describes his call to the vocation of poet thus: 'A flame, as Lord Byron said, seemed to kindle up my entire frame, along with a strong desire to write poetry; and I felt so happy, that I was inclined to dance . . .' In 1878 he made an abortive journey to Balmoral to try and see Queen Victoria. He was turned back at the gatehouse, but not before he had given some taste of his power as a poet. In 1887 he sailed to New York but was unable to get any theatrical or musical engagements. Back in Dundee he performed in circuses. He died having attained the dubious honour of being the world's worst poet. However, so sublimely bad is his doggerel that he has achieved a certain immortality, and continues to be recited with genuine enjoyment.

The Edinburgh writer with the most colourful lifestyle must surely be **Robert Louis Stevenson** (1850-94), who was born the son of the joint engineer to the Board of Northern Lighthouses. He first studied engineering at Edinburgh University,

Robert-Louis Stevenson

but abandoned this for law and became an advocate in 1875. He was early plagued with an infection of the lungs which forced him to travel often in search of a healing climate. Stevenson met his future wife in 1876 in an artists' colony in the Forest of Fountainebleau in France. Fanny Osbourne was an American, ten years older than RLS and at the time separated from her husband. In the following year Stevenson made a canoe trip with the son of James Young Simpson through Belgium and France. His *Inland Voyage* was based on this experience. In 1878 he wrote *Travels with a Donkey in the Cevennes,* which describes a trip through France with a very different form of locomotion. In 1883 there followed *Treasure Island,* and when he wrote *Kidnapped* and *The Strange Case of Dr Jekyll and Mr Hyde* (1886), Stevenson was in Bournemouth, where he met the American novelist Henry James, with whom he became friends. In 1888 he chartered a yacht to sail the Pacific. He went to Tahiti (three years before Gauguin) and to Hawaii: there in a hut on the beach he finished *The Master of Ballantrae.* Then to the Gilberts and Samoa and finally Australia. As a result of this trip Stevenson settled on Samoa, where he built a fine house, farmed his estate and continued to write. His *Weir of Hermiston* was unfinished at his death in 1894. *Treasure Island* is an unrivalled adventure story, and *Dr Jekyll and Mr Hyde* a supreme study of the divided self, deriving, as well as from a powerful imagination, from the mixed experience of affection for Edinburgh and reaction against its oppressive Presbyterian respectability. Did he also remember the outwardly respectable but nocturnally criminal Deacon Brodie?

Helen Brodie Cowan Watson (**Helen Bannerman**) was born in Edinburgh in 1862, the daughter of a Free Church minister. Her father was an expert in the study of shells and compiled a study of the material brought back by the *Challenger* expedition which explored the waters of the southern hemisphere in 1873-76. He taught his daughter several languages: Portuguese, French, Italian and German, and she showed considerable ability in art and music.

When Helen was two the family moved to the Scots Church at Madeira and ten years later returned to Edinburgh. As· a child Helen enjoyed drawing cartoons, and writing jokes and stories, and she had a taste for bloodthirsty if improbable plots. Women were not then admitted to St Andrews University, but she passed a special external degree for women in languages and literature, and then studied in Hanover and Torre Pellice, Italy. In 1889 she married Will Bannerman, who was posted as medical officer to a regiment in India, taking his bride with him. Her husband was promoted to District Surgeon and devoted himself to researching into plague, which at that time ravaged the country.

Helen had two daughters, and it was during a voyage with them to the calm of the hills that her first book, *The Story of*

Little Black Sambo, was born. She bound the volume herself and sent it off to her daughters. The book was first published commercially in 1899 and by 1903 had become so popular that eight British editions had appeared. Helen herself, having sold the copywright for £5, had no other financial return from her book.

In 1901 *The Story of Little Black Mingo* followed and in 1902 *The Story of Little Black Quibba.* Other works followed to a total of ten books. The letters she wrote to her children from India at their schools in Britain were bound into 17 volumes full of anecdotes and observation of nature (she was a contemporary of Beatrix Potter). Subsequent editions of her books, especially American ones, introduced illustrations which destroyed the ethnic dignity of her stories by introducing an alien element of offensive racial prejudice, which was never in the original. Helen Bannerman died in Edinburgh in 1946 at the age of 84.

Hugh MacDiarmid (1892-1978), although born in Langholm, had a long association with Edinburgh, starting with his coming in 1908 to be a student teacher at Broughton Higher Grade

Hugh MacDiarmid

School, a profession he abandoned for journalism. He has come to be known as the begetter of the 'Scottish Renaissance', dating from the 1920s when, in single-minded isolation, he began to attack the contemporary state of Scottish culture – or lack of it – as he saw it. He exposed the defeated provincialism of a formerly independent nation which had lapsed into acceptance of the sentimentalities of the 'Kailyard' school of novelists – all very arch, coy and falsely countrified: a degenerate version of Burns, brought on by ignorance of Scotland's own past and of European and international culture. Besides the Scottish establishment, he saw England as the chief agent of provincialisation of Scotland, and therefore as an enemy, and his thinking – a blend of Communism and Scottish nationalism – was found abrasive and too extreme by many, but it was probably what it took to mount and sustain a campaign on behalf of an altered state of national consciousness. He was expelled from the Communist Party in 1938 because of his continued membership of the Scottish National Party which he had helped to found (1928), as had Compton Mackenzie, a Catholic convert. Always keen to display in his poetry an awareness of the international scene, he simultaneously pressed into service the Scots tongue (or Lallans) for its reminder of roots and for its expressiveness. His most famous poem is 'A Drunk Man Looks at the Thistle'. Abrasive, extreme and provocative, he continues to provoke disagreement as to his true literary stature (T. S. Eliot was an unlikely supporter), but he was the stuff – a literary Luther? – of which cultural change is made.

Compton Mackenzie (1883-1972), the novelist, settled in Edinburgh late in life – in Drummond Place – but quickly established himself as a doyen of the literary scene. Author of a notable autobiography, he is probably best remembered now for his novel *Whisky Galore,* a comic masterpiece later made into a famous film, and drawing on his experiences of living in the Hebrides: he had settled in Barra in 1928. He also helped to found the Scottish National Party.

Muriel Camberg (**Muriel Spark**) was born in Bruntsfield in 1918 and attended James Gillespie's School for Girls where she won a poetry competition held in honour of the centenary of Sir Walter Scott and was crowned Queen of Poetry. In 1936 she went to live in South Africa and then Rhodesia. She returned to Britain in 1944 to the Political Intelligence Department of the Foreign Office where she invented news items to discredit the enemy. After the War she wrote critical biographies of nineteenth-century figures and edited the letters of the Brontës, Mary Shelley and Cardinal Newman. In 1951 she won an *Observer* Short Story Competition with a story about the apparition of an angel on the Zambesi river. Subsequently she won the Italia Prize and was awarded the James Tait Black Memorial Prize by Edinburgh University. In 1967 she was made OBE. She lives in Rome.

As a child she gave early promise of a literary bent by composing torrid love letters that she signed with names of fictitious men and hid under the sofa cushions in the hope of shocking her mother. Her interest in people and their talk was an early one, as she herself notes: 'Since ever I can remember, I've had the habit of going over conversations which I've overheard, or in which I've taken part, and re-casting them in neater form'.

Her best-known work is the novel *The Prime of Miss Jean Brodie*, which has been made into a play and into a film. Modelled loosely on Muriel Spark's teacher at Gillespie's, Miss Christina Kay, the character of Jean Brodie reflects her creator's own cultural rebellion. Miss Spark tells us that 'I attended James Gillespie's School in Edinburgh. One day I was given a document called a Leaving Certificate, so I took the hint and I left'. However, she also admits that Gillespie's allowed her to get on with her writing and put no pressure on her to play hockey. While she likes Edinburgh, she finds the City is not conductive to creative writing. She describes it as 'the saturnine Heart of Midlothian, never mine'.

There follows a literary scamper: Daniel Defoe (1660?-1731), author of *Robinson Crusoe* (derived from the real-life shipwreck of the Scotsman Alexander Selkirk from Fife), was in Edinburgh as an English government spy in the period leading up to the Union of England and Scotland in 1707. Tobias Smollett (1721-71) visited his sister in Edinburgh, and describes the city in his novel *Humphry Clinker*. Oliver Goldsmith (1730-74) studied medicine at Edinburgh University for two years, as did Peter Mark Roget, since famous for *Roget's Thesaurus*. Thomas de Quincey (1785-1859) lived in Edinburgh from 1820 until his death and wrote his *Confessions of an English Opium Eater* there. He died in Edinburgh and is buried in St Cuthbert's Church cemetery. Thomas Carlyle (1795-1881), destined for the church, studied at Edinburgh University, turning instead to the teaching of mathematics at school. Abandoning this, he returned to Edinburgh to study law – unsuccessfully – turning thereafter to writing. He met his future wife, Jane Welsh, in Edinburgh, and settled there for ten years in 1825, leading a precarious literary existence and, through Francis Jeffrey, having contributions accepted by the *Edinburgh Review*. Later, when famous, he became Rector of Edinburgh University in 1865. We have already met Conan Doyle, born in Edinburgh and creator of Sherlock Holmes (see under *Doctors*). Kenneth Grahame (1859-1932), author of *The Wind in the Willows*, was born in Edinburgh, the son of an advocate, but when he was five his father died and the family moved south. John Buchan (1875-1940), whose most famous novel, *The Thirty-Nine Steps* (1915), has so far been made into three films (the first by Hitchcock), worked as an editor for the then Edinburgh publishing firm of Thomas Nelson (since shut down and removed from Edinburgh by the late Roy Thomson, the Canadian who also brought *The Scotsman*), and, when famous, returned as Lord High Commissioner to the General Assembly of the Church of Scotland in 1933, and Chancellor of the University in 1937. In 1932 he published his biography, *Walter Scott*. In 1917, while convalescing in Craiglockhart Hospital from wounds, Siegfried Sassoon (1886-1967) and Wilfrid Owen (1893-1918) wrote a new bitter kind of poetry of war, contrasting with its former glorification. Owen even managed to teach at Tynecastle School.

A pleasing literary footnote concerns the firm of Waverley Cameron, who have been in their premises at Blair Street, Edinburgh since 1788, and who for generations were famous for their **'Waverley Pen'**:

> They come as a boon and a blessing to men,
> The Pickwick, the Owl and the Waverley Pen.

Testimonials such as the following were received:

> In Lahore for my Plain Tales I used a slim,
> octagonal-sided, agate penholder with a
> WAVERLEY nib.
>> (Rudyard Kipling)
> I must return to my lone WAVERLEY.
>> (Robert Louis Stevenson,
>> Samoa, Oct. 6th, 1894)

> This is my first trial of a new Steel pen,
> which I find is not so good as my old
> 'WAVERLEY'.
>> (Edward Fitzgerald of *Omar
>> Khayyam* fame)

So famous was the jingle that it led to parodies such as the following:

> They come as a boon and a blessing to men,
> The blackout, the torch and the cute little W.R.E.N.
> *(Stars and Stripes,* Oct. 4th, 1944)

Waverley Cameron are still going strong, but of course with a much altered and diversified range of products, but should the pen-nib make a comeback, they say they will be ready.

Lord Provosts

The exact date of the founding of the Burgh of Edinburgh is not known. However, the first alderman of the burgh mentioned by history is William de Dederyk (1296). By 1376 the chief office in the Burgh was that of *prepositus* (provost), held by John de Quhitness. In 1487 James III granted a charter which created the title of *Lord* Provost and added the further duty of being sheriff of Edinburgh. Some three hundred years later Lord Cockburn had a low opinion of the Town Council and its method of operation. The Council chambers were in a 'low-roofed room, very dark and very dirty, with some small dens off it for clerks'. 'Within this Pandemonium sat the town-council, omnipotent, corrupt, impenetrable.'

Perhaps the most notorious of all Edinburgh's Lord Provosts was Sir Andrew Ramsay, who served two terms in that office (1655-58 and 1662-73). He held the office for the longest recorded number of years and his tenure was noted for time-serving and corruption. He was responsible for two most unpopular acts: the purchase of the Citadel at Leith and the acquisition of the right to levy duty on ale and wine (both granted by his patron the Earl of Lauderdale).

John Coutts, Provost in 1730, was a commission agent and a dealer in grain, later a negotiator of bills and involved in banking. He is said to have been the first Provost to entertain strangers in his own house instead of in the local taverns at the town's expense. He had Jacobite leanings and eventually died near Naples.

Sir James Stirling held the office on three occasions: 1790-92; 1794-96; and 1798-1800. He was the son of a tradesman, possibly a fishmonger. In his youth he went to the West Indies to work on a plantation and rose to become secretary to the Governor of Jamaica. He became a director of the Bank of Scotland, Master of the Merchant Company and President of the Chamber of Commerce. He is said to have dealt harshly with rioters, and in 1792 a mob tried to destroy Sir James

Stirling's house in the New Town, forcing him to take refuge in the Castle. He was very tall and thin: once a countryman coming to the City caught sight of Sir James and asked, 'Is that the Lord Provost? I thocht it was the corspe runnin' awa' wi' the mort-cloth'.

William Creech (1745-1815) was Lord Provost from 1811 to 1812. He was by profession a bookseller, and his shop and business had once belonged to Allan Ramsay ât the east end of

William Creech

the Luckenbooths. He served on the jury in the trial of Deacon Brodie and was the first secretary of the Edinburgh Chamber of Commerce, a position he held for many years without remuneration. He was a co-founder of the influential Speculative Society. Creech was a born storyteller and conversationalist: his 'levées' at his home in Craig's Close in the morning and in his shop during the afternoon were legendary. Cockburn tells us that Creech's shop was 'the natural resort of lawyers, authors and all sorts of literary idlers who were always buzzing about the convenient hive. All who wished to see a poet or a stranger or to hear the public news, the last joke by Erskine, or yesterday's occurrence in the Parliament House, or to get the publications of the day, congregated there'.

Creech was also a publisher who put the works of Adam Smith and David Hume into print. He loved theologicl controversy and had as a young man accompanied Lord Kilmaurs on a tour of the Continent. Kilmaurs introduced Creech to the poet Robert Burns, and in 1787 Burns' second (Edinburgh) edition of his poems was published by Creech. At first Burns was very taken with him: 'of all the Edinburgh literati and wits, he writes most like a gentleman . . . His social demeanour and powers, particularly at his own table, are the most engaging I have ever met with'. But Creech angered the poet by holding back payment from the sale of his poems, until at length Burns, breathing vengeance, attacked him in print:

A little, upright, pert, tart, tripping wight
And still his precious self his dear delight;
Who loves his own smart shadow in the streets
Better than e'er the fairest she he meets.

This may have been more than personal spleen. From another quarter it is recorded that 'He was a careful cautious man, perhaps even mean. He was very unpopular during his term of office because of his habits of parsimony and economy which restrained him from the lavish hospitality to which Edinburgh was accustomed in its Lord Provosts'.

George Drummond was an enlightened anti-Jacobite Whig who fought at the Battle of Sherrifmuir in 1715 and at the time of the '45 commanded the First or College Company (who, in

George Drummond

spite of Drummond's inspiring show of determination, deserted when they had got no further than the West Port). Although born in Perthshire in 1687, he came to Edinburgh as a young man and was educated in the schools of the City. At the age of eighteen his skill in mathematics and calculation led to his being asked to examine the Scots accounts in connection with the negotiations for the Treaty of Union. After 1707 he was made Accountant-General of Excise, and in 1715 a Commissioner of Customs. In the following year he became a member of the Town Council.

In 1725 he was first elected Lord Provost and set about raising funds to build an Infirmary for the City. Four years later a small house was opened for patients, and in 1738 (by a charter of George II) building began on its first site (in Infirmary Street) of the hospital which was to achieve international fame as the Royal Infirmary. Drummond, who was the greatest benefactor of the University during the fifty years he managed the City, held the office of Lord Provost for six terms, his final one being at the age of 75.

Drummond was the organising force behind the proposal for a New Town, and in 1753 an Act was passed concerning the construction of public buildings and the widening of the streets. One of the main prerequisites for expansion to the north of the Old Town was the draining of the Nor' Loch. This was completed in 1759. In the following year the Royal Exchange (later the City Chambers) was finished on the High Street of the Old Town to provide accommodation for the merchants of Edinburgh who from time immemorial had done their business in the High Street round the Mercat Cross. Covered arcades were provided for shops and coffee houses to encourage the merchants to make use of the building. Drummond was also the inspiration behind the building of St Cecilia's Hall in the Cowgate as a concert hall for resident and visiting musicians. In 1763 he laid the foundations of the North Bridge, three years before his death at the age of eighty.

The breadth of interest in commerce, education, public health and the fine arts; the evident concern for the welfare of the whole City which Drummond so patently showed, make him an outstanding figure in the development of Edinburgh from crowded burgh on its ancient site to a spacious modern city. The competition for the plan for a New Town in 1776, ten years after Drummond's death, was the continuation and the culmination of his life's work.

Sir James Miller had the unique distinction of being the only man ever to have been Lord Provost of Edinburgh and Lord Mayor of London. He was educated at Broughton and

Sir James Miller

Heriot's; at the age of twenty-two he had already made £55,000, an enormous sum at the time. Originally trained as an architect, he was only twenty-one when he branched out on his own. He was the founder of James Miller and Partners and served on the Town Council from 1936 to 1954, representing St Andrew's ward. During the Second World War his firm built a number of buildings of value to the war effort, including that for the electronics firm Ferranti at Crewe Toll which was completed in seventeen weeks. He was Lord Provost of Edinburgh from 1951 to 1954 and received a knighthood in 1953. As Lord Mayor of London he delivered over one thousand speeches during the years 1964 to 1965.

He loved sailing, and when his son was killed he built the topsail schooner *Malcolm Miller* to his memory. He was a member of the Royal Forth Yacht Club and also outfitted the *Auld Reekie*, a Clyde puffer, for scouts and youth clubs. He took a keen interest in Highland affairs and instituted the Murrayfield Highland Games and was chieftain of the Highland Gathering in 1973. He died in 1977.

Sir Andrew Murray was born in Edinburgh in 1903, the son of a solicitor. He was educated at Daniel Stewart's and George Heriot's, where he was sports champion in 1922. He became a member of the Town Council in 1928, standing for North Leith, and in that capacity he worked hard for disadvantaged sections of the community, the young and the old, organising an advice bureau among other achievements. He was City Treasurer in 1942 and seven years later became a Companion of the Order of St John of Jerusalem. He was appointed Lord Provost in 1947, an office which he held till 1951, and it was shortly before he took up office that the Edinburgh International Festival of Music and Drama came into being. After 1945 he revived the Leith Pageant and in 1950 publicly declared his aims in office to be: the strengthening of the family unit, the maintenance of good employment and the development of international friendship. He travelled widely, to more than twenty countries. He was Edinburgh's ambassador at large, its genial dynamo. Sir Andrew died in 1977, only a day after Sir James Miller.

Jack Kane was born in Stoneyburn, West Lothian. At the age of eight his father was killed in an accident in a coal pit. He was educated at Bathgate Academy and was early involved in trade

Jack Kane

union activity. After leaving school he became a clerk on a building site. This, coupled with a strong social conscience, opened his eyes to the injustice which was the lot of very many working families. He was deeply influenced by the poverty he saw around him in Niddrie Mains in Edinburgh, and remembers in particular a mother who was forced to carry her sick child from Niddrie Mains to Edinburgh: the child was dead on arrival at the hospital. He represented Liberton from 1938 on the Town Council and was Councillor for Liberton and Craigmillar from 1949, working hard to improve the conditions of life of people in those areas. From 1972 to 1975 he became the first Labour Lord Provost of Edinburgh and the last Lord Provost of Edinburgh Corporation before the reorganisation of local government following the Wheatley Commission recommendations. Lord Provost Kane was awarded the OBE but turned down a knighthood because he felt it should not be given automatically to every Lord Provost. Jack Kane has left a lasting monument to the people of Craigmillar in the Jack Kane Centre where thousands of Edinburgh people, young and old, can enjoy sport and other community activities. Over a long period of time he has also been closely involved with the Workers' Educational Association, in, for example, Pre-Retirement education. He has also served as Chairman of Trustees of the National Galleries of Scotland.

Music Hall and Variety

For many years a vigorous undercurrent of popular musical entertainment flourished in the 'penny gaffs' and the 'free and easys of the town. This tradition, nourished and invigorated by amateur and semi-professional talent as well as the full-time practitioners, lives on today in the pubs and clubs which advertise talent competitions and employ part-time entertainers.

At No. 63, Princes Street during the 1870s and '80s a sing-song was to be found every night. This was the home of Bryce's, which was reached down some steps from the street. Bryce's consisted of a long subterranean room in which rows of small tables were placed on each side. At one end, on a raised armchair with a table in front of him, Norman Thomson, the chairman, presided. To his right sat the orchestra: John Inglis on piano, Joe Hart on the violin. With a rat-tat-tat of his hammer and the cry of 'Order, gentlemen' the chairman asserted his authority. For thirty years Norman Thomson, a shoemaker, exercised his office and sang his favourite song, 'Scots wha hae', in a rich bass voice. Seated in front of him were his clientele of shopkeepers, clerks and spurred cavalry soldiers in scarlet tunics and gold braid. R. S. Pillans, later a well-known Theatre Royal comedian and pantomime dame, cut his first teeth before the audience at Bryce's, and Peter Strachini was often to be found there with his bird imitations. There was no charge for entry, and a large schooner of beer cost a mere four pence.

In the 1890s smoking concerts were very popular, particularly in the sports clubs, but they could not rival the perennial entertainment of penny gaffs such as Connor's or Ferguson's at the foot of Blackfriars Wynd. Both consisted of long and dirty canvas enclosures with raised wooden planks for seats. The scenery and fittings of the small stage were rough and ready. Foul-smelling paraffin lamps lit up the auditorium, which was invariably packed. Here in the 1870s were to be seen melodramas such as *Sweeney Todd*, *Rob Roy* and *Belphegor the Mountebank*. In Connor's, Ned Holt occasionally acted Hamlet and was often to be seen in his threadbare suit and worn-out boots wearily trudging to his abode in White Horse Close.

Robert Louis Stevenson on many occasions walked from his house at Swanston to the penny gaff in the Caledonian Railway Goods Station (Thomas Brash's) to spend his weekly pocket money of half-a-crown. There he mixed with thieves, seamen, chimney sweeps, all sorts. At Ferguson's penny gaff the call-boy could be seen running out frequently during the performance to the nearby tavern for ale and porter, Morgan's beer shop in Blackfriars Wynd. The performance would begin with shouts of 'Up wi' the hippen (curtain)' from the impatient customers. Tweedledum Paddy, an Irishman from Glasgow, having captivated his audience by the verisimilitude of his dying collapse, would repeat the feat several times to shouts of 'Gie's anither fa!'

During this period one of the most popular entertainments was the Harlequinade. Harlequin would come on with his magic slap-stick and dance across the stage with the graceful Columbine. Then there were shouts of 'Here we are again' as Joey the Clown and old Father Pantaloon came on and the fun began: strings of sausages, butter slides, red-hot pokers, bustling policemen who always came off second best, trap doors, sudden dives through shop-windows and the grand climax of the stage crowd, shouting and jostling.

In 1886 John Henry Cooke's Circus played at the Palladium; one of the highlights was Mazeppa riding a galloping horse with a 'victim' tied to the animal. Newsome's Circus provided Dick Turpin's thrilling 'Ride to York'.

The heyday of Variety was from 1900 to 1920, but the pantomime was also a very popular annual event, and continues so to the present, with stars such as Stanley Baxter. The Edinburgh Theatre (later known as Poole's Synod Hall) spared no expense in décor. The decorations were superb: crimson and gold on a white background flashed from the dress circle and boxes. The roof was gorgeously painted, the stage curtain was rich in colour and costly in texture. The attack on the doors of the theatre for its first panto, *Bluebeard*, was like a rugby scrum.

In 1911 Edinburgh's most horrendous theatrical tragedy took place when the Great Lafayette, an illusionist, was burnt to death at the Empire, Nicholson Street when the draperies and hangings caught fire. He was later buried with great ceremony at Piershill Cemetery. A year later Sir Edward Moss, the impresario, died from natural causes and was buried in Portobello. Moss was responsible for the Theatre of Varieties opened in Chambers Street in 1877 and for the famous Waverley Market Carnival which began in Christmas 1885 with such exotic artistes as Duncan's performing dogs, Spessardy's bears, Hocheschmidt the world-famous catch-as-catch-can wrestler, and Rosa and Josepha Blazek, the original Siamese twins.

By the 1930s the Pierrot shows run by a tall, fresh-looking, ageless man with a flower in his buttonhole (André Letta) were all the rage on Portobello's seaside promenade. In 1931 a young man later to become one of Britain's favourite romantic singers worked at Portobello for two seasons: Donald Peers had originally come to repaint Piershill Barracks in 1925 and on that occasion made the contacts which led to his subsequent engagement.

Sir Harry Lauder is today a figure of contradiction: his baroque caricatures of the humours of Scotland either endear or cause revulsion. As to his success, there can be no disagree-

Sir Harry Lauder

ment: chatting once to Caruso, Lauder was amazed at the astuteness of the Italian tenor over royalties. His own songs had been signed away often for a pound a song. When one considers that the biggest record sellers in the world were

Melba, Caruso and Harry Lauder, the Scotsman's reputation for meanness can be seen to be particularly ironic.

Lauder was born in 1870 in a very humble birthplace at Portobello by the sea. His father, who was a potter turning out bottles for lemonade and jam, was to have a family of eight children. In his spare time he trained professional runners. After a time the family moved to Musselburgh to be closer to the pottery where Lauder's father worked; Harry took up caddying on Musselburgh Links.

When Lauder was twelve years old the family moved to England, as his father had taken up an offer of employment there. In 1882, however, he died, and the family moved back to Scotland, this time to Arbroath where Harry soon took a job in Gordon's Mill as a 'half-timer', spending one day at school and the next at work, in alternation. Educated by the schoolmaster 'Stumpie' Bell (so called because he only had one leg). Lauder worked at the flax-spinning but also joined the Band of Hope where he learned to sing hymns and songs and do recitations. At the age of thirteen he won a singing competition.

The following year the family moved once more, to Lanarkshire, where Harry became a miner, first a 'trapper' opening and closing the wooden doors which controlled the air currents, and then a pony driver.

By 1894, however, Lauder, through talent and determination, had become a professional entertainer in Glasgow and now sported the Astrakhan collar coat which it had always been his goal to acquire as the badge of success. In the next year he toured Scotland with the violinist Mackenzie Murdoch, and then toured for six weeks as a comedian, but also as a baggageman, billposter and stage carpenter: he learned the craft of the theatre from back to front. His first big break came when he was signed for the Argyle Theatre in Birkenhead. There he sang Irish songs in the first place and only put Scots songs into his encores.

In 1900, at the age of twenty-nine, he went to London and after some anxious weeks was suddenly summoned to replace a 'turn' who had gone sick from Tom Tinsley's *Gatti's in the Road*. Lauder hit his audience with everything he knew: dressed in tartan trousers, yellow spats, brown boots, coloured waistcoat and black frock-coat, he sported a black and green tie and a badly-fitting tile hat. The critics were pleased: 'This man Harry Lauder brings the scent of the Scottish heather over the footlights into the smoke-laden atmosphere of music-hall'. Seven years later Lauder's popularity was such that he was able to make the first of his many trips to the United States: his initial appearance on coming off the boat at New York was disconcerting. One agency rep observed, 'He's four foot an' no more in height, has thick rimless eyeglasses and looks like a real country bumpkin in a shabby old tartan coat and baggy pants'. However, he was piped ashore by Highland pipers and drove off in a tartan-decked automobile. Lauder played the New York Theatre in Times Square at a fee of over $4,500 a week. In 1908 he was at the Lincoln Square Theatre and followed his huge successes with a total of twenty-two trips to North America, being welcomed into the highest levels of American society, and making friends with such notable figures as Henry Ford.

He was now earning more than any other star. One of his supporting artists was the unknown songwriter Irving Berlin, later to become one of the world's household names. Lauder's philosophy was simple: 'If, by bein' a simple Scots comic, and singin' bonnie humorous songs, I can do my wee bit to help make the world a brighter place, and help mysel' along the road at the same time, well, then, I'm richt glad to lend a hand'.

After receiving the news of his son's death during the First World War, Lauder set off to entertain the troops at Boulogne hospital base and then sailed to the USA where his friendship with Theodore Roosevelt, Calvin Coolidge, Woodrow Wilson and Warren Harding symbolised his great support with the American people. His other friends included Andrew Carnegie, Sir Thomas Lipton the grocer boy from Glasgow, and Charlie Chaplin, whom he met in California.

When, after the Second World War, Winston Churchill was to be given the Freedom of Edinburgh, he insisted that Sir Harry Lauder be present to sing 'Keep Right on to the End of the Road'. Lauder died in 1950.

Johnny Victory was one of the few Scots music hall comedians to emerge from Edinburgh. Born in 1922, he was the son of Peter Victory who transferred from selling fish to running taxis (hence his gag-line 'Now they tell me that as a comic I'm a good taxi-driver wasted'). His style was one of heavy humour, but he was a popular figure all over Scotland, having got his first break at the Palladium in 1946. In 1967 he moved to Belfast as the closure of the Palladium meant a lot less work for him. He was injured on stage in a panto in Belfast, but managed club and cabaret appearances in Ireland and a Continental tour. He was Honorary President of the Hibs Supporters Association and worked with the East of Scotland Bookmakers Association on a number of charitable ventures. He was found dead in his caravan at Loanhead in 1968.

Chic Murray, one of Scotland's most inimitable comics, died in Edinburgh in 1985 at the age of sixty-five. Born in Greenock, a former shipyard worker, he started in showbusi-

Chic Murray

ness singing and playing the piano. With his wife Maidie, who he married in 1945 (they were divorced in 1974), he formed a double-act, 'the tall droll with the small doll'. The peak of their success was in 1956 when they appeared in the Royal Variety Show at the London Palladium. In 1964 they bought a hotel in Edinburgh. Maidie gave up show business to run it and Chic went solo.

He broke into films with the James Bond movie, *Casino Royale*. More recently he appeared as the headmaster in Bill Forsyth's award-winning film, *Gregory's Girl*, and in 1983 played the Liverpool Football Club manager, Bill Shankly, in a musical play, *You'll Never Walk Alone*. Shortly before he died Chic Murray had begun renovating a cottage in Colinton, with the idea of making Edinburgh his base, a City which had taken him to its hearts from the days of his appearances in the Empire.

Philosophers

David Hume (1711-76) was the greatest of Scotland's philosophers. He was born in Edinburgh, and when he was only two years of age his father died and the young David Hume was left to be brought up by his mother. Largely self-educated, he attended the University of Edinburgh, but he left without graduating. Intended for the legal profession, at the age of 18 he decided to make philosophy his career and eventually moved to London in 1734 and from there to France, where he stayed for three years to write the manuscript of his first and greatest work, the *Treatise of Human Nature*, an attempt to introduce the experimental method of reasoning into moral subjects. Hume's conclusions made him unpopular with many sections of the Church of his time: in Hume's opinion we have only the evidence of our senses that an external world exists outside ourselves. Everything is subjective, there can be no objectivity. Man's belief in individual identity is also an illusion, for how can we be the objects of our own senses? The *Treatise* marks the high point of scepticism; we cannot trust our senses, our memory or our imagination. Everyone who reasons or believes in anything is a fool. Hume tried twice to become a professor, once in 1744 at Edinburgh and again in 1751 at Glasgow. He was unsuccessful on both occasions. He travelled to Canada as Advocate-General of all the forces under General St Clair (a distant relative) and as Secretary of St Clair's military embassy to Vienna and Turin in 1748-49. Finally in 1752 he secured the status he desired through appointment as Keeper of the Advocates' Library in Edinburgh. He boasted that he could 'cover the floor of a large Room with Books and Pamphlets wrote against him'.

In 1763, during an embassy to Paris, he fell under the spell of Madame de Boufflers, a former mistress of a prince of the Royal blood and is said to have declared his love to her with considerable ardour. During this period he made friends with the French philosopher Rousseau, whom he received in Eng-

The David Hume Monument, in Old Calton Burying Ground, by Robert Adam

land in 1766 and found to be decidely neurotic. Hume was appointed Under Secretary of State for the Northern Department, but after eleven months returned to Edinburgh where he died in 1776 in what was humorously named St David's Street, after the greatest sceptic of them all! Notorious for his want of religious conviction – or at any rate for his attacks on revealed religion – he died a source of disappointment to certain clergymen who had hoped for a deathbed conversion, instead of which he met his end with tranquillity and without their ministrations.

Adam Smith (1723-1790), a native of Kirkcaldy in Fife, was the founder of the classical school of economics, who first came to fame, while professor of moral philosophy at Glasgow University, with his *Theory of Moral Sentiments* (1759). He had lectured at Edinburgh University on rhetoric and belles lettres,

Adam Smith

and remained a frequent visitor. His most influential work, *The Wealth of Nations* (1776), postulated the theory of the division of labour and emphasised that value arises from the labour used in production. He believed that in a *laissez-faire* economy self-interest could coincide with the public good. 'Jupiter' Carlyle records of him that 'though perhaps only second to [David Hume] in learning and ingenuity, [he] was far inferior to him in conversational talents. It may comfort modern readers to know that Carlyle, although an admirer of the *Theory of Moral Sentiments*, considered that continuing classic, *The Wealth of Nations*, 'tedious and full of repetition'.

Adam Ferguson (1723-1816), born in Perthshire and educated at Perth Grammar School and St Andrews University, after service as a chaplain with the Black Watch, with whom he

Adam Ferguson

saw service at Fontenoy and displayed conspicuous courage, succeeded David Hume as Librarian of the Advocates' Library in 1757, resigning two years later to become successively Professor of Natural Philosophy and Professor of Moral Philosophy at Edinburgh University, thus demonstrating the brilliance and diversity of intelligence that was remarked upon by his contemporaries. With his *Essay on the History of Civil Society*, which ran into several editions and was translated into most European languages, he may be said to have founded the modern discipline of sociology.

Cockburn paints the following picture of him: 'Our neighbour on the east was old Adam Ferguson, the historian of Rome, and [Dugald] Stewart's predecessor in our moral chair – a singular apparition. In his younger years he was a handsome and resolute man. Being chaplain to the Black Watch, he could not be induced even by the positive orders of his commanding officer to remain in his proper place in the rear during an action, but persisted in being engaged in front. Time and illness, however, had been dealing with him, and, when I first knew him, he was a spectacle well worth beholding. His hair was silky and white; his eyes animated and light blue; his cheeks sprinkled with broken red, like autumnal apples, but fresh and healthy; his lips thin, and the under one curled. A severe paralytic attack had reduced his animal vitality, though it left no external appearance, and he required considerable artificial heat. His raiment, therefore, consisted of half boots. lined with fur, cloth breeches, a long cloth waistcoat with capacious pockets, a single-breasted coat, a cloth greatcoat also lined with fur, and a felt hat commonly tied by a ribbon below the chin. His boots were black; but with this exception the whole coverings, including the hat, were of a Quaker grey colour, or of a whitish brown; and he generally wore the furred greatcoat even within doors. When he walked forth he used a tall staff, which he commonly held at arm's length out towards the right side; and his two coats, each buttoned by only the upper button, flowed open below, and exposed the whole of his curious and venerable figure. His gait and air were noble; his gesture slow; his look full of dignity and composed fire. He looked like a philosopher from Lapland. His palsy ought to have killed him in his fiftieth year; but rapid care enabled him to live uncrippled, either in body or mind, nearly fifty years more. Wine and animal food besought his appetite in vain; but huge messes of milk and vegetables disappeared before him, always in the never-failing cloth and fur.

'Domestically he was kind, but anxious and peppery. His temperature was regulated Fahrenheit; and often, when sitting quite comfortably, he would start up and put his wife and daughters into commotion, because his eye had fallen on the instrument, and discovered that he was a degree too hot or too cold. He always locked the door of his study when he left it, and took the key in his pocket; and no housemaid got in till the accumulation of dust and rubbish made it impossible to put the evil day off any longer; and then woe on the family'.

Pioneers and Explorers

Following a long history of Scottish activity in Europe as merchants, mercenaries, scholars and churchmen, the first major Scottish settlement elsewhere was in Ulster in 1605. James VI did particularly well out of the Virginia plantations, and two main waves of Scottish settlement are recorded in the New World: at the beginning of the seventeenth century Nova Scotia, New Galloway and Insuli Caroli were founded; and at the end of the seventeenth century other important colonies were East New Jersey, Stuart's Town and the ill-fated Darien Scheme. William Paterson's plan to make money from a settlement on the Isthmus of Darien between North and South America did not have the notable success of that other Scottish banker and entrepreneur, Edinburgh-born John Law of Lauriston, who founded New Orleans and helped establish great colonial prosperity for France in North America.

John Campbell was born in Edinburgh in 1766. After a good classical education at the High School he became an apprentice goldsmith and jeweller. Most of his free time, however, was spent visiting the sick and dying poor, for he was a devout Presbyterian. In 1789 he made a decision to prepare himself for the ministry, and began to establish Sabbath schools and to preach in villages and outlying country areas. He was chosen to be one of the directors of the Edinburgh Missionary Society.

He studied in Glasgow at the turn of the century, and after a preaching tour of the Highlands set off for Africa on the first of his journeys which was to take him, 3,000 miles through Africa. He was described as 'a dumpy Scottish minister who traversed the African wastes with a black umbrella to ward off the sun'.

In 1818 he again sailed for Africa for a ten months' expedition which saw him discover the course of the Orange River and the source of the Limpopo. Beginning his journey, he writes that 'The scenery was extremely grand and interesting, being marked by stupendous cliffs, rugged rocks, and spiral-topt mountains of great elevation. Their bases were covered with mimosa trees, the flowers of which appeared like innumerable golden balls suspended from the branches. The Hex River, with rumbling noise, was heard forcing its way along the jungle . . .' But there was a less attractive side to life in the interior: 'Old people being considered useless beings are universally despised. An old woman was lately allowed to starve at Lattakoo for want of food, after which they dragged her body, as if she had been a dog, to the outside of the town, that she might be devoured by wolves . . .'

Campbell returned to Britain in 1821, arriving at St Helena en route. There he 'delivered a 'unicorn's horn' and other African curiosities (such as a blue asbestos stone found beyond the Orange River) for the Admiral, Sir H. Lowe and his distinguished charge, the exiled Emperor Napoleon Bonaparte.

William Cargill (1784-1860) was born in Edinburgh, the son of a Writer to the Signet. After education at the Edinburgh High School he bought a commission in the 84th Regiment, then stationed in Bengal. Following the battle of Assaye (1803) he became a lieutenant in the 74th Highlanders and served with them throughout the Mahratta War. In 1810 he sailed with his regiment for the Peninsular War. He was severely wounded at the battle of Busaco and invalided home. He rejoined his regiment at Madrid, and, after promotion, fought during the entire Peninsular campaign, with special gallantry at the battle of Toulouse in 1814. He sold his commission in 1820.

After setting up an unsuccessful business as a wine merchant in Edinburgh, Cargill turned to banking and, on moving to London, became involved in the New Edinburgh (Otago) colonisation scheme in New Zealand. With the Disruption of 1843 and the establishment of the Free Church in Scotland, there was pressure to make the colony an exclusively Free Church settlement. Cargill published a pamphlet in 1847 which modelled the proposed colony on the New England Pilgrim Fathers. The colony was established in 1848 at Otago and in due course became Dunedin, chief city of the provincial district of Otago on the South Island. The early streets were named after those of Edinburgh, and the name of the city itself, 'Dunedin', was the Celtic word for Edinburgh.

Cargill played a controversial but central part in the growth of the colony. He was too autocratic and undiplomatic to be a good administrator. He was an indistinct speaker and suffered from deafness. But for all that, he played a unique role. He trudged around the colony 'in an undress of Ayrshire grey, a broad blue bonnet on his head, with a flaming red toorie in the centre, a stunted black pipe in his mouth, a stout walking stick in his right hand, and a shepherd's tartan plaid thrown over his left shoulder'.

The son of an Edinburgh schoolmaster, **Alexander Gordon Laing** was born in the City in 1794. After leaving Edinburgh University (at the age of 15) he became a schoolmaster in

Major Alexander Gordon Laing

Newcastle, and returned six months later to work with his father who ran a private academy. After joining the Prince of Wales Edinburgh Volunteers, he left teaching for the army and went to Barbados in 1811, where his mother's brother was serving. His uncle obtained for him an ensign's commission in the York Light Infantry (West Indian Regiment) which he joined in Antigua.

Two years later he was invalided back to Scotland with a liver complaint and in 1819 promoted to lieutenant and sent to rejoin his regiment in Sierra Leone. In 1821, a mere fifteen years after the abolition of the slave trade, Laing was chosen to lead a mission to Zambia and the Mandingo country. He travelled 200 miles inland through unexplored country to Falaba and to the source of the Rokelle River. He was within three days of the source of the Niger. Unable to secure further promotion. Laing gave up his military career and turned his mind to the problem which most concerned him: the question as to whether (as was widely believed at the time) the Nile and the Niger were the same river. Laing was convinced that they could not be the same and set out (with Colonial Office backing) to complete Mungo Park's work by finding the main course of the River Niger.

Laing obtained his supplies in Malta and sailed for Tripoli. Among his many feats on this his last expedition was an astonishing journey from Wadi Ahennet to El Muktar's camp with ten sabre cuts in his head, a musket bullet in his hip, and both legs injured. In this condition he covered 400 miles of the worst desert in the world with no one to help him but a few Africans. Laing was not impressed by the Missionary Society and its agents. He writes: 'It has happened to myself to have seen one missionary lying drunk in the streets; to have known a second living with a negress, one of his parishioners; and a third tried for the murder of a little boy whom he had flogged to death'. He recorded his experience of missionaries in his *Travels in West Africa*.

Laing was the first recorded white man to reach the fabled city of Timbuctoo, the capital of central Africa. He arrived there on 13th September 1826 and left a week later, having been free to inspect every part of the town and even enter the mosques. Halfway to Arawan, on 24th September his guide ordered his servants to kill him. This was done probably while Laing was asleep. His head was cut off and his papers, letters and books were torn and thrown to the wind in case they contained some magic.

Sir James Hector (1834-1907) was born in Edinburgh, the son of a Writer to the Signet as William Cargill had been. He also attended the High School (after Edinburgh Academy) and worked for a time in his father's office. He then studied medicine at the University and also attended lectures in natural science on an extra-curricular basis, assisting the professors of botany and zoology. He graduated in 1856 and was chosen as geologist and surgeon on a Government expedition to investigate communications in western Canada, to explore unknown country and to look for passes over the Rocky Mountains.

Hector spent two adventurous years in Canada: Kicking Horse Pass, which carries the Canadian Pacific Railway, was named after a narrow escape from death on Hector's part, and a monument to him marks the spot. Later he investigated Vancouver Island and goldfields and mines in western America. On his return to Edinburgh he was awarded the Fellowship of the Royal Society of Edinburgh and, in 1861, the Royal Geographical Society's gold medal.

He was appointed geologist to the Provincial Government of Otago, New Zealand, and during this phase of his life undertook a series of arduous explorations on foot and in 1863 by schooner-rigged yacht through the islands and fiords. In 1864 he was appointed Director of the Geological Survey for the whole of New Zealand and became scientific adviser to the Government. He was also Director of the Colonial Museum and Manager of the Institute for the Advancement of Science and Art. In these posts he supervised the issue of catalogues of New Zealand plants and animals and analysis of minerals, ores and soils. He was created KCMG in 1887 and was honoured by the Geological Society of London and by the German Emperor.

John Murray was born in 1841 in Ontario, Canada of Scottish parents. He entered Edinburgh University, first as a medical student, but following a wide variety of other courses: literature, chemistry, natural history, law. He assisted Professor P. G. Tait, the physicist, in his laboratory, and came into contact with James Clerk Maxwell and Lord Kelvin.

In 1868 he was a surgeon on a whaler and spent seven months in the Arctic, working ashore on Jan Mayen Island in the Greenland Sea. He was a member of the *Challenger* Expedition to the Antarctic and on its return worked on the publication of its results, editing them between 1880 and 1909. Chief assistant in the *Challenger* office in Edinburgh in 1876, Murray became Director from 1882 to 1895. Among his works was *The Origin and Structure of Coral Reefs and Islands* (1880) and *Deep Sea Deposits* (1891). As well as being a marine zoologist, he was a pioneer of modern oceanography. In 1897 to 1909 he undertook a survey of the Scottish freshwater lochs and was one of the founders of the Ben Nevis Observatory and the Millport biological laboratory. He postulated the existence of an antarctic continent, which subsequent investigation confirmed, and three years before his death in 1914 he took part in surveys of the North Atlantic.

The *Challenger* voyage was organised by C. W. Thomson (1830-82). He had been educated at Edinburgh University and was Professor of Natural History there from 1870. His *The Voyage of the Challenger* was published in 1877.

Born in Edinburgh in 1853, **Sir Leander Starr Jameson,** South African statesman, came from a family which had made its fortune in whale-oil and soap boiling in the French war. His

Leander Starr Jameson

father was a Writer to the Signet who had had some success with poetry and drama. His grand-uncle was the Professor of Geology at Edinburgh University. When his father inherited a legacy in 1860, he bought two newspapers in Sudbury. These eventually failed and the family moved to London where, in 1870, Leander began his medical studies at University College and gained the gold medal in Materia Mędica.

His career really began when he left for South Africa in 1878 to be a partner in a medical practice in Kimberley, the famous gold-town. There 'Dr Jim' met up with the young English claim-holder Cecil Rhodes, a man who was to play a decisive part in his life: Jameson engaged in pioneer work and was made administrator for the South Africa Company at Fort Salisbury.

Jameson was fortunate in being able to cure the President of the Orange Free State from Bright's disease, but he was a non-nonsense individual who tolerated fools only with difficulty. To a fanciful lady who complained of a pain in her back, Starr replied: 'rub it with a brick'. He was a proverbial and enormously popular figure who drove around in a billycock hat in a smart victoria with two very fast black horses. He performed miraculous operations and marvellous cures. He was famous for the dances he gave and the boxing-matches where he was the bottleholder, and was a skilled poker-player.

In 1889 he resigned his medical practice to accompany a trader who was to deliver 500 rifles and 50,000 rounds of ammunition to Lobengula, King of the Matabele. Lobengula suffered from gout, for which Jameson gave him injections. The king's pain was relieved, and he granted Jameson permission to dig for gold. Jameson had seen gold dust carried in vulture quills by natives from the interior and went north to prospect in the tributaries of the Zambesi. The expedition covered about 430 miles: 230 by horse, 50 on foot and 150 by rowing.

Jameson's most famous exploit was his abortive 'Raid' in 1895-6 when he tried to come to the aid of the Outlanders – in dispute with the Boer government – with 600 men. Ambushed by the Boers at Krugersdorp, eventually the 250 men Jameson had left were surrounded by 3,000 Boers and forced to surrender. Jameson was sentenced to be shot, but President Kruger refused to sign the order for his execution. Jameson continued in public administration, and with the help of Cecil Rhodes became Progressive Premier of Cape Colony, being created a baronet in 1911.

Three of the greatest British explorers had connections with Edinburgh. Born at Kinnaird in Stirlingshire, James Bruce (1730-94) studied law at Edinburgh University. In 1768 he began a journey of exploration from Cairo to Abyssinia and discovered the head stream of the Blue Nile in 1770. Mungo Park (1771-1806) studied medicine at Edinburgh and worked as a ship's doctor, making two journeys up the Niger, in 1795 and 1799, before being killed by natives in 1805. Sir Ernest Shackleton (1874-1922) was secretary of the Royal Scottish Geographical Society from 1904 to 1905. He took part in Scott's National Antarctic Expedition with the *Discovery* in 1901 and made the first expedition of the *Nimrod* around the Ross Sea in the Antarctic in 1907. Shackleton, who was buried at the whaling-station in Grytviken on South Georgia in 1922, was awarded the Livingstone gold medal of the Royal Scottish Geographical Society.

Politicians

In 1828 **Thomas Babington Macaulay** (1800-59) wrote to his mother from Edinburgh: 'My Edinburgh expedition has given me so much to say that, unless I write off some of it before I come home, I shall talk you all to death, and be noted a bore in every house which I visit'. Macaulay had made the acquaintance of Francis Jeffrey (for those *Edinburgh Review* he was to write). Macaulay continues: 'When absolutely quiescent, reading a paper, or hearing a conversation in which he takes no interest, his countenance shows no indication whatever of intellectual superiority of any kind. But as soon as he is interested, and opens his eyes upon you,' the change is like magic. There is a flash in his glance, a violent contortion in his frown, and exquisite humour in his sneer, and a sweetness and brilliancy in his smile, beyond anything that ever I witnessed. He possesses considerable power of mimicry, and rarely tells a story without imitating several different accents. His familiar tone, his declamatory tone, and his pathetic tone are quite different things. His house is magnificent. It is in Moray Place, the newest pile of buildings in the town, looking out to the Forth on one side, and to a green garden on the other. It is really equal to the houses in Grosvenor Square. Fine, however, as is the new quarter of Edinburgh, I decidedly prefer the Old Town. There is nothing like it in the island'.

In 1839 Macaulay was elected MP for Edinburgh. His victory speech, for all the rhetoric, reads like the words of a man with a genuine affection for the City: 'From an early age I have felt a strong interest in Edinburgh, though attached to Edinburgh by no other ties than those which are common to me with multitudes; that tie which attaches every man of Scottish blood to the ancient and renowned capital of our race; that tie which attaches every student of history to the spot ennobled by so many great and memorable events; that tie which attaches every traveller of taste to the most beautiful of British cities; and that tie which attaches every lover of literature to a place which, since it has ceased to be the seat of empire, has derived from poetry, philosophy, and eloquence a far higher distinction than empire can bestow'.

William Ewart Gladstone (1809-98), who became Leader of the Liberal Party in 1866 and Prime Minister two years later, had strong Edinburgh connections. It is claimed that Thomas Gledstanes, who bought Gladstone's Land in the Lawnmarket in Edinburgh in 1617 (now a Scottish National Trust property), was an ancestor of the Liberal Prime Minister. Be that as it may, Gladstone's immediate family on his father's side were Edinburgh folk. St Thomas Parish Church in Leith is closely connected with the family: Gladstone's grandfather was a corn merchant in Leith at Cornhill and for forty years an elder there; one of his grandfather's brothers was parish schoolmaster of North Leith from 1769 to 1799; another brother was managing partner in the Edinburgh Roperie and Sailcloth Company in Leith and a third brother worked in its counting-house. Gladstone's own father had his earliest commercial experience in the same counting-house before going to Liverpool to make his fortune in shipping.

The hotel table on which Gladstone wrote the notes for his political speeches in the Midlothian Campaign is in the possession of the Scottish Liberal Club in Edinburgh. Gladstone opened the Scottish Liberal Club in Edinburgh in 1880, and a bust of the Prime Minister in his second term of office was given a place of honour there in 1885, a year which also saw the re-erection of what was left of the original medieval Edinburgh Mercat Cross (only the cental column remained) in a fine new structure in Parliament Square, the cost of which was borne by Gladstone as a mark of gratitude to the City of Edinburgh.

Gladstone had reason to be pleased with Edinburgh, where many of his most powerful speeches were delivered. In the winter of 1880, during the first Midlothian Campaign, thousands of Edinburgh people crowded into Princes Street to welcome him, although the day was dark and cold and it was raining. He rode from Waverley Station to Dalmeny House in an open carriage in company with Lord Rosebery, followed by mounted policemen. Gladstone's head was bared, a spectator remembered many years later, and he made a swaying figure with his waving grey locks, the image of an old lion.

The biggest halls in Edinburgh proved too small to hold his potential audience. At a mass meeting in the Waverley market twenty thousand people came to hear him speak, some from as far afield as the Hebrides. When he spoke in the Corn Exchange in the Grassmarket, the meeting began with the Old Hundred and 'Scots Wha Hae'. The comment was made by a visiting journalist that it was not 'singing, it is more like worship'.

James Connolly (1870-1916), famous now as an Irish Labour leader, was born in Edinburgh's Cowgate and educated at St Patrick's School. At the age of eleven he began work as a

James Connolly

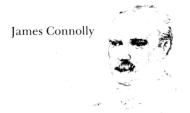

printer's 'devil', washing paint-smeared rollers, making tea and sweeping the floor. His reading was done by the light of embers whose charred sticks he used as pencils. At twelve he worked in a bakery and two years later in a mosaic-tiling factory. When he was fourteen he joined the Second Battalion, the Royal Scots Regiment, pretending he was older than he really was, and was stationed in Cork where he gained first-hand knowledge of the Irish problem.

Connolly stood for the Scottish Socialist Federation as a local election candidate in Edinburgh in 1894 and 1895. In the Edinburgh *Labour Chronicle* of 1894 he wrote the following critique of political life in the City: 'The conduct of the Edinburgh School Board, coupled with the conduct of the Town Council in refusing to insert the fair wages clause in a most important contract, should help to clear the cobwebs from the eyes of the intelligent voters and enable them to appreciate the necessity for an infusion of new Socialistic blood into all our public bodies. For some time to come the work of Socialists on all such bodies will not be so much to pass new laws as to infuse into their administrator the spirit of the new life, to use all power to inaugurate the reign of justice, to convert our industrial system from a machine for making profit into an instrument for sustaining life, to transform our politics from the government of men into the wise and well-ordered administration of things, to relegate to the limbo of exploded superstitions the old doctrine of freedom of contract between affluence and starvation, and thus, by constantly placing our doctrines and our efforts upon the same platform as the class interests of the workers, to create such a public feeling in our favour as shall enable us to bridge the gulf between the old order and the new, and lead the people from the dark Egypt of our industrial anarchy, into the Promised Land of industrial freedom'.

Connolly spent some time in the United States, engaging in trade union activity, and then in Ireland, with James Larkin, organised the great transport strike in Dublin. He organised socialist 'armies' and with the Irish nationalist movement Sinn Fein took part in the Easter Rising of 1916. He was arrested and executed by firing-squad on 12th May that year.

Wendy Wood (1892-1981) was born in Kent, the granddaughter of a Highland crofter on her mother's side and with her roots in the Welsh Border on her father's. The family early

Wendy Wood

in her life moved to South Africa, where her father was employed by a Swedish brewing company. When she was twelve she came to Scotland and two years later attended a Scottish boarding-school.

A fervent nationalist, in 1916 she formed the Scottish League, and became a member of the Home Rule Association, which began that year. When the Scottish National Party was born in 1928, Wendy Wood became a member. She had become a regular speaker at Edinburgh's Hyde Park Corner: the Mound. The Youth Movement of the SNP, the Scottish Watch, was her work and was inspired by her at its foundation in 1931. Her most decisive public act of defiance and protest came in 1932 when she and some others brazened their way past fifty soldiers who were on guard at Stirling Castle, removing the Union Jack and replacing it with the Scottish Lion Rampant. Her public life was a series of cleverly orchestrated gestures designed to put across points in which she passionately believed. In 1936 she was appointed Publicity Officer of the Organising Committee of the Scottish representatives to the British Congress. She tried to persuade the Federated Union of European Nationalities to bring what she claimed were violations of the Treaty of Union to the notice of the Council of Europe and the United Nations Organisation. Bitterly opposed to the drain of brain and muscle from Scotland through emigration, in 1936 she made a bonfire of immigration papers and brochures for Australia outside the Australian Immigration Office and painted the slogan 'Don't Go' on the doorstep.

She founded the Scottish Patriots in 1949, and in 1953 extracted a promise from Sir Thomas Innes the Lord Lyon that the Royal numeral E II R would be taken down from decorations in Princes Street, and that there would be no more such displays on letter-boxes or Royal Mail vans, since the Queen was Elizabeth I of Scotland.

In 1960, while attending the Assembly Hall with Sydney Goodsir Smith to see a performance of his epic play *The Wallace*, she arranged for a patriot girl to present the actor who played William Wallace (Iain Cuthbertson) with a lion rampant flag and to ask him to sing 'Scots Wha Hae' (which he and all the audience did). The following year she addressed the General Assembly of the Church of Scotland in the same Assembly Hall asking the Church to support Home Rule for Scotland. When King Olaf of Norway was due to visit Edinburgh in 1962 another E II R sign appeared high over the

North Bridge. Wendy Wood immediately went home, blew three eggs, filled them with waterproof ink (purple, red and black), plugged the eggs with plasticine and threw them one by one at the offending sign. She rapidly found herself in the cells – not for the first time – but when the case came to Court, it was dropped because she threatened to call the Lord Lyon as a witness to the justice of her case. Four years later she contrived to have the Postmaster-General of the time, Antony Wedgewood Benn, issue a Burns stamp from the Philatelic Section of the GPO in Edinburgh. A stamp to commemorate the Bicentenary of the New Town was followed by a stamp in 1968 to commemorate the death of William Wallace. In 1967, as leader of the Scottish Patriots, she had applied to the Lord Provost for permission to burn the Union flag on St Andrew's Day.

The refusal of the Government in 1971 to set up a Scottish Convention in Edinburgh, which she considred a betrayal of promises already made, saw her begin a fast to the death, which however she called off after six days. A lively and provocative figure till the day she died, her great cry was that 'The time of Scotland's freedom is coming'.

John Cormack (1894-1978) was an Edinburgh institution, a weekly crowd-puller at Edinburgh's Speakers' Corner at the foot of the Mound. His virulent attacks on what he saw as the prenicious influence of Roman Catholicism in Scottish life were based on his personal experiences in Ireland. Born in Edinburgh, the son of Highland parents and brought up in the Baptist tradition, he joined the Argylls as a boy soldier in 1909, fought in the trenches during the First World War and saw action in Ireland during the wars of Independence from 1919 to 1921. He then left the Army and began to work for the Post Office in Edinburgh.

Every Sunday he was to be seen at the Mound from the early 1930s to the 1960s preaching his openly sectarian view of Scottish life. He formed Protestant Action and was elected to Edinburgh Town Council in 1934 as a member for Leith North. In the following year he publicly condemned the granting of the Freedom of the City to the Roman Catholic Prime Minister of Australia, Joseph Lyons. His supporters were later active in causing a disturbance at a women's eucharistic meeting in the Waverley Market during which the Roman Catholic Archbishop was mobbed and four priests had to be rescued. Six out of thirteen Protestant Action candidates were returned in the Town Council elections of 1936, and Cormack was to be seen in the City in an armoured car with the message 'Kormack's Kaledonian Klan' proudly displayed. In 1938 he was again returned for South Leith, a seat he held till 1962, when he retired from politics. In practical matters a conscientious councillor, his sectarian utterances, with the passage of time, rendered him an increasingly obsolete and isolated figure.

John P. Mackintosh was born in 1929 and educated at Melville College, Edinburgh. He studied Modern History at Edinburgh University before going on to Oxford and Princeton. In 1953 he was appointed assistant lecturer in History at Glasgow, and then taught successively at Edinburgh, the University of Ibadan in Nigeria and at Strathclyde, from which he resigned as Professor of Politics in 1966 on entering the House of Commons as MP for Berwick and East Lothian. Shortly before his untimely death in 1978 he was appointed Professor of Politics at Edinburgh.

Professor Mackintosh held the seat for Labour from 1966 to 1974, when he was narrowly beaten. He regained it shortly after and held it to his death. He had joined the Labour Party in 1948 and as an MP he had his differences with the Wilson and Callaghan governments: in 1976 he and Brian Walden walked off the floor of the House rather than support the Government over the Dockworth Regulation Bill. He also ran a five-year campaign to extend the Labour Government's grudging devolution proposals for Scotland. A maverick at Westminster (partly because he was a man of the centre in politics), he had prodigious energy and was a skilful debater and speaker on television and radio. Mackintosh was a reconciler and a man of charm and charisma as well as of principle. Among his best-known writings are *The British Cabinet* (1962) and *British Government and Politics* (1970). In many ways John Mackintosh was lost to British politics and academic life in his prime and would undoubtedly have continued to rise in stature had he lived.

Youngest of the leading political figures associated with Edinburgh is **David Steel** (born in 1938), current leader of the Liberal Party, who was educated at George Watson's and Edinburgh University where he graduated MA in 1960. He has represented Roxburgh, Selkirk and Peebles as MP since 1965 and was the youngest Member of Parliament at the time of his election, and in 1977 the youngest member of the Privy Council. David Steel has also conducted a distinguished career as a presenter and interviewer on radio and television.

David Steel

Pop

When **Jackie Dennis** was a fifteen year-old he appeared in the Empire Theatre impersonating adult performers. He was immediately acclaimed as an infant prodigy. Jackie sang 'Coming through the Rye' to jazzy rhythm, and with him on the bill were Larry Grayson and the John Barry Seven. Jackie shot from the obscurity of Grierson Gardens and an apprenticeship in plumbing to fourth position in the charts with 'La Dee Dah' and twenty-ninth place with 'Purple People Eater' (both in 1958). In the early '60s teenage girls mooned around chalking 'I love Jackie' on walls, and Jackie himself, dressed in his kilt, went over to the States to appear on the Perry Como Show.

However, things changed quickly for the young star, for when he returned from a six-week tour of Australia in 1960 he found he had been completely forgotten by the public. Soloists like Dennis, Marty Wilde or even Tommy Steele had been overtaken by groups such as the Beatles. Jackie set off on a career singing in working men's clubs, commenting bitterly: 'My whole show business life which began the day I left Leith Academy . . . has been like a travelling telstar. I've zoomed up into the heavens and come back down to earth'. In his heyday he was earning £650 a week. When he slipped out of the public eye he was left with a cafe in Tranent, a second-hand car and a regular Christmas card from Perry Como's manager. Nevertheless he did not give up: 'I've still got my friends in show business. They've all stuck by me, and friends are the most important thing in the world to me. I love the life and I'd never be forced to give it up. I'd rather sweep the stage than resort to the job I was destined to take when I left school. Could you picture ME as a plumber?'

But in 1972 he was in a club listening to a girl trying to sing 'Ave Maria'. Everyone was talking and shouting orders. The compere jumped onto the stage, hammered on the table and shouted: 'Shurrup, shurrup. Give't poor cow a chance'. Jackie immediately phoned his manager and said 'That's it. I've had enough', and returned to Edinburgh to take up a job in the Civil Service.

The Bay City Rollers were an Edinburgh phenomenon which burst on the pop scene in 1971 with their hits 'Keep on Dancing' and 'Shang-a-Lang'. With Leslie McKeown on vocals, Stuart Wood (Woody) and Eric Faulkner on guitar, Alan Longmuir on bass and his brother Derek on drums, the Rollers took the country by storm in their white gym shoes and tartan scarves, in the manner of Jackie Dennis and Rod Stewart.

The story of the Rollers, however, is really the story of their manager – Tam Paton, a miner's son from Prestonpans, a potato humpher who had the sheer nerve and the push to make the Rollers succeed. It started when he met two kids in the Palais dance hall; they asked him to be their manager. Paton remembers them as 'atrocious musically at the time', but the girls shouting and screaming for the two (Derek and Alan Longmuir) convinced him that they had potential. He booked the Bee Gees for one night in Rosewell Miners' Institute just so that he could slip the Rollers in as a support band. Twelve hundred people turned up and the Rollers were on their way, but Tam himself was beaten up and lost £350.

A lucky break came when Dick Leaky, the American owner of Bell Records, came over to Glasgow. His plane was diverted by fog, and it was Paton's job to run him to the West, but not before he had taken him to hear the Rollers and signed them up. In the period 1971 to 1973 things went badly: three records flopped, but the Rollers won the Luxemburg Song Festival, stripped to the waist and painted gold. Paton next had the bright idea of getting hold of the names and addresses of the 60,000 girls aged 14 to 16 who were the members of the Dave Cassidy and the Osmonds' fan club. He arranged a Roller photo session and sent out small postcards of the group with the invitation 'Buy 'Remember'' (the Rollers' latest). By 1974 the Rollers had copied Slade's use of tartan and there were five hit albums in the UK. In 1977 'Saturday Night' was No. 1 in the USA and the Rollers toured the States, Australia and New Zealand, but the group broke up shortly afterwards. So the Rollers disintegrated, and the Bay City fell silent.

A more durable talent was **Paul Jones,** educated at the

Paul Jones

Edinburgh Academy. He began with Manfred Mann before branching out on his own as a singer and later as an actor. In more recent years Edinburgh has seen the genesis of the Fire Engines, Paul Haig, the Exploited, the Questions and the Revillos who were formed in 1976 soon after the two members of the group, Eugene Reynolds and Fay Fife, met at Edinburgh College of Art. A number of other groups have shot into the limelight through appearances at the Edinburgh Festival Fringe: one of these was the Flying Pickets. And of course it should be noted that chart-topping singer Barbara Dickson once made Edinburgh her home when working as a civil servant.

Born in the middle of the Second World War, **Stuart Henry** received his education at Daniel Stewart's College, Edinburgh before training at drama college in Glasgow. After a spell in repertory at Edinburgh's Gateway Theatre he became a professional disc jockey in 1966, first with Radio Scotland. A thirteen-week contract with the BBC in London followed, and from there he went to Radio Luxembourg where he has been ever since. In 1979 he was diagnosed as suffering from multiple sclerosis but has continued to work as a broadcaster with the help of his wife. Although confined to a wheelchair, Stuart Henry was recently able to come over to Scotland to present an award to the Disabled Scot of the Year.

Printers and Publishers

Printing began in Scotland as a commercial process with the granting of a patent to Andrew Myllar and Walter Chapman by King James IV. Following the Reformation, the General Assembly of the Church of Scotland lent its authority to the new process when it gave £200 for the purchase of printing equipment in 1562 to bring out a metrical version of the Psalms. In 1680 there is mention of an 'invasion of Dutch printers'. Native enterprise was shown again by Thomas Ruddiman, a Banffshire schoolmaster, who had obtained employment in the Advocates' Library, and then in 1706 joined with the printer and bookseller Robert Fairbairn to publish editions of the poems of Gavin Douglas and William Drummond, as well as the works of Allan Ramsay and George Buchanan. In 1730 Ruddiman became Keeper of the Advocates' Library.

James Donaldson, 'bookseller' (1751-1830), was born at the West Bow, Edinburgh and succeeded his father as proprietor and editor of the newspaper the *Edinburgh Advertiser* in 1774, which enjoyed an especially wide circulation during the excitements of the French Revolution. His printing office in the Old Town was situated in the Stripping Close at Castle Hill, so called because criminals were stripped before being flogged at the different public wells – a practice that went on until 1805.

He left the bulk of his fortune – over £200,000 – to found a school for 300 poor children, which became Donaldson's School for the Deaf. A splendidly ornate building in the Tudor style, it was designed by William Henry Playfair and was visited in 1850 by Queen Victoria and Prince Albert. Legend has it that Queen Victoria wanted to buy it as a royal residence but was refused, which didn't go down well, but nearer to fact is the remark, 'Your school is finer than any of my Scottish palaces'.

Archibald Constable (1774-1827) transformed the world of publishing through his generosity to authors. He had begun as a young assistant in a bookshop in the City and by 1802 has started the *Edinburgh Review* with Sydney Smith, Francis Jeffrey, Henry Brougham and Francis Horner. He helped to publish Walter Scott's poems and entered into a London partnership, but was bankrupt a year before his death in 1827.

William Blackwood (1776-1834) was born in Edinburgh and – a Tory – founded *Blackwood's Magazine* in opposition to the Whig mouthpiece, the *Edinburgh Review*. It was to become a leading British periodical and remained in family editorship until its demise in 1976. Blackwood had a keen eye for new talent. John Galt's *The Ayrshire Legatees*, for instance, first appeared in *Blackwood's Magazine*, and as a publisher Blackwood reissued many works in book form that had first appeared in the magazine. In 1818 he published Susan Ferrier's *Marriage*. Later he published the *New Statistical Account* of Scotland (1840s), an extensive undertaking embarked on, it was said, as much out of a patriotic impulse as from desire for profit. Although a Tory and opposed to parliamentary reform, he was a keen advocate of civic improvements in Edinburgh.

Thomas Nelson (1822-1892), son of the founder of Thomas Nelson & Sons, was born in Edinburgh and educated at the High School. The staple of the firm was the reissue, inexpen-

sively, of standard authors, and he is credited with the invention, in 1850, of the rotary press. The firm was subsequently to be acquired by the Canadian, Roy Thomson (1894-1976), who also acquired *The Scotsman* newspaper. Nelson's were removed from Edinburgh, but *The Scotsman* remains.

Robert Chambers and his brother **William** (1800-83) (later twice Lord Provost) set up in business together and published

Lord Provost William Chambers

Chambers' Encyclopaedia and *Chambers' Journal*. Robert was a dedicated author of a wide variety of non-fiction, such as *A Biographical Dictionary of Eminent Scotsmen, Domestic Annals of Scotland* and the valuable sourcebook, *Traditions of Edinburgh*. William initiated many city improvement schemes involving extensive slum clearance, resulting in a significant reduction in Edinburgh's annual death rate. He also put large sums of money into the restoration of St Giles Cathedral. His statue stands in Chambers Street, driven wide and straight through what had become an insanitary huddle of old dwellings.

William Creech (1745-1815) (whom we encountered as a Lord Provost) was prominent among Edinburgh publishers, as was **William Smellie** (1740-95), who brough out the first edition of the *Enclyclopaedia Brittanica* in 1871. With Burns he sang bawdy songs at the Crochallan Fencibles, a drinking club in the local inn run by Dawnay Douglas. Smellie had been educated at Duddingston Parish Church and the High School and had developed a voracious appetite for knowledge which gave him a truly encyclopaedic mind. Burns writes of him:

> Shrewd Willie Smellie to Crochallan came;
> The old cock'd hat, the grey surtout, the same;
> His bristling beard just rising in its might,
> 'Twas four long nights and days to shaving night;
> His uncomb'd grizzly locks, wild staring, thatch'd;
> A head for thought profound and clear, unmatch'd;
> Yet tho' his caustic wit was biting-rude,
> His heart was warm, benevolent and good.

Which brings us to **John Ritchie Findlay** (1824-1898), born in

Arbroath, the grand-nephew of John Ritchie, one of the founders of the *Scotsman* (1817), who became its proprietor. He provided the money – over £70,000 – for the erection of the building in Queen Street, Edinburgh that was to house the National Portrait Gallery and the National Museum of Antiquities. He was secretary for six years of the Society of Antiquaries of Scotland and was also a benefactor of the National Gallery of Scotland. His Edinburgh residence in Rothesay Terrace overlooked the Dean Village, where he built, as flats for working people, Well Court, a complex grouped round a square with a community hall and a clock tower, and possibly reflecting some of the social planning ideas of Patrick Geddes. Designed by Sydney Mitchell, it was said to present Findlay with a view from his house that would remind him of 'romantic Nuremberg'.

Four generations of **Bartholomews** have made notable contributions to cartography. John Bartholomew's grandfather introduced layer colouring for relief representation in maps; his father developed this technique, the outstanding example of which was the Royal Scottish Geographical Society's *Atlas of Scotland* published in 1895.

John Bartholomew (1890-1962) had studied cartography at Edinburgh University, and at Leipzig and Paris universities. In 1914 he joined the Gordon Highlanders, saw action in France and Flanders, and was wounded and three times mentioned in dispatches. He was on Sir Douglas Haig's staff and later became a Staff-Captain in Intelligence, working on coding and deciphering. He was awarded the Military Cross for bravery. He was a pioneer in the mechanics of production whose *Times Survey Atlas of the World* (1922) became justly famous. He provided the Geography Department of the University of Edinburgh with a better-equipped library and laboratories and funded the appointment of a professor. He was devoted to the Royal Scottish Geographical Society, being Honorary Secretary for thirty years and succeeding his father in his post. He was also a Trustee of the National Library of Scotland, was on the council of the National Trust for Scotland and was awarded the Gold Medal of the Royal Scottish Geographical Society. In 1960 as Cartographer Royal he was awarded a CBE.

The heyday of Edinburgh publishing gradually declined

from its Victorian and Edwardian peak to the sale in 1962 of Nelson's to Lord Thomson and of Oliver and Boyd to the *Financial Times*. Nevertheless, there have been encouraging signs of new life in Edinburgh publishing to which the growing membership of the Scottish Publishers' Association testifies.

Royalty

Mary Queen of Scots (1542-1587) did not have the statecraft of her mother, Mary of Guise, nor the acumen of her great rival, Queen Elizabeth of England. Yet the contradictions and contrasts of her life have made her the focus of many plays and

Mary Queen of Scots, by Nicholas Hilliard

historical novels. At the age of fifteen she married the Dauphin of France. Three years later in 1561 she landed in Leith, no longer Queen of France and a widow. Mary fascinated: she could sing, play instruments, dance, ride a horse, hunt, sew and embroider. A Catholic, she arrived in a Scotland in the grip of Reformation. In spite of her attractive personality, Mary's life from this point seems to have consisted of her making one ill-judged decision after another (in her personal life as well as in affairs of state). She married her weak cousin Darnley (who was four years younger) and was then suspected of having him blown up in Kirk o' Fields to marry the divorced Bothwell who captured her with 800 men. After the Battle of Carberry, Mary was imprisoned in 1567 in Lochleven Castle, having been forced to abdicate. After her escape and defeat at Langside she fled to England and eventually, after a long exile and imprisonment, was beheaded as a piece of political expediency, dying with great dignity.

A great sinner to some, she became a saint to others. What is clear is that while she was not equipped to rule Scotland, she could captivate, and inspire romantic notions of a rose blooming among thorns: with her going there died French cosmopolitanism and gaiety, however much, another point of view, Scotland has been being used militarily by France as a northern embarrassment against England.

Mary's son, **James VI** of Scotland, succeeded Queen Elizabeth as James I of England in 1603, having, unlike his mother, proved an astute ruler of Scotland. Also unlike Mary, he was a

James VI

Protestant, and therefore – the enticements of English wealth apart – he could view England as a natural ally in the fight against the Catholic powers of Europe. He genuinely believed in the concept of 'Britain', in which – a man of considerable intellect – he was much ahead of the vast majority of his subjects, both English and Scottish. Visionary this idea might be, but from Edinburgh's point of view, with his going there went a court from her midst, a drift of Scottish nobles from Edinburgh to London, and a consequent impoverishment of life in Scotland's Capital, both cultural and material. Scotland now began to enter England's orbit, a process which, in political terms, was completed in 1707 with the Union of Parliaments, leading to the demise of Parliament in Edinburgh and the north-south peregrinations, ever since, of Scottish M.P.s to Westminster. Inevitable perhaps in a world of *realpolitik* and, with England poised to create the British Empire, materially beneficial to Scotland. But Edinburgh, bereft of Court and

Parliament ever since, may be said to parade the trappings
instead of the substance of a Capital, although still a Presbyterian – Church of Scotland General Assembly – and legal – the
Scots legal system, as distinct from the English – Capital;
besides being a thriving financial centre, generally reckoned
second only to London in Europe. But has something of
ancient importance gone when, in 1953, in contrast to 'James I'
of Great Britain, Queen Elizabeth is presented to Scotland as
'the second' when Scotland never had 'a first' and when, after
the full ceremonial of a coronation at Westminster Abbey, that
Queen attends a ceremony in St Giles, Edinburgh in a coat and
with a handbag over her arm, preceded by the Ancient
Honours (or Regalia) of Scotland – crown, sceptre and sword
of state – everyone else in full ceremonial garb?

On Tuesday September 17th 1745 **Prince Charles Edward
Stuart** (1720-88), intent on recapturing the throne from the
House of Hanover, and leading the Jacobite Rising, entered the
King's Park at the head of his army. He rode to Holyrood Palace
to be welcomed by a crowd of twenty thousand people wild with

Prince Charles Edward Stuart, in youth – and in old age

enthusiasm for the heir of their ancient royal house. A
contemporary description tells us that 'He was in the prime of
youth, tall and handsome, of a fair complexion; he had a light-
coloured periwig, with his own hair combed over the front. He
wore the Highland dress, that is, a tartan short coat without the
plaid, crimson velvet breeches, and military boots; a blue
bonnet was on his head, and on his breast the Star of the Order
of St. Andrew'. Others observed that he had a melancholy air
and looked more like a fashionable gentleman than a conquer-
ing hero. He was duly proclaimed King James VIII and

Charles Prince Regent at the Mercat Cross.

On the 19th the Prince left Edinburgh for Duddingston (now part of Edinburgh) where he stayed the night in a cottage opposite the west entrance of Duddingston House. He had arranged for transport to be sent out from Edinburgh for the wounded of the impending battle with Sir John Cope and also secured the help of many medical men, both Jacobite and Whig. The night before the battle the Prince slept in a field wrapped in his plaid. The surprise attack of his soldiers left only some one hundred and seventy Government infantry alive and uncaptured out of two thousand captured or dead. The battle was over before Alexander Carlyle could get out of bed in his father's manse at Prestonpans to see it. The Edinburgh surgeons tended the worst cases locally while the rest of the wounded (some six hundred Government troops and seventy Highlanders) were taken to the Royal Infirmary and the Edinburgh Charity Workhouse. Over a thousand prisoners were housed in the Canongate Kirk and the Canongate Tolbooth. Most of the captured Highlanders came over to the Prince's side. On the day after the battle the Jacobite army marched in triumph through Edinburgh led by pipers playing the Prince's favourite tune, 'The King shall enjoy his own again'. The victorious clans came next, followed by the prisoners and the wounded in carts at the rear. The parallels with the triumphs of victorious Roman generals must have been apparent to many. But the Prince was still at Prestonpans supervising the care of the wounded. He spent that night at Pinkie House in Musselburgh and returned to Edinburgh the next day.

One of the greatest surprises to the citizens of Edinburgh was the culture and good manners of the Jacobite officers. Alexander Carlyle remarked on the civility of the victorious officers, such as Lochiel (who had been responsible for the quick-witted and bloodless capture of the City in the first place). The discipline of the common soldier in the Prince's army also gave rise to astonishment. During the occupation there was no drunkenness, and there were no riots on the part of the Highland army.

Not everyone was pro-Stuart, however: Provost George Drummond tactfully went to London to woo a wife; the poet

Allan Ramsay retired with a diplomatic illness to Penicuik; the judges had fled from Edinburgh some time before; and the two Edinburgh banks had sent all their cash and securities to the Castle for safe-keeping.

The Edinburgh clergy were given freedom of worship by the Prince, himself a Catholic. At the West Kirk the old minister Mr Macvicar did not deviate from his habitual form of worship and offered up this Sibylline prayer in the presence of the Prince: 'Bless the King; Thou knowest what King I mean. May the crown sit long easy on his head. And as for this man that is come among us to seek an earthly crown, we beseech Thee in They mercy to take him to Thyself, and to give him a Crown of Glory'. The Prince laughed at his honest temerity and left it at that.

By and large, however, Whigs and Jacobites co-existed peacefully. 'Of the ladies', it has been written, 'two-thirds proclaimed themselves Jacobites, and one-third of the men were of the same persuasion.' Edinburgh contributed passively to the Jacobite forces in the form of tents, military stores and arms, and the Jacobites, for their part, were content during the course of the seven weeks' occupation to go about their business in their distinctive Highland dress of a white cockade, a plaid waistcoat and a Highland sash. Later, after Culloden and the defeat of the Rising, there was an Edinburgh mania for Jacobite tartan. Ladies wore it as plaids, gowns or riding habits and made it into quilts, curtains, even shoes and pin-cushions. Charles himself did not wear the kilt at any time in Edinburgh. His dress was either the tartan trews or breeches, and with both he always wore boots, .thus contradicting the claim made by many an Edinburgh lady that she had danced with the Prince. Moreover he appears to have been distant in the company of ladies and diffident if not embarrassed. He preferred the military life to that of a fashionable gallant, in spite of appearances to the contrary.

Charles did not succeed in capturing Edinburgh Castle, where the eighty-five-year-old General Joshua Guest doggedly held out. The Jacobites used Allan Ramsay's Goose-Pie house to fire on the Castle sentries, and a blockade was applied. General Guest replied with midnight sorties and by bombarding the town, killing a number of citizens. The blockade was lifted on October 5th, and the Prince was even able to persuade officials of the Royal Bank to remove £6,100 from the Castle.

In spite of a rumour of an assassination attempt on the Prince on the 3rd of October, he continued to find favour with the ladies of the town, being showered with gifts of plate, valuables, tablecloths and napkins. Not many Edinburgh men enlisted in his service, however: only two lawyers, for example. But the medical men did so in greater numbers: the Jacobite army enlisted forty-four surgeons and physicians from Edinburgh.

After the Prince's departure for Dalkeith on the 1st of November, there were mixed reactions and recriminations in the town. A new Town Council was elected and promptly voted the freedom of the City to the Duke of Cumberland, who was to defeat Charles at Culloden in 1746, spending a solitary night thereafter at the Palace of Holyroodhouse. Provost Archibald Stewart was tried for being a suspected Jacobite sympathiser on the grounds of his obvious indecision and his Jacobite name, but he was unanimously acquitted. After Culloden rumours of a Jacobite victory were rife until the true outcome of the battle was known. We are told that 'Balls and dances were held by the disaffected ladies whose mirth was interrupted about one in the Sunday morning by a round from the great guns of the Castle, answered by discharges from the men of war in the Road (Leith Roads) on receipt of quite contrary news'. The Stuart cause was ended. 'Edinburgh had not much cause to be proud of her conduct in 1745', it has been observed. 'If she did little for King George II, she did less for Prince Charles.'

The Palace of Holyroodhouse has had its ups and downs. Here is the bedroom of Mary Queen of Scots, and the room in which her Italian secretary David Riccio or Rizzio, with whom she was suspected of having an improper relationship, was murdered by her jealous husband, Lord Darnley, and a group of noblemen. A brass plate marks the spot where he lay dying from fifty stab wounds. In 1633 Charles I, succeeding James VI, was crowned there but then, back in London, stirred up a hornet's nest by attempting to impose Anglicanism on Presbyterian Scotland, leading to the famous episode in 1637 when, it is said, Jenny Geddes, who sold cabbages in the High Street, threw her stool at the hapless cleric who attempted to conduct

Holyrood Palace

an Anglican service in St Giles. Following Charles I's execution by beheading in London in 1649 at the end of the English Civil War, Charles II was promptly proclaimed King of Scotland in Edinburgh in 1650, but the Scots had backed a loser, and were invaded by a victorious Cromwellian administration. The palace was damaged by fire while occupied by Cromwellian troops but, after the Restoration of **Charles II** in 1660, was restored to the design, still surviving, of Sir William Bruce. Charles it was who also inspired the series of paintings there by the Dutchman Jacob de Witt of Scottish sovereigns starting from 330 B.C.

Charles II, in Parliament Square, said to be the oldest equestrian statue in Britain (no less!). They number over a hundred, and as likenesses are naturally inventions, not accurate portrayals. Charles's equestrian statue, cast in Holland in 1685, can be seen in Parliament Square, behind St Giles Cathedral. The Town Council had intended one of Cromwell, but on Charles's Restoration astutely changed their minds! Charles's brother James, Duke of York, held court at Holyroodhouse from 1679 to 1682, restoring some of the life and ceremony the want of which had been felt since James VI had left for London in 1603, but he subsequently proved a disaster as James II of England (VII of Scotland), pursuing intolerant Roman Catholic policies which were unacceptable in England and Scotland alike. He was ousted by the Protestant Dutchman, William of Orange, who was to be followed by a succession of Protestant monarchs in London – Queen Anne, George I (from Hanover), George II and George III – none of whom showed any interest in Scotland: it took a Stuart – Prince Charles Edward, in 1745 – to hold court at Holyrood house again during the Jacobite Rising. A colourful episode followed when the Comte d'Artois, brother of Louis XVIII of France, took up residence there from 1796 to 1799 in the wake of the French Revolution. Then, in 1831, having become **Charles X of France** but having been forced to abdicate, he was back again. Dogged by massive debts, he found not the least of the Palace's advantages to be that it served as a debtor's sanctuary, protecting him from his creditors, from whom however he was immune on Sundays, when he would emerge to scatter largesse among the poor. Also, his presence with his court was good for business in the Canongate. So when at last he sailed away from Leith, he got a rousing send-off. **Queen Victoria** was an occasional visitor at Holyroodhouse, although her passion was for Balmoral, Deeside and the Highlands – a phenomenon known by some as 'Balmorality'. Nowadays Queen Elizabeth (II or I?) spends an annual residence at Holyroodhouse. In her absence the Palace is used as the official residence of her Lord High Commissioner to the General Assembly of the Church of Scotland, and throughout the year the Hereditary Keepers of the Palace of Holyroodhouse are the Dukes of Hamilton, a post they have held since 1646. When in residence, Her Majesty also inspects the Sovereign's Bodyguard in Scotland, the Royal Company of

Archers, and holds a Royal Garden Party to which are invited the notables of the nation.

The major link, however, between the days of Edinburgh's having a monarch in residence (ending with the departure of James VI) and the present when the monarch visits Scotland's Capital annually was the visit of **George IV** in 1822 which, as we saw, owed much to Sir Walter Scott, a fervent royalist and a romantic keen to revive former glory. Relations between

George IV

Scotland and England had not been good: although the Union of the Parliaments of both countries in 1707 put an end to hostilities, English suspicions, indifference and – when, if ever, indifference changed to attention – condescension had been marked by a protracted absence from Scotland by the ruling British monarch: not since the time of Charles II (1650) had there been a visit, and the Jacobite Risings, particularly that of 1745 led by Prince Charles Edward Stuart, had hardly endeared Scotland to the English.

Perhaps no one knew how the visit of the sixty-year old George IV, of the House of Hanover, to Scotland, ancestral land of the ousted House of Stuart, would go, but in the event it was a triumph, perhaps a theatrical one, but then again perhaps it took the element of theatre/tartan to capture the public imagination and to set the two former nations on the road to reconciliation and – less desirably – begin the craze for tartan and things Highland as though they represented Scotland as a whole, Lowland and Highland. Scott, great man though he be, may have a lot to answer for! Victoria fell for it, Harry Lauder battened on it, television on New Year's Eve/

Hogmanay perpetuates it: Brigadoon. But at least Scotland was being noticed again after a long spell of feeling left out in the cold, and so the whole visit inspired a rapturous reception. It achieved a climactic symbolism when there was a state procession to Edinburgh Castle – the Regalia of Scotland (sword of state, sceptre and crown) were carried before the King.

A word about the Regalia – the **Honours of Scotland,** on view still at Edinburgh Castle. At the instigation of Sir Walter Scott – again – these symbols of Scottish nationhood had been discovered where it was suspected they were, in a locked chest

The Crown of Scotland

in the Castle, their purpose gone since 1603. The crown is believed to include the circlet of Robert the Bruce who, defeating the invading English at Bannockburn near Stirling in 1314, ensured Scotland's independence. The sceptre was presented to James IV (1473-1513) by Pope Alexander VI and it was remade for James V (1512-42). The sword of state was presented to James IV by Pope Julius II in 1507. Smollett wrote: 'Of these symbols of sovereignty the people are exceedingly jealous. A report being spread, during the sitting of the union Parliament [1707] that they were removed to London, such a tumult arose that probably the lord commissioner would have been torn in pieces if he had not produced them for the satisfaction of the populace'. The statue of George IV now stands at the intersection of George Street and Hanover Street, and the street where both the National and Public Libraries stand is named George IV Bridge.

Finally, the **Order of the Thistle.** This ancient order of chivalry is said to have existed under James V (1512-42).

Disappearing at the Reformation (1560), it was revived by James VII in 1687 and then again re-established by Queen Anne in 1703. The order consists of the Sovereign and sixteen Knights, and takes as its emblem the Thistle of Scotland. It formerly met in the Chapel Royal at Stirling Castle, and subsequently at Holyrood Abbey which, after the Reformation, had a chequered career, falling eventually into ruin in the eighteenth century. Eventually, in 1911, after abandonment of plans to restore the Abbey, the Thistle Chapel was opened in St Giles Cathedral, a small but jewel-like addition designed by Sir Robert Lorimer, architect also of the National War Memorial at Edinburgh Castle (1928) which, unlike the memorial to the Napoleonic Wars, on Calton Hill, was seen through to magnificent and moving completion. The Napoleonic memorial, or National Monument, to a design by W. H. Playfair after the Parthenon on the Acropolis in Athens, ran out of funds and came to be known as 'Edinburgh's Disgrace'.

Soldiers, Sailors and Airmen

The Scots – a small nation – have always been warlike: survival was never handed to them on a plate. Among the anonymous Scots who travelled to soldier in foreign lands there was many an Edinburgh man. In France Charles VII established the Scots Foot Guard and Archers in 1425, and the Garde Ecossaise was formed around the year 1445. The Scots Gendarmes made up part of the royal bodyguard and were later to fight for the French against the Duke of Marlborough.

Sweden was another country where Scots made a notable contribution. The Scots Brigade was the spearhead of Gustavus Adolphus' army at the battle of Leipzig in 1631. After the battle many towns and castles in Germany had governors who were Scots.

Fighting in the Dutch Wars of Independence in 1568 were a fair number of Scots and, in 1572, companies were raised in Scotland to fight for the Netherlands. Later, Daniel Defoe gave his opinion that the Scots were the best soldiers in Europe and should serve Britain 'instead of cutting each other's throats in the service of foreign princes'. In 1782 the Scots Dutch Brigade was disbanded, having been the last large force of Scotsmen in the army of a foreign power.

Popular legend has it that the origins of the **Royal Company of Archers** stretch back to the days of King James I (1394-1437) when they were the Sovereign's personal bodyguard. In 1603 we hear of representatives of the Guard shooting for the Silver Arrow at Musselburgh. The established date of formal foundation of the Company of Archers is 1676. It was set up for noblemen and gentlemen to encourage 'the Noble and Useful Recreation of Archery, for many years neglected'. The first Captain-General was John, First Marquis of Atholl. In 1704 a Royal Charter from Queen Anne gave 'perpetual access to all public butts, plains and pasturages legally allotted for shooting arrows with the bow, at random or at measured distances'. In return the Archers were required to render yearly to Queen Anne and her successors (if asked for only) 'one pair of barbed arrows'.

In 1714 came the first public march of the Archers from Parliament Close to Holyrood, then to Leith Links to shoot for the Silver Arrow, and finally through Leith to the accompaniment of the firing of ships' guns. The Archers shot either at the clout (180 yards) or at the butts (100 feet), and Archers' Hall, built in 1776, with its glazed shooting gallery, gave plenty of scope for practice.

On the visit of George IV in 1822 (stage-managed by one of the Archers, Sir Walter Scott) they had assumed a quasi-military role as The King's Body Guard, by which title they were now to be known. When Queen Victoria sailed up to Scotland twenty years later the Royal Archers stood on parade in field uniform in the Riding School in Lothian Road. However, the Queen was twenty-four hours late and the Archers spent the whole day waiting in vain. Worse was to come. When the Queen did finally land at Granton with a squadron of escorting ships, the Archers had been alerted and were marching to meet her in fours. The Queen was tired and set off from Granton immediately, escorted by Dragoons before and behind. The Archers tried to take up a position on either side of the road at Warriston, competing with the 'prancing Dragoons'. They followed the Queen's carriage manfully but at Parson's Green the Queen set off at a rapid rate for Dalkeith, and the Archers abandoned the fruitless chase. All turned out well in the end, for the Queen issued a direct order for the Archers to accompany her for the rest of the visit and she wrote in her Journal: 'The pressure of the crowd was really quite alarming, and both I and Albert were quite terrified for the Archers' Guard, who had very hard work of it, but were of the greatest use'.

Today the Royal Company is four hundred strong and regularly performs its function as Royal Bodyguard whenever the Queen is in residence at Holyroodhouse and engaged in official duties. The Archers are still to be seen shooting in competition in the time-honoured style, a living reminder of Scotland's proud history.

The Trained Bands – citizens recruited to help keep order in times of trouble – were instituted in 1580. By 1626 there were eight companies of 200 men each. The chief officers of the Trained Bands formed themselves into a Society in 1663. Their uniform was a dark blue coat, plain yellow buttons, a white vest, nankeen breeches and white silk stockings. The Society was by 1789 a secret one, with its own secret word of parole and favourite meeting-place (often Fortune's Tavern or the Laigh Meeting House). In 1769 the Trained Bands had been summoned by tuck of drum to muster at Leith Links in order to fight against the Covenanters at Bothwell Bridge. Later they guarded large numbers of Covenanter prisoners in Greyfriars Churchyard. Although their last meeting was in 1798, a symbolic vestige of the Trained Bands remained in the periodic appointment of a Captain of Orange Colours (the 1st Company) by the Town Council. Among such Captains were the philosopher and economist Adam Smith, Hugo Arnot the historian of Edinburgh, and William Creech the publisher and Lord Provost.

In 1689, to secure Edinburgh for William of Orange, the **Earl of Leven,** by beat of drum, in two hours raised a regiment of 800 men, known as 'Leven's' or 'The Edinburgh' Regiment. In 1887 it received its present title of the King's Own Scottish Borderers, and it has the unique right, as 'Edinburgh's Own', to march through the City with bayonets fixed and drums beating.

Fixed to the wall above Mid Common Close in the Canongate is the figure of the Emperor of Morocco dressed in a turban and a necklace. There are a number of explanations as to why this curious effigy should be there; one of them has all the hallmarks of a story from the Arabian Nights. The story goes that during the riots and the violence which followed the coronation of Charles I in 1633, the home of the Lord Provost, Sir John Smith, who was unpopular, was set on fire by the mob. A ringleader of the street riots was captured, and he turned out to be **Andrew Gray,** an Edinburgh University student, younger son of the Master of Gray, Sir William Gray, brother-

H

in-law to the Provost. In spite of the entreaties of his family, young Andrew was found guilty of arson and sentenced to death. The night before his execution the scaffold was being erected at Mercat Cross in the High Street. Andrew enlisted the help of a friend who gave drugged liquor to the Tolbooth guard. Andrew escaped into a close leading down to the Nor' Loch and a boat took him across the water. He travelled quickly to Leith and then away to sea, disappearing over the horizon.

In 1645 Edinburgh was smitten by the plague. The High Street, once full of traders and townsfolk, was deserted. Grass grew between the cobbles and the stench of death lay all around. At the height of the epidemic a strange foreign warship appeared off the coast and anchored in Leith Road. Old salts who saw her said she was an Algerian pirate vessel, of the kind that struck dread into the hearts of merchantmen all over the Mediterranean. A fierce crew of armed men clambered into a small boat which the warship let down into the water. The boat landed at Leith, and all could see that the armed foreigners were led by a powerfully built Moor. They marched up the Canongate to the Netherbow Port and demanded to be let into the town. The Provost and the magistrates asked for time to negotiate with the warlike strangers, but so many of Edinburgh's fighting men had died in the plague that they were forced to give in to the Moor's demand for a large ransom.

Lord Provost Smith was asked to hand over his eldest son as a guarantee of good faith. However, since his only child was a daughter, he offered to give her in exchange for no harm coming to the town. He explained that his daughter was even then ill with the plague. The Moor softened at this news, and told the Provost that he had a marvellous medicine. He promised that if the medicine did not cure the Provost's daughter, he would leave Edinburgh without doing any harm to the inhabitants. His offer was accepted, and the Provost's daughter was taken to a house in the Canongate, as the Moor refused to enter the town. The girl was cured and the Moor revealed himself as none other than the young Andrew Gray once sentenced to death. He had returned to carry out vengeance on the inhabitants of Edinburgh. By now he realised that the Provost was a relation of his by marriage. Andrew

Gray fell in love with the Provost's daughter, they were married and lived happily ever after in a house in the Canongate. On the wall of his house Andrew placed a statue of his former patron and friend, the Emperor of Morocco, and the house is known as Morocco Land.

General Tam Dalyell of the Binns (c. 1599-1685) learned his soldiering in the service of the Czar of Russia against the Poles and the Turks. He left his mark permanently on the memory of Edinburgh by the way in which he defeated and captured the Covenanting army at the battle of Rullion Green in 1666. Eighty Covenanters were taken off to the City to be tried. Some were hanged, others tortured, and others deported to the West Indies.

The mere mention of his name was enough to strike fear into those he opposed: 'He never wore a peruke; nor did he shave his beard since the murder of Charles I. His head was bald, which he covered with a beaver hat, the brim of which was not three inches broad. His beard was white and bushy, and yet reached down almost to his girdle.' His devotion to his profession led to his raising the Royal Scots Greys in 1681, and it was Sergeant Charles Ewart (1769-1846) of this regiment who, at Waterloo, captured the Imperial Standard of the 45th Invincibles and was promoted Ensign. He was reinterred on the Esplanade of Edinburgh Castle in 1938, and has also given his name to a public house nearby in the Lawnmarket.

James Graham, the Marquis of Montrose (1612-50), was an astute general who outwitted the Covenanting armies between 1644 and 1645. Montrose was implacably opposed to the Marquis of Argyll (known as 'Gillespie Gruamach' or cross-eyed

James Graham, Marquis of Montrose

Archibald). Montrose suspected him of wanting to rule Scotland in place of King Charles I. Argyll was the most powerful member of the Committee of Estates which ruled Scotland at the time, and he attacked those who would not sign the Covenant. In spite of Montrose's flair for generalship and his success in what appeared to be impossible tactical conditions (he defeated a Covenanter army three times the size of his own using only his 'naked, weaponless, amunitionless men'), he was finally defeated in Sutherland and found wounded and exhausted amid the bogs and icy streams. In Edinburgh he was sentenced to death, and the Town Guard escort which led him to the place of execution was commanded by Major Thomas Weir (later tried and executed as a wizard). Montrose was sentenced 'to be carried to Edinburgh Cross (the Mercat Cross), and hanged up on a gallows Thirty Foot high, for the space of Three Hours, and then to be taken down, and his head to be cut off upon a Scaffold, and hanged on Edinburgh Tolbooth; his Legs and Arms to be hanged up in other public Towns of the Kingdom, and his body to be buried at the Place where he was executed'. As he passed up the Royal Mile Montrose came to Moray House and the cavalcade stopped: looking up he caught sight of his enemy Argyll through the shutters. He died with gallantry and dignity.

Argyll, having crowned Charles II at Scone, took sides with Cromwell against him, and was finally defeated in his turn and beheaded in Edinburgh in 1661.

The first arrival of Oliver Cromwell in the City was in 1648 when he had dined with Argyll at Moray House, and he dined there again two years later. On that occasion his soldiers did great damage: 'The College Kirk, the Gray Freir Kirk, and that Kirk callit Lady Yesteris Kirk, the Hie Scule, and a great pairt of the College of Edinburgh were all wasted, thair pulpites, daskis, loftes, saittes, windois, dures, lockes, bandis [hinges], and all uther thair decormentis, war all dung doun to the ground by these Inglische sodgeris, and brint to asses'.

'Jock' Porteous, after whom were to be named the notorious **Porteous Riots** of 1736, was the son of a tailor in the Canongate. He was trained by his father to follow his profession, but at an early age showed signs of disruptive behaviour and rebelliousness, so much so that it is said he would attack his father in his temper. His father, who could put up with him no longer, sent him off to be a soldier in Queen Anne's time, and so it was that he found himself serving with the Scots Dutch Brigade in the States of Holland. In Flanders his only warlike act was reputed to have been the shooting of a hen for amusement. He was suspected of having cut the throat of his captain after the latter had given him a beating. Porteous left the army shortly after and returned to his home town. At the time of the 1715 Jacobite rising the number of Edinburgh's Town Guard was increased, and the trained bands and the volunteers were also given arms. To the poet Fergusson the Town Guard were 'black banditti', and John Porteous on his return to the City was selected as the Guard's drillmaster on the strength of his service in the Low Countries. Although records suggest that Porteous did his job well, he was removed from the post in 1716 (possibly for an outburst of temper), but reinstated two months later. In 1718 he was made ensign of the Town Guard, which was composed of some 100 men divided into three companies, each commanded by a captain-lieutenant. In 1726 Porteous was appointed captain-lieutenant and paraded in front of his men in their military coats and cocked hats, carrying muskets, bayonets and Lochaber axes (a sort of halberd with a hook). The headquarters of the Guard was the Guard House, a long, low, ugly building which stood in the middle of the High Street to the west of the Tron Kirk until its removal in 1875. Scott wrote that it 'might have suggested the idea of a long black snail crawling up the middle of the High Street'. The Guards themselves were posted at night as sentinels at the time when Edinburgh was still a walled city, and the corps was mainly composed of soldiers discharged from the Highland regiments.

From his appointment Porteous is said to have been unnecessarily harsh and cruel and to have abused his authority. He was contemptuous of the common people, and they knew to beware of him. A broad-shouldered, muscular man, with a gentle-seeming but pockmarked face, he was the only man they and the Guard feared, and this ability to intimidate seems to have won him the full support of the Town Council.

Porteous' fortunes took a turn for the worse when a smuggler named Andrew Wilson appeared on the scene.

Wilson's criminal career has a streak of Keystone Cops in it. The people of Scotland sided with smugglers and hated the excisemen because they saw the taxes as yet another instrument of oppression from London. Wilson cornered a collector of excise in his lodgings after he had gone to bed. He and his friends began to break down the door, but the collector jumped out of the window with a bag of money, unfortunately leaving his trousers behind. He lay hiding under some straw until morning, dressed only in his nightshirt. Meanwhile Wilson and his accomplices were taken to the Tolbooth and sentenced to be hanged. At that time convicted criminals were hanged in the Grassmarket at the foot of the West Bow. The gallows was placed in a massive block of sandstone with a triangular socket-hole. After Wilson was hoisted up on the gallows, the magistrates present went to a tavern overlooking the gallows for the 'deid-chack', the customary execution meal. After half an hour the criminal was cut down, the signal being given by the magistrates pointing a white rod out of the tavern window. As he went to cut Wilson down, the hangman was stoned and one of the mob cut the rope. Immediately a shower of stones and dirt was thrown at the Guard, who opened fire in retaliation, killing three and wounding twelve, and then withdrew up the West Bow chased by the crowd. They fired again and three more were killed.

Porteous, put on trial for the episode, was found guilty but reprieved by the Queen. The Edinburgh mob were so incensed that they went on the rampage, stealing the keys of the West Port and nailing and locking the gates, then streaming down the Cowgate and locking all the other gates to stop the regular troops from getting into the town. They broke into the Guard House and took 90 firelocks, Lochaber axes and the town drums, freed a number of prisoners and tried to break into the Tolbooth with sledgehammers, but when this proved impossible they set fire to the gates with barrels of tar. Captain Porteous was dragged into the street, a coil of rope was taken from a shop in the West Bow, and he was strung up on a dyer's drying-frame (about 15 feet high). After he had hung for three minutes, the crowd stripped off his nightgown, broke his arm and shoulder with a Lochaber axe, burnt his foot and then jerked him up and down for an hour. Finally they nailed down the rope and left his body hanging till five o'clock in the morning. A violent man, but also a violent town. The story is told in Scott's *Heart of Midlothian*. Porteous is buried in Greyfriars Churchyard.

John Paul Jones, known as 'the Pirate', was born in Kirkcudbrightshire in 1747. He was apprenticed at the age of twelve to a Whitehaven merchant and made a number of voyages to America where he had an elder brother in Virginia. Having been a mate on a slave-carrying ship, he inherited his brother's property in 1773 and changed his name, John Paul, to John Paul Jones. In 1775 he volunteered for service with the American fleet and was posted to Europe two years later. In September of that year Jones arrived off the coast of Eyemouth and later seven miles off Dunbar, then passed close to Leith on his way to Kirkcaldy. The people of Leith worked furiously through the night to prepare for the expected invasion. Old cannon were rolled into position, barricades were built and soldiers and seamen manned the coastal defences along the front. Jones by this time had learned that Leith was virtually defenceless and that the guns at Edinburgh Castle could not be turned to fire in the direction of the port. He planned to demand £200,000 from the citizens of Leith, and with this in view had written the following letter: 'The Honourable J. Paul Jones, Commander-in-Chief of the American Squadron now in Europe, etc., to the Worshipful the Provost of Leith, or, in his absence, to the Chief Magistrate who is now actually present and in authority there. The British marine force that has been stationed here for the protection of your city and commerce, being now taken by the American arms under my command, I have the honour to send you this summons. I do not want to distress the poor inhabitants; my intention is only to demand your contribution towards the re-inbursement which Britain owes to the much injured citizens of the United States. Leith and its port now lies at our mercy; and did not our humanity stay the hand of just retaliation, I should without advertisement lay it in ashes'. Fortunately the letter was never sent, for the wind changed (some said through the prayers of a local minister), and the Americans were forced to move on. Jones served also in the French and Russian navies, and died in Paris in 1792.

Colonel William Inglis was born in Edinburgh in 1764, the son of an Edinburgh surgeon. After joining the 57th Regiment when seventeen, he served in America, then in various campaigns in Flanders, Normandy and Brittany. By the age of

Colonel William Inglis

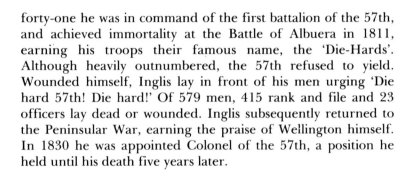

forty-one he was in command of the first battalion of the 57th, and achieved immortality at the Battle of Albuera in 1811, earning his troops their famous name, the 'Die-Hards'. Although heavily outnumbered, the 57th refused to yield. Wounded himself, Inglis lay in front of his men urging 'Die hard 57th! Die hard!' Of 579 men, 415 rank and file and 23 officers lay dead or wounded. Inglis subsequently returned to the Peninsular War, earning the praise of Wellington himself. In 1830 he was appointed Colonel of the 57th, a position he held until his death five years later.

Lieutenant-General William Crockat was gazetted an ensign in the 20th Regiment of Foot in 1807. He distinguished himself on the field of battle at the battles of Vimera, Corunna and Vittoria in Spain. After the French Wars were over, he and his regiment were sent to St Helena where he was the last officer to be in charge of Napoleon, the 'caged eagle of St Helena', who died in his custody. Crockat was despatched to Britain to bring the news of Napoleon's death. After a period spent in India, he retired to Edinburgh in 1830 where he lived, till his death in 1874, in Inverleith Row.

Douglas, first Earl Haig (1861-1928) was born in Edinburgh, and after an education at Clifton and at Brasenose College, Oxford, he went to Sandhurst in 1883, then travelled to India with the 7th Hussars. Although he had failed the examinations

Earl Haig

for the Staff College and suffered from colour blindness, his career was meteoric. He served with the Egyptian cavalry in the Omdurman campaign in 1898 and was a brigade-major in the Boer War before commanding the First Calvalry Brigade at Aldershot and being posted to South Africa. From 1900 he was a column commander in the Cape Colony and Regimental Lieutenant-Colonel with the 17th Lancers, after only fifteen years' service. In 1903 he was Inspector-General of Cavalry in India, and in the following year became a Major-General. He went to the War Office in 1906 as Director of Military Training, and then returned to India in 1909 as Chief of the General Staff.

At the time of the First World War he took two divisions to France as the First Corps and enhanced his reputation as a leader at the First Battle of Ypres. He was subsequently appointed Commander-in-Chief. In spite of the arithmetical progression of his career to this point, his reputation suffered as a result of decisions he took during the War. Although he had courage and skill in directing the battle and played an important part in the defeat of the enemy, arguably he failed to make himself aware of the tactical situation on the ground and pointlessly committed the lives of many of his men where there was little chance of success. After the War he worked tirelessly for the development of the British Legion and the United Services Fund. His equestrian statue stands on Edinburgh Castle Esplanade.

Two anecdotes are recorded by John Kay about **Admiral Duncan.** In 1792 a mob entered George Square to protest over

Admiral Duncan

Duncan's neighbour, Dundas', opposition to the reform of the electoral system. A straw figure of Dundas was burnt on a pole. Duncan, although aged sixty-one, was a strong, athletic man of giant stature. 'Armed with a crutch', writes Kay, 'belonging to old Lady Dundas, which he seized on rushing out of the house, he laid about him among the crowd with great vigour; and even after the head of the crutch had been demolished, he continued to use the staff, until compelled to reteat by the overwhelming inequality of numbers'.

After Duncan's naval victory over the Dutch at Camperdown in 1797 a whole brigade of volunteers, between two and three thousand strong, entered George Square and marched in slow time in front of the Viscount's house. He saluted them and the naval car carrying Duncan's flag, the body of seamen following with cavalry and infantry. At the end of the North Bridge the people took the horses from the Admiral's carriage and drew it through the New Town. In the evening there was an entertainment in Fortune's Tavern held by the Lord Provost and magistrates, and the Freedom of the City was presented to Viscount Duncan. His portrait, by Reynolds, hangs in the National Gallery of Scotland.

There have been a good number of ships with the name HMS *Edinburgh,* as befits a City boasting the Port of Leith. The first ship to be called *Edinburgh* in the Royal Navy was a Fifth Rate of thirty-two guns which had started life as the *Royal William* in the Scottish Navy and was taken over at the Union in 1707 when it was renamed HMS *Edinburgh.* It ended its life being sunk at Harwich to act as a breakwater, in 1709. The second *Edinburgh* began its career as the *Warspite,* built in

Blackwall in 1666. It was a Third Rate of sixty-four guns and became the *Edinburgh* in 1715. Its most famous engagement was the capture of the French privateer, *Le Duc de Chartres*, in the Channel in 1746. The second *Edinburgh* was broken up in 1771. The third *Edinburgh* was launched in the Thames in 1811, a Third Rate with seventy-two guns. It took part in the blockade at Anzio in 1813, the driving of the French out of Spezzia in 1814, the blockade of the Syrian coast and the bombardment of St Jean d'Acre in 1840. Five years later it was fitted with a screw and an engine, much to the crew's disgust. After various exploits in 1854 and 1855 (the capture of Bomarsund and the blockade of the coast of Courland), the *Edinburgh* was sold to Messrs. Castle. When HMS Majestic was launched in 1882 it was promptly changed into another HMS *Edinburgh*. This was a real ship of the line, a first-class battleship which saw service in the Mediterranean between 1887 and 1893. After a spell as a coastguard ship at Queensferry it was sold in 1910. There were various other ships with names such as HMS *Duke of Edinburgh* (in action in the Red Sea War and at Jutland) and the *Edinburgh Castle*, an armed merchant cruiser.

Twenty-eight years were to pass from the sale of the HMS *Edinburgh* in 1910 to the launch in 1938 of the next ship of that name by Swan Hunter at Tyneside. The new 10,000-ton cruiser was launched by Lady Gumley, the wife of Sir Louis Gumley, Lord Provost of Edinburgh, in the presence of a party of representatives from Edinburgh Corporation. Some time later the Edinburgh Women Citizens' Association and the National Council of Women joined forces to make a White Ensign and a Union Jack for the new cruiser, and in 1939 the City of Edinburgh presented a number of gifts to the ship's company when HMS *Edinburgh* sailed into port (these included silver candlesticks and a challenge cup). During the first air raid on Scotland of the Second World War German aircraft attacked the cruiser in the Firth of Forth, but she survived.

The City of Edinburgh adopted another vessel in 1941 during Warship Week. This was HMS *Howe* which, after serving through the War, ended its life in 1958 when the 35,000-ton King George V Class battleship ran aground on a mudbank in the Firth of Forth and had to be towed to the breaker's yard at Inverkeithing. The ship's bell, however, was rescued and presented at a Remembrance Day Service by Vice-Admiral J. D. Luce, Flag Officer (Scotland), to the Rev. Dr Harry Whitley of St Giles Cathedral.

It was in April 1942 that HMS *Edinburgh* left Scapa Flow to take up convoy duty over the 2,000-mile route via Iceland to Murmansk in Russia, a route known as The Gateway to Hell. The *Edinburgh's* geared turbine engines were capable of more than thirty-three knots; she was fitted with asdic equipment for detecting submarines and radar devices; and she had four triple turrets of six-inch guns and was armed with twenty-one-inch torpedoes. She set sail into thick fog to rendezvous with the convoy. On board was a cargo of steel plates to repair the crippled HMS *Trinidad* which lay in the dry dock at the Kola Inlet. On the way they were attacked by U-boats: the *Empire Howard* was hit by three torpedoes and her cargo of trucks slid into the sea as the ship sank. Depth-charges had to be laid into the swimming survivors for fear of the U-boats. Finally HMS *Edinburgh* arrived in Russia.

Shortly before she set back again along the convoy route, the cruiser took aboard five tons of Russian gold ingots (said to have belonged to the Czar in the days before the Russian Revolution). This was in payment for the military equipment America was supplying to Russia to fight the Germans at Moscow and Stalingrad. Some murmured that it was blood money. When HMS *Edinburgh* was spotted by a Junkers 88 reconnaisance plane, she began to take avoiding action with a zigzag course. In spite of this, U-boat 456 hit her with two torpedoes, one amidships at the forward boiler room and one aft which ripped off the stern. Attempts were made to tow her back to Kola and the *Edinburgh's* one remaining turret was still able to return devastating fire at some German destroyers the convoy encountered. Finally she was again torpedoed on the 2nd of May. The wounded were transferred to another British ship. Passengers on the *Edinburgh* included many Poles released from Russian prisoner of war camps (General Sikorski's secretary died in his bunk), Czechs interned by the Russians, and British Army and RAF instructors. Eight hundred men escaped to the minesweepers and the Edinburgh was deliberately scuttled with the bodies of fifty-seven men on board. In 1981

Jessop Marine Recoveries Ltd faced fierce public criticism for disturbing the wreck of the *Edinburgh* which the Admiralty had stipulated must be teated as a war grave. In spite of the delicacy of the operation and its controversial aspects, the crew of the salvage vessel raised forty million pounds' worth of gold ingots from a depth of nine hundred feet. Four years later the latest HMS *Edinburgh*, a Type 42 destroyer, was commissioned at Leith.

The Dukes of Hamilton have played a prominent part in Scottish history and have a special connection with Edinburgh, being the Hereditary Keepers of Holyroodhouse. The fourteenth Duke, while the Marquis of Douglas and Clydesdale and MP for East Renfrewshire, was chosen as the chief pilot for the Houston Mount Everest Expedition in 1933 when he and Flight Lieutenant David McIntyre flew over the highest peak in the world. The Marquis, a former Scottish Amateur Boxing Champion (Middleweight), was the youngest squadron-leader in the Auxiliary Air Force and commanded the 602 (City of Glasgow) Bomber Squadron. In May 1941 the Duke of Hamilton, as he had become, was the surprised host of Hitler's deputy, Rudolph Hess, when Hess landed in Scotland in order to secure a peace settlement with Britain. The Duke had been called up at the beginning of the Battle of Britain and became Station Commander at Turnhouse Aerodrome, Edinburgh with responsibility for an Air Sector which covered most of the eastern and central belt of the country. Later he was Commandant of the Air Training Corps in Scotland. In later years the .Duke was Lord High Commissioner to the General Assembly of the Church of Scotland from 1953 to 1955 and again in 1958, thus playing a prominent part in Church events in Scotland's Capital.

To return to the War: on 16th October 1939 two waves of German bombers passed over Edinburgh on their way to attack the naval dockyard at Rosyth on the Forth. The Spitfires of the 603 City of Edinburgh (Fighter) Squadron of the Royal Auxiliary Air Force were scrambled and in the ensuing dogfight four Heinkels were destroyed – the first enemy planes of the Second World War to be brought down in Britain.

The European military tradition of the Tattoo has its origins in the seventeenth and eigthteenth centuries in the Low Countries (the scene of continual armed conflict) when the regimental drums and pipes would be heard marching through the streets signalling all military personnel to return to camp. Military historians are divided over the differences between Tattoo and Retreat. Manuscript copies of Retreat calls exist, dating from some three hundred years ago. What is clear is that by the beginning of the nineteenth century the army bands of Russia were probably the finest in Europe: they incorporated religious hymns into the ceremonial as an expression of the deep devotion of the ordinary Russian soldier. The Catholic armies of Austria and the predominantly Lutheran forces of Prussia followed the Russian example. In 1809 Beethoven composed three military marches as Tattoos, one of which became the March of the Yorcksen Corps in 1813. By the turn of the twentieth centry the Tattoo as a military spectacle was the pride of Germany, Austria, Britain and France. Today's Tattoos are smaller and more compact than those at the beginning of the century but they continue to incorporate the playing of the Last Post and the singing of an evening hymn to the accompaniment of massed bands.

The **Edinburgh Military Tattoo** began with drill displays at the Ross Bandstand in Princes Street Gardens. The Tattoo arrived on the Castle Esplanade in 1948 but began its association with the Edinburgh Festival in 1950 when the finale took the form of a performance of Handel's Music for the Royal Fireworks conducted by Sir Thomas Beecham. It is often thought that the Tattoo consists only of displays by the Army. In fact the other branches of the armed forces have played important parts. The Navy, for example, has demonstrated an interception at sea, a ladder display, cutlass drill and hornpipe dancing; the Royal Marines have appeared almost annually, playing with the massed bands, and have demonstrated an assault on the Castle, for instance, with a dramatic descent from the Half Moon Battery to the Esplanade using rope techniques. The Royal Air Force have made musical contributions, and have shown the work of the Alsation dogs of the RAF police and the gymnastic prowess of the Airobats. One of the most popular aspects of the Edinburgh Military Tattoo is the generous splash of tartan which is a feature of the event. Scottish regiments are either Highland (wearing the kilt) or Lowland (wearing tartan trousers known as trews). The survival of Highland dress was due entirely to the Army, for from the year 1746 when the Disarming Act came into force (following the abortive Jacobite Rebellion), to its repeal in 1781, only soldiers in the service of the Crown were permitted to wear the tartan. Scottish military dress originated with the formation of the Black Watch as a regiment in 1739, and the Highland dress worn by the Scottish regiments was always the Government or military tartan consisting of a belted plaid and red coat. The colours of collars and cuffs differed between regiments but musicians and pipers often wore tartan other than that of their regiment as in the case of the Royal Stuart tartan conferred on some regimental musicians by the Sovereign.

The Lone Piper playing on the ramparts of the Castle and spotlit in the dark is characteristic of the eerie romanticism of the Edinburgh Military Tattoo which maintains close links with the Army School of Bagpipe Music (part f the Army School of Piping located in Edinburgh Castle). Scottish dancing is a feature too: Highland dancing gives a chance to show agility and skill around the broadsword for the men or solo dancing for the women as in dances from the Hebrides. Lowland dances are more spacious and involve a greater number of dancers. Again, it was the Scottish Regiments of the British Army that formed the strongholds of Scottish dancing (especially the Highland). When it is considered that some two hundred and fifty thousand spectators attend the Edinburgh Tattoo each year, its impact as a means of communicating Scottish life and culture can be seen to be unrivalled (especially when a vast television audience is taken into account).

Producers of the Tattoo have from time to time introduced historical re-enactments into the programme, such as incidents in the history of the Order of the Knights of St John of Jerusalem; Queen Victoria presenting colours; and the installation of Lord George Hamilton as Constable, Governor and Captain of Foot at Edinburgh Castle in 1714. Invaluable as a source of advice for such *son et lumière* events has been the Castle's own United Services Museum

More than seventy overseas contingents have taken part in the Tattoo, adding their own special style to the proceedings, including the Fanfare à Cheval of the Garde Républicaine de Paris; the ever-popular Gurkha pipe bands; the Danish Life Guards in their blue and scarlet; the Janissaries of Turkey with their medieval military music and drill; the US Marine Corps; the Evzones of the Greek Royal Guard; a Breton Pipe Band; the running band of Italy's Bersaglieri; the Sri Lankan dancers with elephant; the enormously popular Maoris with their song and dance (already well-known from the Rugby field); the Banner Display team from Cori in Italy; and the Royal Band and Dancers of the Sultan of Oman.

A recent encouraging development vis-à-vis the age-old and increasingly terrifying business of armed confrontation has been what have come to be known as the Edinburgh Conversations, get-togethers between Russian and Western foreign policy and defence specialists. The Conversations take place annually, alternating between Moscow and Edinburgh, and one of the leading organisers is **Professor John Erickson,** head of the Department of Defence Studies at Edinburgh University.

And by way of parting shot: a tourist attraction at Edinburgh Castle is always **Mons Meg,** the huge late medieval siege

Mons Meg

cannon made for King James II in 1455. It was once believed that she had been made locally for the siege of Threave Castle in Kirkcudbrightshire, but now she is thought to have been made at Mons in Flanders. In 1558 she was fired on the occasion of the marriage of Mary to the Dauphin of France – the cannonball was found two miles away. Mons Meg burst when firing a salute for King James VII, the former Duke of

York, in 1682. She was removed to London in 1754 but, through the efforts of Sir Walter Scott, was returned to Edinburgh in 1829. In 1985, having returned to London yet again, this time for restoration, she yielded new information about herself: the thirteen-foot, four-inch long gun with the twenty-inch bore was weighed. Answer: 5.94 tons. (It is interesting to note that, by way of a sort of metallurgical entente cordiale, at about the same time the statue of Eros from London's Piccadilly Circus came to Edinburgh for restoration – to Charles Henshaw & Sons.)

Sport

Athletics

It was not till 1883 that the Scottish Amateur Athletics Association (SAAA) saw the light of day and held its first meeting at Powderhall, Edinburgh. Before that time bodies such as the Edinburgh University Athletic Club had held competitions which included such bizarre events as putting the cannon ball and the stilt race. Athletes in those early days would try their hand at any event: in 1883 the international rugby forward W. A. Peterkin of Edinburgh University A.C. won the 100 yards in 10.5 seconds, went on to win the 440 in the afternoon and came within a hair's breadth of winning the shot-putt. Peterkin was a man of parts: he studied medicine at the University but failed to complete the course and emigrated to Texas in 1884. He possessed a fine baritone voice and was a popular figure on London concert platforms.

The real sprint star, however, was Alfred Reynolds Downer, who although born in Jamaica in 1873, arrived in Edinburgh at an early age and was educated at George Watson's and the Edinburgh Institution (Melville College). In 1893 he won the 100, 220 and the 440 yards at the SAAA championships and repeated this feat the two following years. His fastest times were 9.8 seconds for the 100 yards and 19.8 for the 220, both world bests in 1895. The next year Downer was banned from amateur athletics and became an outstanding professional: in 1897, for example, he held the world professional record for the 400 yards (44.8 seconds). He was a fairly dissolute character and his life was a chequered one: D. A. Jamieson writes, 'In his short life – he died when in his thirty-ninth year – Downer quaffed to its deepest from the goblet of life – and in its dregs he found much bitterness'. He died in 1912 and was buried in Morningside Cemetery.

Eric Liddell was one of the finest athletes ever produced by

Eric Liddell

the British Isles. Although born in China (1902), it was in his family's home town of Edinburgh that he first showed his true athletic prowess. While a trialist for the Scotland rugby team he scored ten tries in his first two trials and then went on to be chosen for the team where his speed and agility made him a formidable weapon in the Scottish armoury. In the same year (1922) he won the 100 and 220 yards in the Scottish Championships and the Crabbie Cup for the most meritorious performance. He went on to win for the next three years and in 1923 also won the 100, 220 and 440 yards in a Triangular International Contest. In July 1923 he broke the 100 yards British record. The following year he won the Harvey Cup as the best champion of the year at the Stamford Bridge British Championships, winning the 100 yards in 9.7 seconds and the 220 in 21.6 seconds. At the Paris Olympics in 1924 he refused to take part in the preliminary heats for the 100 yards because, as they were being held on a Sunday, his religious principles prevented him from taking part in sport on the Lord's Day. Nevertheless, he won a bronze medal in the 220 and a gold medal in the 440.

In July of that year he graduated BSc from Edinburgh University and was crowned with a wild olive wreath like the Greek champions of old, in whose mould he was formed. He returned to China in 1925 to carry out his life's work as a missionary, and after twenty years' service, died at the end of the Second World War in a Japanese internment camp. Much of his strength of character is captured in the film *Chariots of Fire*.

Born in 1953, **Allan Wells** attended Fernieside Primary School before going on to Liberton High School. He was a member of the Boys' Brigade and as a youngster did not make

Allan Wells

a very auspicious start: he got his older sister to write away for a Charles Atlas body-building course on his behalf but gave up the idea when he heard the price (£5). According to his mother, the secret of Allan's success was the bananas she fed him: bananas are a perfect combination of enzymes and minerals. At the age of nineteen he damaged his big toe on his right foot and the operation to correct the damage left him with a v-shaped section missing and made him believe that he would never walk again. However, he persevered with training which he found 'exhausting and incredibly monotonous and boring' and used the old professional runner's form of training, the speedball which he was able to hit around 4,000 times in 18 minutes. By this time he was able to say that 'There's something wrong with an athlete who doesn't enjoy it. If you hate the training, it would be sadistic to go on'.

When he first joined Edinburgh Southern Harriers, Wells started as a long-jumper but took up serious sprinting in 1976. In 1978 his wife Margot was a semi-finalist in the Commonwealth Games as well as the 100 metres hurdles champion for Scotland. Wells worked as a marine engineering apprentice instructor until he moved into public relations as success began to come on the track. He won two Golds and a Silver at the

Edmonton Commonwealth Games in 1978, but his supreme achievement was in the controversial political atmosphere of the Moscow Olympics in 1980 when he beat Cuba's Silvio Leonard in the Lenin Stadium with a time of 10.25 seconds and a fraction of an inch of his torso. This was the first Scottish Olympic sprint Gold since Eric Liddell's in 1924 and the first British sprint Gold since Harold Abrahams also in that year.

Lately, popularising athletics still further, has come the Edinburgh Marathon, now an established annual event, and 1970 saw the Commonwealth Games held in the specially built Meadowbank Stadium, seating 15,000 and also incorporating a multi-sports centre. The Games returned there again in 1986.

Boxing

Ken Buchanan was a connoisseur's boxer with a textbook left jab. Born in 1946, 'King Ken' or 'Baby-face' Buchanan boxed for the Sparta Club in his leisure time from learning the

Ken Buchanan

joinery trade; he was Scotland's Featherweight champion from 1954.

In 1969 he decided to quit the ring but a year later he beat Ismael Laguna in 110° of heat in San Juan, Puerto Rica to become World Lightweight Champion. In his dressing-room after the fight Buchanan dived into his bath keeping hot and cold compresses over his eyes, and a fanatical Scottish fan insisted on pouring a case of champagne into the bathwater. However, this victory was not recognised because he had boxed for the World Boxing Association title when the British Boxing Board of Control recognised only the World Boxing Council.

The following year he again met Laguna, this time in Madison Square Gardens, New York. Laguna smashed Buchanan's left eye in the third round and the resulting lump had to be sliced open with a razor-blade by his manager and the bruised blood squeezed away. It was his homecoming to Edinburgh after beating Ruben Navarro in Los Angeles in February 1971 that stays in the memory: 'King Ken' with his £25,000 prize was welcomed with champagne and bagpipes. Thousands of fans crowded into Waverley Station and along Princes Street as he drove by in an open coach. Banners proclaimed the message 'Welcome Home Champ'. When he finally won his Lonsdale Belt in 1973 by beating Jim Watt, Buchanan was described as an 'incensed terrier, chasing . . . viciously with heavy thumping punches'. His inspiration for a boxing career had come from watching a film about Joe Jouis when he was eight years old.

Football

The origins of football are shrouded in the mists of time. However, we do know that James I of Scotland frowned on such frivolous pastimes which he believed to be much less important than encouraging archery as a defence against foreign invaders like the English. In more relaxed times King James IV is recorded as having paid two shillings in 1497 to buy footballs. It was not till almost three centuries later that football as an organised sport emerged in Edinburgh. In 1873 the Heart of Midlothian Football Club was founded, to be followed two years later by the Hibernian Football Club.

The most celebrated Hearts players were the **Terrible Trio:** Conn, Bauld and Wardhaugh. Willie Bauld from Edinburgh was the 'King of Tynecastle' in the heyday of the midfield trio during the 1954-55 season when they won the Scottish Cup for Hearts for the first time since 1906: Bauld scored a hat-trick. After many honours he eventually left football to become a shopkeeper and died tragically in 1977. Hibs, for their part, had a forward line known as the **Famous Five:** Smith, Johnstone, Reilly, Turnbull and Ormond. Gordon Smith was an Edinburgh man, known as the 'perfect gentleman of football'. Smith achieved five League Championship medals, and scored over 300 goals in some 900 matches, playing for both Hibs and

Scotland. Smith, who also played for Hearts from 1959 to his retiral in 1964, holds two records: he won League Championship medals with three different clubs and made a winger's record score in a match (five goals). Lawrie Reilly was another Edinburgh-born member of the Famous Five. He was Hibs' most capped player and won 38 international caps between his signing of Hibs at the age of 16 in 1945 (when he was an apprentice painter) and his retiral through the after-effects of a cartilege operation in 1958. 'Last Minute Reilly' (as he was known because of his ability to pull a late goal out of the bag when it mattered most) played on the wing and then at the centre where his goal-scoring powers were devastating. One of Scotland's most famous goalkeepers was the late Tommy Younger, who began with Hibs in 1948 and then moved to Liverpool in 1956; his giant frame made him a difficult man to beat, and he won 24 caps for Scotland.

Golf

Golf has been played in Edinburgh from at least the year 1457, when James II introduced a statute against it lest, like football, it interfere with archery. Nevertheless James IV is recorded as playing it in 1503, and in 1642 Charles I is recorded as having been in the middle of a game of golf on Leith Links – said to be second in seniority to St Andrews only – when he was interrupted by news of the Irish Rebellion. The Duke of York (later King James VII) was resident at Holyroodhouse during the period 1681 to 1682. He was challenged by two English noblemen to make up a foursome with a Scottish player. John Paterson, a shoemaker and the best golfer in Edinburgh, was picked by the Duke, and after a memorable contest Paterson and the Duke won. With the proceeds of the match Paterson was able to build a comfortable house for himself in the Canongate. By the eighteenth century golf had become so popular that players banded themselves into clubs: the Royal Burgess Golfing Society (1735), the Honourable Company of Edinburgh Golfers (1744) and the Bruntsfield Links Golfing Society (1761).

The earliest description of the game dates from 1687, as do

the earliest verses, but it is the mock-heroic poem 'The Goff', by the solicitor Thomas Mathison (1743), which celebrates the fascination of the game:

> Goff, and the Man, I sing, who, em'lous, plies
> The jointed club; whose balls invade the skies;
> Who from Edina's tow'rs, his peaceful home,
> In quest of fame o'er Letha's plains did roam.

Tobias Smollett, in *Humphrey Clinker* (1771), acknowledges the social prestige of golf as he observed it in Edinburgh:

> I never saw such a CONCOURSE of genteel company at any races in England, as appeared on the course of Leith. Hard by, in the fields called the Links, the citizens of Edinburgh divert themselves at a game called golf, in which they use a curious kind of bats tipped with horn, and small elastic balls of leather, stuffed with feathers, rather less than tennis balls, but much harder. This they strike with such force and dexterity from one hole to another, that they will fly to an incredible distance. Of this diversion the Scots are so fond, that when the weather will permit, you may see a multitude of all ranks, from the senator of justice to the lowest tradesman, mingled together, in their shirts, and following the balls with the utmost eagerness. I was shown one particular set of golfers, the youngest of whom was turned of fourscore. They were all gentlemen of independent fortunes, who had amused themselves with this pastime for the best part of a century, without having ever felt the least alarm from sickness or disgust; and they never went to bed, without each having the best part of a gallon of claret in his belly. Such uninterrupted exercise, with the keen air from the sea, must, without doubt, keep the appetite always on edge, and steel the constitution against all the common attacks of distemper.

Some golfers were particularly ingenious in the wagers they made against each other. Take the case of the following, noted by Henry Mackenzie, the Man of Feeling:

> Golf, a favourite amusement of Edinburgh, was played on Bruntsfield Links, tho' the crack players preferred those of Leith. I recollect a wager laid by a celebrated golfer, that he could strike a ball from one of the windows in the building at the end of the Luckenbooths looking down the street, in six strokes to the top of Arthur's Seat, the first stroke to be from the bottom of a stone basin. He won his bet; the first stroke striking the ball to the Cross, and the second reaching the middle of the Canongate.

The first great Edinburgh golfer was **Freddie Tait,** born in 1870, the son of an Edinburgh professor. Tait, a muscular six-footer, was superintendent of army gymnasia in Scotland and

F. G. Tait

acclaimed as the greatest amateur golfer of his time. In 1893, on the Old Course at St Andrews, on a calm frosty day, he drove his tee shot 250 yards, after which it rolled for another hundred. Tait was amateur champion at Sandwich (1896) and Holylake (1898), and won the Scottish Amateur Championship twice at St Andrews. A lieutenant in the Black Watch, he was wounded in the South African War in 1899 and was killed leading a reconnaissance a year later.

Tommy Armour, known as 'The Silver Scot' and 'The Iron Play King', was the outstanding Edinburgh player in this century. A member of the Braid Hills Club, in his day he was reckoned the world's best iron player. Armour served in the Tank Corps during the First World War and was wounded in one eye, leaving his sight permanently impaired. Nevertheless he went on to win the French Amateur Championship and the Gleneagles Hotel Tournament in 1920, and became the US PGA champion in 1930. He was unique in that he played for Great Britain in the preliminary match of the amateur international in 1921 and then represented the US in an unofficial preliminary to the Ryder Cup, having emigrated to America and turned professional. In 1924 he won the British Open, the US Open and the US PGA title. Three years later he again won the US Open, and the British Open again in 1931. He spent twenty years at Boca Raton in Florida and was a familiar figure there sitting with his drink under an umbrella supervising the development of golfers young and old. He died in 1968 at the age of seventy-two.

In and around Edinburgh, it should be noted, there are no fewer than twenty-four golf courses, private and public, the most internationally famous of which is nearby Muirfield, a regular venue of the British Open, and now the home of the Honourable Company of Edinburgh Golfers who, founded at Leith Links in 1744, moved there in 1891. A course much admired by Jack Nicklaus, it was his model for the course of the same name which he designed in the USA.

In 1986 one-time Bathgate fireman **Eric Brown,** one of Scotland's greatest golfers, died suddenly at his home at Juniper Green in Edinburgh aged 61. At the height of his career in the '50s the Open title eluded him on at least three occasions, but it is by his combative match-play that he is remembered better still, having never lost an encounter in the Ryder Cup, and subsequently becoming an inspirational Ryder Cup captain.

Horse-Racing

One of the earliest records of organised horse-racing in Edinburgh is to be found in an entry for 1504 in the accounts of the Lord High Treasurer for Scotland. Edinburgh, therefore can claim to have been the host of one of the oldest recorded race meetings in the world.

In 1773, when the first official Racing Calendar appeared, there were only two race meetings in Scotland: at Kelso and at Edinburgh.

The annual Edinburgh fixture was held for over three hundred years on the sands at Leith. A Royal Plate was presented to the Edinburgh Races in 1728 to be competed for by six year olds.

The Royal Caledonian Hunt (founded in 1777, with its headquarters in Edinburgh) had suggested to the Lord Provost in 1812 that a more fitting site for the Races should be landscaped on the Bruntsfield Links by clearing it of trees. However, a new venue was eventually found in 1816 when the meeting was transferred from Leith Sands to the grassy links of

Musselburgh, a flat, oval course one and a quarter miles long. The Edinburgh Gold Cup of one hundred guineas – now £4000 – was introduced in the following year and from that time racing continued to flourish under the auspices of the Lothians Racing Club and its President, the Earl of Rosebery.

Motor Racing

In the motor racing season 1956 and 1957 the Edinburgh-based **Ecurie Ecosse** filled the first two places in the Le Mans 24-hour race, thus bringing international recognition to the headquarters of the team in Merchiston Mews. Behind this success the driving force was an Edinburgh accountant, the late David Murray. Educated at the Royal High School, Murray went on to Edinburgh University and qualified as a CA in 1934. Murray drove for Scuderia Ambrosiana, the Maserati-sponsored equipe which entered for the European Grand Prix. In 1947 he drove a Q-type MG and won first place in Leinster. Four years later the genial, fast-talking Murray, with his flair for showmanship, founded Ecurie Ecosse, which was affection-ately referred to as 'The Haggis Bashers'. In 1962 Murray smashed the record for 2½-litre engines at Monza with a speed of 152 miles per hour per lap. Sharing the wheel of the winning Ecurie Ecosse D-Type Jaguar on both occasions at Le Mans was Edinburgh racing driver Ron Flockart. Flockart (born in 1923) was educated at Daniel Stewart's and took a BSc at Edinburgh University before joining the Army where he became a captain in REME which involved him in organising and riding in motor cycle sand races in Egypt. After a fine career as a racing driver Flockart was killed in Australia.

Richard Noble was born in Edinburgh in 1946. He was educated at Winchester and Oxford and then took up employ-ment in a chemical company. Coming from a military family, he seems to have been born with a sense of adventure. At the time of John Cobb's death on Loch Ness while attempting the world water speed record, Noble decided he would take up the challenge to be the fastest man on earth. By 1977 he had begun to test his Thrust 1 vehicle with which he hoped to break the world land speed record. However, he had a 130 mph crash and had to sell the car as scrap for £175. He built Thrust 2 and in 1980 broke six UK records at Bonville Flats in Utah. In 1982, while he was travelling at 300 mph on an RAF runway, the parachute brake knotted. Noble had to swerve and crash into a wood. In the interim he trained as an aeroplane pilot as this seemed to be highly relevant to the way his vehicles performed. After a long wait he succeeded in getting the financial backing he so desperately needed, and on October 4th 1983 in Nevada he reached a speed of 638 mph in Thrust 2, and so became the first Briton since Donald Campbell to hold the world land speed record.

Mountaineering

Thomas Graham Brown (1882-1965) was born into an Edinburgh medical family. In 1903 he took a science degree at Edinburgh University and three years later qualified as a doctor. After serving with the Royal Army Medical Corps on the Balkan Front he was appointed Professor of the new department of Physiology at the University of Wales, his specialism being neuro-physiology (the mechanism of muscular reflexes). While his medical career was distinguished, Brown was chiefly famous for his achievements in mountaineering. While appreciating the magnificence of mountain scenery, he was a rigorously scientific climber, who irritated his colleagues by stopping at intervals on his climbs to take notes and photographs in order to compile a scientific record of the ascent. In his day he was known as 'der beste Kenner des Mont-Blanc', and from 1924 to 1939 'Tim G.B.', as his friends knew him, climbed every year either in the Alps or further afield. During the 1930s his achievements surpassed those of any other climber from the UK.

His greatest climb, was the 'Triptych' of three routes up the Brenva face of Mont Blanc. In his book, *Brenva*, he describes the moment of revelation when the possibility of the three climbs first suggested itself: 'Complicated as is the Brenva face, and broken as are its ribs, the magnificent wall nevertheless has a grand simplicity from the mountaineer's point of view: *One direct route to Mont Blanc, one direct route to Mont Blanc de*

Courmayeur, and one direct route to the high pass between the two summits. When this picture of the Brenva face finally revealed itself to me in its complete form, it did so as a great triptych, a thing scarcely to be matched in its fullness and splendour'. Brown was a bachelor whom Robin Campbell described thus in his Edinburgh flat: 'He was a small man and seemed smaller still in his room, hunched over his calabash in an oversized armchair surrounded by towering bookshelves, his pale face caught by the glow from the electric fire. He smoked more or less continuously and accumulated around his chair a comfortable barrier of used matches, burnt-out dottle and empty tins of Three Nuns tobacco, which added piquancy to the layers of fish-supper wrappers and abandoned copies of the Times'.

Dougal Haston was born in Currie, Midlothian in 1940, in what is now part of Edinburgh District. His father was a baker, and young Dougal was introduced to climbing by Alick

Dougal Haston

Buchanan-Smith, now a Conservative MP, and then leader of a local youth club. Haston joined his first mountaineering club at the age of fourteen and climbed in Glencoe. At sixteen he became a member of the Mountaineering Club of Scotland. He conquered the Eiger seven years later in 1963 and ran a climbing school at Glencoe two years after that. Already he was demonstrating his great psychological resilience and his immense strength. In contrast to the days when he had learned his climbing first on the railway bridge walls at Currie using six-inch nails as pitons and a clothes line as a rope, Haston gave up his studies in philosophy at Edinburgh University in 1966 to devote himself professionally to the sport he loved. He made the first direct ascent by the North Face of the Eiger (a feat he describes in his autobiography *In High Places*), a far cry from his early days on Salisbury Crags, Glencoe and Ben Nevis.

On his annual visits to the Alps he had climbed the North Face of the Matterhorn, but 1970 saw him as a member of the UK team climbing the South Face of Annapurna in the Himalayas. Along with Graham Tiso (the designer of mountaineering equipment) and David Bathgate, a master joiner, he was one of three Edinburgh men on the 1972 British Expedition which was forced to abandon an attempt on Mount Everest. In 1975 he made the first ascent by the South-West Face of Everest, in spite of the death of his colleague, Mike Burke. Death was ever-present on these climbs which stretched the limits of men and technology.

Haston achieved the first ascent of Mount McKinlay in Alaska in 1976 and in the same year was presented with the Livingstone Gold Medal of the Royal Scottish Geographical Society at a ceremony in the Usher Hall in Edinburgh which was followed by a lecture with slides by Haston and two others to an audience of more than two thousand.

He had settled in Leysin in the Swiss Alps in 1966 when he took over as Director of a ski-school when his predecessor was killed on the North Face of the Eiger. In 1977 he was skiing alone less than seven thousand feet up the Swiss Alps near Leysin in the Col du Luisset when he was tragically killed in an avalanche. He had been preparing for an expedition to Pakistan and Nepal and for an attempt on K2, one of the highest summits in the Himalayas. Dougal Haston, one of the top two or three climbers in the world, was buried in a small Alpine cemetery. In 1978 a bronze plaque was erected in his memory on the railway bridge wall above the Water of Leith walkway in Currie.

Rugby

It was in 1823 that William Webb picked up the ball and ran with it while a schoolboy at Rugby. The game was played for the first time in Edinburgh during the year 1855, when the Edinburgh Academy took it up and three years later formed the first Scottish Rugby Club. By 1870 the Scottish Rugby Union was in existence, comprising Edinburgh Academy, the

Royal High School, Merchiston, Edinburgh University and two West of Scotland clubs. In the following year the first International against England was played at Raeburn Place (which Scotland won).

In more recent years Edinburgh has been fortunate to produce rugby players of the calibre of Ken Scotland (also capped for his country at cricket), Douglas Morgan and the great **Andy Irvine,** who, with 51 Scottish caps, has played on the wing and at full-back, and kicked Scotland to victory on numerous occasions. Irvine, who played for Scotland from 1972 to 1982, scored over two hundred and fifty points for the

Andy Irvine

national side, gained fifty-one Scottish caps and played in three British Lions tours. He was probably the most exciting and lethal attacking full-back in the world and could change the course of a match with his thrilling acceleration and an armoury of unexpected jinks and deceptive swerves. His value as a kicker was often proved, as in 1980 when he turned an impending 14-4 victory for France into a Scottish triumph in the last fifteen minutes of the game with sixteen points (a goal, two tries and two penalties).

On 17th March 1984 the Scottish Rugby team won the Grand Slam against a powerful French team, thus completing an unbeaten season which gave them the Calcutta Cup against England and the Triple Crown. This was the first time since 1938 that Scotland had achieved the Grand Slam, and it was fitting that it should be theirs on the national rugby ground, Murrayfield Stadium in Edinburgh.

Skiing

Skiing first seems to have arrived in Scotland through the efforts of the Scottish Mountaineering Club, founded in 1889. One of its members, Harold Raeburn, ascended Blackford Hill, the Braids and even the Pentlands in 1893, using a stout pair of Norwegian skis. The founding of the National Ski Club for Scotland in 1907 gave more formal impetus to the sport. Its members first met in the Scottish National Antarctic Expedition's room in Surgeon's Hall, called together by Dr William Bruce, the Antarctic surgeon who had been in charge of the high altitude observatory on Ben Nevis. By 1936 Edinburgh folk were to be seen in their dozens during the heavy snowfalls of that November skiing enthusiastically. In more recent times Edinburgh has seen the development of a new uplift by Bill Blackwood, who tested his prototype at Turnhouse. It was the opening in 1965 of the Hillend artificial ski slope, however, that opened new horizons for Scottish skiers. Under the guidance of the Austrian Hans Kuwall Scottish skiers were given the opportunity to develop a much higher level of skill in spite of the relative lack of real snow. One of these is **Martin Bell** who began skiing at the ag of six, mostly at Hillend. A pupil at George Watson's, Bell later went to the Austrian ski school at Stamms. The result was to turn him into Britains top alpine skier at the age of twenty one, the youngest of the world's top thirty downhillers, thirteenth in World Cup points in the 1985-86 season.

Swimming

If you had happened to pass through Portobello in past years, like as not, you would have caught sight of a stocky, broad-shouldered figure in an open-necked shirt, shorts and sandals carrying a shopping-basket. The Iron Man, **Ned Barnie,** was part of Portobello history, a monument to guts and determination.

Formerly head of the Science Department at David Kilpatrick School in Leith, Ned Barnie was a champion Channel swimmer three times in 1950-51. He was once the oldest person to swim the Channel and as far as history records was the first person to swim the Firth of Forth, having made two double crossings between Granton and Burntisland in 1924. In 1950 he was fifth in the France to England race and that August was the first man to swim the Channel both ways in one season. All this despite the fact that doctors told him in 1925 that he would probably never swim again. Every January he had a habit of taking a New Year's Day dip in the Firth of Forth, cracking the ice if necessary: 'It's more refreshing', he confided once, 'when there's a little frost in the air'. The secret of his long life and endurance is to be found in the regular training he always undertook: on Sunday mornings when others were in bed, he would be off hiking over the Pentlands, and every morning before work, he would cover between twenty and a hundred lengths of Portobello Baths. In retirement his philosophy for success (and it appeared to work) was: a healthy attitude of *mind*. Ned Barnie died in December 1983.

Born in 1924, **Peter Heatly** was educated at Leith Academy and Edinburgh University, where he took a BSc in Engineering and began a long and successful career as a civil engineer. He was able to combine a distinguished record as a swimmer and diving champion in an amateur capacity with his professional practice as an engineer. He has taken an active interest in swimming pool design, for example, and, as Chairman of the Scottish Sports Council, has had a decisive influence on the development of sport in Scotland. As a member of Portobello Amateur Swimming Club he was Scottish and ASA Diving Champion and an Internationalist from 1937 to 1958 and Scottish Freestyle Champion and record-holder over several distances from 1942 to 1947. Heatly was a member of Scotland's Commonwealth Games Team, winning a gold medal for diving in 1950, 1954 and 1958. In the Olympic Games held in London in 1948 he came fifth in the high diving competition. After the end of his career as an international competitor, he held a number of key administrative posts for the Commonwealth Games and was a member of Edinburgh Town Council. His contribution to sport was recognised in 1971 when he was appointed CBE in the New Year's Honours List.

J

Although born in Ceylon, **David Wilkie** was sent to Edinburgh at the age of eleven to be educated as a boarder at Daniel Stewart's College. Wilkie, whose birth sign was Pisces (the sign of the Fish), spent his Sunday afternoons at Warren-

David Wilkie

der Baths. 'Life', he recalls 'was sheer hell' at that time after the tropical paradise of Ceylon. He tried to avoid swimming training as much as possible but was eventually found out and persuaded to carry on. His first big final as a swimmer was the 200 metres at the 1970 Commonwealth Games in Edinburgh. He took a bronze medal there and two years later in the Olympic Games at Munich took the silver, also in the 200 metres breaststroke. This achievement led to his being made a Life Member of the Warrender Swimming Club where he was affectionately known as 'Jungle Boy', because of his tan and his early life in Ceylon.

In 1973 he picked up a gold in the 200 metres breaststroke and a bronze in the 200 metres medley·at Belgrade. Wilkie remembers the former event vividly: 'I was delirious, shocked out of my mind to think I had broken the world record'. He had, of course, also broken the European, the Commonwealth, the British and the Scottish records. By this time Wilkie had gone to the University of Miami in Florida on a scholarship to study marine biology. The following year saw him take two golds at the European Championships in Vienna as well as a silver. In the same year he achieved another two golds and a silver in the Commonwealth Games at Christchurch. Two years later came his surprise achievement when he broke the 200 metres breaststroke record in the Montreal Olympics.

In all, Wilkie, who was awarded the MBE for his services to swimming (in 1974), had 15 major swimming medals: 8 gold, 4 silver, 3 bronze. He held 30 major records (3 World, 9 European and 18 Commonwealth) and was never beaten over 200 metres in the breaststroke from September 1973 to 1976, when he retired.

With the holding of the Commonwealth Games in Edinburgh in 1970, Edinburgh acquired the splendid, purpose-built Royal Commonwealth Pool, which has lifted swimming facilities into a new, international dimension.

Street Life

Sellers of Food and Drink

Of all Edinburgh's many legendary characters, it was the street vendors who were the most numerous and colourful. At a time before the development of modern large-scale distribution techniques it was the hardy street vendor striding from house to house or standing in the markets who provided the hundred and one necessities and luxuries of living. The more mundane household goods or repair services were supplied by wandering tradesmen. A great number of them took up their stances in the markets or outside important buildings shouting their wares. These included the caddies (carriers of water, parcels, news or town guides), ballad-criers, travelling cobblers, sellers of fruit and vegetables (the kailwives) and fishwives, all of them competing with their own distinctive cries, loudest at night. The traditional cries continued up to about 1870, but from that time they began to disappear, and, like songbirds, were heard no more.

From time immemorial the High Street of Edinburgh was full of noise and confusion as the street traders shouted their wares. The Luckenbooth shops and the Krames' open stalls both crammed against the north wall of the Kirk of St Giles and filled up with people forcing their way through the mud and filth of the 'Stinking Stile', as that narrow arcade was called. There was always the danger of having a housewife's slops dropped on your head from the houses above.

Right up the 1870s the old street cries gave colour and romance to the town. When the clock at the Tron Kirk struck eight at night the chorus of cries reached its climax, for this was the official signal for selling to begin. The laughing crowd threaded their way through the lines of barrows lit with paper lanterns, past the penny shows, the ballad singers and the speech criers. This joyful confusion is seldom to be seen today (outside New Year on the Edinburgh Festival).

254

The trade which had the best remembered cries was that of the fishwife. Everyone in Edinburgh last century knew the cries of 'Cockles and Wulks', 'Wulks an' Buckies' or 'Cockles an' Mussels'. Early each Spring, when the biting wind still blew off the sea, women from Musselburgh, Newhaven and even Dunbar trudged up the steep roads to the City and took up their stances in the Old Town. In spite of the building of a spacious and prosperous New Town the main stances of the vendors continued to be in the High Street. So the fishwives set

 Newhaven fishwife

up their stalls at the street corners, often on upturned wooden boxes, displaying the shellfish in little saucers along with salt, pepper and spoons. Children loved mussels better than sweets and were always seen besieging the women at the roadside. The most haunting of the shellfish cries was that of 'Caller Oysters'. From September to April the oyster sellers came, often to the New Town, for it was mainly there that the popular oyster cellars were to be found. For much of the eighteenth century oyster parties were all the rage as, the cellars being hidden from public view, an atmosphere of frivolity and abandon was generated which most red-blooded citizens preferred to the staid decorum of the assemblies with their slow-moving gavottes. In the cellars the merrymakers would often invite the oyster girls to join in the fun, and the heavy petticoats of the fishwives would be kicked in the air amid the whoops and yelps of reels and strathspeys. But the oyster-beds in time disappeared from the Forth, and the stances of the oyster-girls beside the theatres of the City were left empty. The cry of 'Caller Ou' was heard no more.

The popular fishwives who for so long provided the City with crabs and herrings were a hardy breed. Maggie Dickson, for example, was hanged in 1724 for concealing the birth of a still-born illegitimate child. The hangman allowed her to hang for the required time and even jerked her legs, as was the custom, to make sure no life was left. She was nailed into a coffin, and on her way to her burial at Inveresk her friends stopped at an inn to refresh themselves. On leaving the inn some time later, one of the company thought he heard a strange noise coming from the coffin. The lid was hurriedly prised open, a vein was bled and some spirits were poured down Maggie's throat. That evening she had recovered sufficiently to speak and was soon receiving financial contributions from all and sundry who came to marvel at her recovery. As she had been officially pronounced dead, she was allowed to go free and, known theeafter as 'half-hangit Maggie', lived to a ripe old age as an innkeeper, dying finally in the arms of one of her many lovers.

The fishwives had the reputation of having the manners and the strength of men. Three of them are recorded in the Old Statistical Account as travelling the twenty-seven miles from Dunbar to Edinburgh barefoot with loaded creels in the space of five hours. They played golf before it was fashionable for women to do so, and, on Shrove Tuesday, the married fisherwoman played the spinsters at football, a game which the married ladies usually won. Three days after the birth of a baby many of them would go out again with the creel. Some of them came from Musselburgh and some from Newhaven. The visitor to the Newhaven Inn often passed by the closes between the fisherfolk's houses. The reek of tan would be in the air; floats, fishing-lines and oilskins hung on the stairs among the innumerable dark blue stockings of the women who sat baiting their lines and gossiping. The working dress of the fishwives was a thick blue petticoat, a blouse and a serge gown over it, and a blue apron with a white stripe. In bad weather a small head shawl was worn with a blue and white checked pattern. The creel itself was in two parts: in the lower larger half the fresh fish was carried; in the top half – the 'skull' – knitting and other odds and ends were stored, or it could be used as a hand basket. Often the fisherwives carried as much as 250 pounds on their backs in their wickerwork creels. On special occasions the Newhaven fisherwomen wore yellow and white, or red and white costumes and Paisley shawls. These costumes are said to have been the dress of the Flemish women whose husbands came to Newhaven in 1507 to build the warship *The Great Michael* for King James IV.

Some aspects of the fish trade, however, were far from romantic or colourful. Lord Cockburn tells us that 'our only fish market was in Fish Market Close, a steep, narrow stinking ravine. The fish were generally thrown out on the street at the head of the close, whence they were dragged down by dirty boys or dirtier women; and then sold unwashed, for there was not a drop of water in the place, from old rickety, scaly, wooden tables, exposed to all the rain, dust and filth; an abomination the recollection of which greatly impaired the pleasantness of the fish at a later hour of the day'. In the early 1800s, Henry Cockburn continues, 'our vegetables had to pass through as bad a process. They were entirely in the hands of a college of old gin-drinking women, who congregated with stools and tables round the Tron Church. A few of the aristocracy of these ladies, the burgomistresses, who had established a superior business, the heads of old booths, marked their dignity by an awning of dirty canvas or tattered carpet; and every table had its tallow candle and paper lantern at night. There was no water here either, except what flowed down the gutter, which, however, was plentifully used. Fruit had a place on the table, but kitchen vegetables lay bruised on the ground'.

Most of the street vendors were specialists in one type of merchandise. The radish seller stood in the street singing 'four bunch a penny, the bonnie caller radishes'; further down was the old turnip woman calling to passers-by: 'Neeps like succar. Wha'll buy neeps?' Around the end of March the first of the spring vegetables made their appearance in the streets. There was much 'Rhubarb, fresh rhubarb, tuppence ha'penny a bunch', and 'Wha'll buy my bonnie water-cresses?' All the year round the hawkers of peas and beans supplied the tables of the good Edinburgh folk with their old cry: 'Wha'll buy peas an' beans, hot an' warm, hot an' warm?' On Saturday nights a farm cart came loaded with hot potatoes smothered in butter and oatmeal. These were known as 'mealy tatties' and were often used to make up the popular dish of 'tatties an' herrin'. At

Hogmanay there were scores of hawkers' barrows along each side of the High Street, some of which bore new-laid eggs and rolls of fresh butter wrapped in a cabbage leaf, besides live hens and ducks, all of which added to the music of the streets. The first fruit seller of the year was always the cherry seller crying 'Wha'll buy ma bonnie cherries, twenty for a bawbee?' or 'Sonsy cherries'. The cherries were carried in a large basket, and the vendor spent the time between sales tying the cherries into bunches of twenty with black thread. The second vendor to appear would be the gooseberry seller chanting 'Ripe berries, the big pint, a ha'penny', and then came the strawberry vendors, often two of them carrying a basket between them, calling 'Ripe strawberries'. In the autumn the town was full of the calls of the apple sellers, one of the most famous of whom was Sarah Sibbald, known as Apple Glory. She sat in Shakespeare Square outside the old Theatre Royal (where the Head Post Office now is). She had met many of the greatest names on the British stage and she talked about them with fierce pride.

The woman vendor best remembered in history was Jenny Geddes, a High Street cabbage seller, whom we have met already. When Charles I tried to introduce English ways of worship into the churches of Scotland in 1623, he appointed a Bishop of Edinburgh and renamed the High Kirk of St Giles 'St Giles Cathedral'. The new order of service and the new prayer book were to be introduced on a Sunday in July, but the majority of the people of Scotland strongly objected to the anglicisation of their liturgy. When the prayer book was to be read for the first time in St Giles, many citizens crowded into the Kirk. The Town Council was there; the magistrates, law lords and two bishops took their places in the large congregation. When the singing of the choir stopped, the Dean, James Hanna, went up the pulpit steps and, after a pause, opened the new prayer book. A hush fell on the congregation as they listened to the first words. Then a voice bellowed: 'Are ye sayin' mass in ma lug?' Next moment a stool sailed through the air, narrowly missing the Dean's head. Pandemonium broke out, and the Bishop was only just able to escape the furious mob. Jenny Geddes is credited by history with having thrown the first stool.

For residents of the City who wanted food cooked in a hurry, the pudding and pie sellers did a roaring trade. They carried their wares in a charcoal grill over their shoulders and in later years displayed them in a stand at the roadside. Black puddings were as popular as white, and most people enjoyed the plain meal pudding. Soup was also available in the streets. In the eighteenth century a man carrying a leg of mutton walked the streets crying 'Twa dips an' a wallop for a bawbee'. This was the signal for the housewives to come to their door with pails of boiling water into which the leg of mutton was dipped, producing the basis of a good broth. Most people, however, could not afford to buy cuts of meat, usually relying on offal such as tripe, pigs' trotters or sheep's heads to fortify their diet. Vendors often carried sheep's heads in baskets through the streets.

Long before the appearance of that modern delicacy, yoghurt, in Scotland, the people of Edinburgh were great consumers of buttermilk, or 'soor-dook' as it was known. Every morning the milkmaids would ride into the City's High Street carrying soor-dook barrels strapped to the saddles of their horses. A favourite summer dish was curds, and during June

'Soor-dook'

and July the vendors sat spooning white chunks of it into their customers' dishes to the cry of 'Curds an' Whey, Curds an' Whey'.

Down the coast at Prestonpans the salt-panners waded into the sea up to their necks to collect the rich brine which was then evaporated in large metal pans heated over coal fires. The resulting fine-quality salt was brought to the City in creels on

the backs of women such as Saut Maggie, who measured out
the salt with a wooden cup which held a quarter of a peck.

Sometimes the muffin man passed by, followed by an army
of children eager for the succulent muffins he carried high
above his head wrapped in a clean white towel. He was also
dressed in white, and householders came from all over to
relieve him of his goods. Sweets, ice-cream, gingerbread and
coconut were bought from street vendors such as Coconut
Tam, a bent little man dressed in black and wearing a bowler
hat. His cry was: 'Cocky nit, cocky nit; a ha'penny the bit, bit,

Coconut Tam

bit. Taste an' try afore ye buy, for that's the way tae make ye
buy'. Thomas Simpson, with his thin-voiced cry, died in 1874 at
the age of 71, and nowadays has a public house named after
him.

Probably the most famous of all characters associated with
street commerce is Greyfriars Bobby; the faithful terrier who
refused to leave the graveside of his master, a Midlothian
farmer, John Gray, who died in 1858 while attending a

Greyfriars Bobby

Wednesday market. Bobby stayed at his master's grave in Greyfriars Cemetery for fourteen years until he died, and his statue in nearby George IV Bridge is now a regular port of call for guided tours and for amateur photographers.

Sellers of Hardware and Services

A vital piece of household equipment was the spit or roasting-jack. A grisly tale attaches to this everyday kitchen utensil. The second Duke of Queensberry (one of the main architects of the 1707 Act of Union) had a mentally-handicapped son who was enormously strong and very tall, but who was hidden away in a room with boarded-up windows in Queensberry House in the Canongate. On the day of the signing of the Union, the 'monster's' keeper went outside for a moment to watch the crowds in the street. Time passed, and when the Duke eventually returned home he found to his horror that his son was sitting in the kitchen roasting the kitchen-boy on a spit.

One of the best-known sellers of roasting-jacks was Laughlan McBain, a hardy veteran of Culloden. McBain manufactured his own jacks and toasting-forks and advertised his wares with such a piercing voice as he paraded from the Cowgate to Parliament Square that the judges and lawyers in the Courts could only persuade him to be quiet by collecting a sum of money large enough to buy his silence.

A further indispensable kitchen aid in the eighteenth century was the heather range which was used to scour pots. Along with ling brushes or besoms, they were sold by vendors who came to town with large baskets on their backs, carrying wooden brush-handles strapped together.

Another popular vendor was the travelling crockery seller. He came round with his cart from door to door. Putting one bowl in each hand, he ground the rim of one against the other, producing a high-pitched squeaking sound, and crying 'Cheeny ahoy'.

Tobacco first came to Edinburgh around 1560, and it spread like wildfire; so much so that the testy intellectual King James VI decided to depose the last vicar of Gullane for the abominable habit, and wrote a virulent *Counterblast to Tobacco*, linking the practice of smoking that drug with all kinds of unspeakable vices. Within a few years, however, tobacco was being indulged in all over Scotland, and gentlemen in coffee houses up and down the Royal Mile smoked their long church-wardens, read the latest gazette from London and discussed the prices on the Exchange. Soon snuff caught on, pinched on the back of the thumb, scented with oil of orange-blossom or burgundy wine. The records of the City Chambers note a number of tobacco-mills and tobacco shops. There were five mills at Colinton, and one at Canonmills, but James Gillespie at 231 High Street was probably Edinburgh's most famous snuff manufacturer, subsequently famous as the founder of James Gillespie's School. His grinder still remains in the possession of the City and also his sign – a negro boy holding a clay pipe, dressed in green trunks, leaning on a barrel marked 'Tobacco'. In the City's tobacco shops the precious commodity was stored in white jars imported from Holland. Juniper wood was kept burning in a dish, and the customer took a glowing ember with a pair of silver tongs to light his clay pipe. Tobacco parties were held for men only, and short Dutch pipes were provided, leaf tobacco in wicker baskets, and pans of peat embers, with an accompaniment of cheese, cold meat, bread and butter. Many inns and coffee houses stocked free clays. The long pipes were placed in open iron cradles after use, suspended by a ring over a charcoal fire and roasted clean. Later they would be ground up for mothballs. Christie's of Leith, which closed in 1962, was the last Edinburgh clay-pipe manufacturer. At one stage a hundred thousand pipes were made there every week.

Housewives, wanting to smarten up their front steps with white pipeclay decoration in the eighteenth and nineteenth centuries, eagerly awaited the pipeclay seller's cry of 'Caystane'. One dealer came around with his wife, his pony and his cart; the pony was as white as the clay he sold.

Blackening, too, was an essential commodity. 'Blacknin' Tam' was a well-known figure in nineteenth-century Edinburgh who carried his wares from house to house in a pitcher from which he would pull out a portion and roll it between his hands into a ball. For heating houses, many Scots used peat, which through-out the year was sold in the City streets. Commonest of all the cries was 'Coals, tenpence the ba', coal'. Chambers, describing

Edinburgh in the time of George III, tells of 'corduroyed men from Gilmerton, bawling coals or yellow sand'. The sand was used for sprinkling on stone kitchen floors, stairs, and the floors of shops and inns. The sandman's cry of 'Ye-sa' was once part and parcel of City life and helped to lull many a child to sleep. Mattresses, before the advent of the 'Continental quilt', were filled with chaff. Especially around Whitsunday the cry of 'Cauf for beds' was to be heard rivalling the cries of the vendors of songbird seed as they trudged through the streets. The sellers of brand-new articles were augmented by the regular visits of those who made a living from repair and restoration: tinkers, for example, crying 'Pots or pans to mend?' or 'Hae ye ony broken pots or pans or ony broken chambers?' and the bellows-repairers shouting 'Old bellows to mend?'

The menders of shoes, china, crystal and stoneware travelled with their families, different members calling different cries in succession, starting on a high note and then gliding down through almost an octave. Pushing his grinding-machine came the knife-grinder calling 'Knives and scissors to grind?' or 'Razors, knives and shears to grind?'

Of all the places of commerce in the City it was the Krames, clustered around St Giles Kirk, that fired the imagination and lived longest in the memory. Lord Cockburn writes that 'In my boyhood their little stands, each enclosed in a tiny room of its

Knife-grinder

own, and during the day all open to the little footpath that ran between the two rows of them, and all glittering with attractions, contained everything fascinating to childhood, but chiefly toys. It was like one of the Arabian Nights' bazaars in Bagdad. Throughout the whole year it was an enchantment. Let any one fancy what it was about the New Year, when every child had got its handsel, and every farthing of every handout was spent there. The Krames was the paradise of childhood'. Beyond the Krames, however, there were also wandering sellers of toys who called 'Here's yer toys for girls an' boys, an bawbee whups for fardins'; and the collector of rags and bones with his barrow, toy balloons and paper flags crying 'Ole cloe'.

Fire was vital for heating and cooking, so the seller of spunks for ignition was sure of a crowd. A spunk was a stick six inches long, smeared with brimstone at both ends, which had to be brought into contact with flint, steel and tinder. In later years the spunk-seller was replaced by the lucifer match-seller with his 'Here's your fine lucifer-matches, only a bawbee the box'. In the nineteenth century a number of match-sellers are recorded such as Sandy Malcolm who had been blinded in an explosion in Noble's works at Falkirk in 1879. He sold matches at the Waverley Market railings. The possibility of fire was, of course, always a recurrent nightmare, especially in the Old Town with

Tronman

its overcrowding: in the old timber houses, crammed together, the smallest spark could and did lead to enormous devastation and loss of life. To prevent this dreadfull catastrophe a band of firefighters known as the Tronmen had been formed. With their flat bonnets, knee-breeches, ladders and coils of rope they provided an essential chimney-sweeping service. The Tronmen, under their Captain of the Chimneys, were often helped by the City's Street Overseers and their Muckmen (street-cleaners) who would convey loads of horse manure in creels (baskets) on their backs to the scene of a fire. Unloaded on the flames, the manure gave off fumes which acted as a chemical extinguisher. After 1824, when a number of great fires had destroyed much of the High Street, Edinburgh set up its first fire brigade, the Edinburgh Fire Establishment, the first municipal fire brigade in Britain, the moving spirit behind which was James Braidwood.

Communication in the City was of the utmost importance. In the seventeenth century newspapers were cried in the streets by boys who also hawked flowers and were employed as link-boys to light pedestrians going from one part of the City to another by night. In 1699 these lads had been required to enrol themselves into a society, which later became known as the Society of Running Stationers or Cadies, with a constitution drawn up by the magistrates. For a uniform the members of the Society had to wear an apron of blue linen which also doubled as a bag. The cadies had the sole privilege of 'dispersing and crying ballads and other periodical perform-ances, prohibiting chair-bearers or others to exercise that office'. Of all the Flying Stationers (who sold broadsheets printed on long strips of brown paper), the best-known was Hawkie, the street speech-crier. The cadies were the indispens-able lubricant of the City's commercial and social activities. They waited in the High Street to show visitors round the town, and to carry messages or parcels. They made it their business to know everything that was happening in the Capital and were on duty day and night, all the year round. Some of their number were known as 'water cadies', but were associated with the Society by occupation rather than formal incorpora-tion. The water cadies were often women carrying small wooden barrels on their backs from which they sold fresh drinking water drawn from the City wells. Cockburn tells us that 'They were a very curious tribe, consisting of both men and women, but the former were perhaps the more numerous. Their business was to carry water into houses; and therefore their days were passed in climbing up lofty stairs, in order to get into flats. The water was borne in little casks, and was got from the public wells, which were then pretty thickly planted in the principal streets; and as there were far more candidates than spouts, there was a group of impatient and wrangling claimants, who, when not eloquent, sat on their kegs. These encampments of drawers of water had a striking appearance. The barrels, when filled, were slung upon their backs, suspended by a leather strap, which was held in front by the hand. Their carriage was made easier by leaning forward, which threw the back outward; and hence stooping was the natural attitude of these sons and daughters of the well. They were known by this peculiarity even when off work. Their backs, which would otherwise never have been dry, were protected by thick layers of hard black leather, on which the barrels lay; and the leather had a slight curl up at its lower edge, which, acting as a lip, threw the droppings, by which they could always be tracked, off to the sides . . . They were all rather old and seemed little . . . The men very generally had old red jackets, probably the remnants of the Highland Watch or of the City Guard; and the women were always covered with thick duffle greatcoats, and wore black hats like the men'. Between 1667 and 1850 special open-fronted sedan chairs were introduced to cope with Edinburgh's uniquely narrow closes. The cadies who carried them waited at street corners, smoking, chewing or snuffing.

Around 1557 an order had been issued that no one should go out into the City after dark without a lantern or a torch or a candle. The link-boys who provided this service were superseded in 1818 by gas lighting when a number of shops and streets were lit by gas jets. The 'leeries' who went from street to street lighting the gas lamps have been immortalised in Stevenson's poem 'The Lamplighter':

> My tea is nearly ready
> and the sun has left the sky;
> It's time to take the window
> to see Leerie going by;
> For every night at tea-time
> and before you take your seat,
> With lantern and with ladder
> he comes posting up the street.

One of the best-known leeries was Leerie Smith who was still remembered in 1938. Every day in times past there was the parade of the lamplighters in Hunter Square, queuing up to receive their quota of oil and wicks to fill their 'crusies' and the 'flambeau' (a thin metal tube stuffed with tow and saturated with oil at the top). Then they would divide up and disperse to their allotted rounds through the streets of the City, with their cheerful and reassuring light.

Street Musicians

Although fiddlers and singers had been expelled from the streets of Edinburgh in 1587 by order of the Town Council, Edinburgh, like most ancient cities, has a long tradition of street entertainment carried on by anonymous or forgotten figures whose dexterity and vocal exertions charmed, pacified or infuriated the passing crowds.

Out of the mists of anonymity step artistes like Davie Arklay and Jamie Main, both blind, who sang for their suppers; poor George Cranstoun, once a teacher of music, who was so small that when he was drunk (which was often) he was pushed into a creel and sent home to his mother: until the day when the porter balanced him on the railings while he rang the door bell and looked round to see him fall to his death in the basement below; and the Nightingale, whose identity long remained shrouded in mystery. She sang in the New Town late at nights, a veil draped over her face. It was often rumoured that she had once been an opera singer, but she turned out to be Kate Powell, educated at a convent, fluent in four languages, a teacher who had begun her career after the death of her husband.

Blind Willie Sangster sat on a stool playing his accordion; George Paterson, who died in 1944, played his fiddle and gave treats to poor children; Herbert Parkin, with bristling red beard, six raincoats and a little spaniel, had trained as a violinist with the Brighton Theatre Orchestra in between puffing his cigars. Jimmy Brown, blind, played the melodeon, and Willie Maxwell performed on the accordion, singing Burns songs.

The last of Edinburgh's hurdy-gurdies vanished in 1966 when Mrs Mary Dunlop died. Previously Angela Varecchi had taken her barrel organ out and about with her monkey, two bull-terriers, a cage with two turtle doves, and her favourite nephew.

Mary Dunlop

At the turn of the twentieth century the German Band with its three or four instrumentalists was all the rage. More recently, John Codona (who died in 1964 aged 71, to be followed by his son) wore his Balmoral hat and played his tenor drum and pan pipes. He was a famous one-man band, a Cameron Highlander who had been gassed in France. It was the most extraordinary experience to see him explode into feverish musical life despite the pain his exertions gave him. In 1979 Donald Dawson, who billed himself as 'The Big Noise', died. He followed the Codonas, but differed from them in having his face made up like a clown's, and wearing colourful socks and trews. At one point he had built up a nine-piece orchestra with a big drum, kettle drum, mouth organ and knee-operated cymbals, playing any five at a time. Less skilful perhaps were pathetic figures such as Mrs Mary Russel, 'Granny Gramophone', who sat outside the Playhouse cinema for ten years until her death in 1954 at the age of eighty. The placard beside her machine read: 'Suffering from severe nervous breakdown'.

Showmen

Like all medieval cities, Edinburgh was a place of seasonal frivolity. With its steep crags, its narrow, twisting walkways, it was a natural theatre, even in later centuries in the broad panoramas of the New Town. In medieval times, on the first morning in May, the townsfolk marched to the Burgh Muir to bring summer home: the procession tumbled along the High Street, a riot of drums, flags, cannons, guisers and dancers, and they returned in the same way, carrying birch branches high above their heads.

During December the Abbot of Unreason presided at Holyroodhouse, and on New Years's Day the King of the Bean ruled. In 1579 the ever-popular plays of Robin Hood were suppressed by order of the Provost and Baillies, and eight years later the Town Council expelled all minstrels, pipers, fiddlers and singers of profane songs from the City. Such rigour did not, fortunately, last; it was not too long before the streets of the City and its environs became once again places of public entertainment.

Annual Fairs were held regularly throughout the year, in July, for example, and at Hallowe'en. In the Grassmarket a weekly grain and livestock market was a great attraction over

A 'Penny Gaff' in the Grassmarket

many decades. The Hallow Fair was held in the Grassmarket from the Bowfoot to the end of the West Port. Here the booths and barrows of the huxters were placed; the smell from scores of paraffin oil jets did not deter the members of the general public from gorging themselves on gingerbread, sliced coconut and black puddings. Ear-splitting music filled the air from the travelling booths with their human monstrosities, the menageries with their lion-tamers, the Fat Lady, the Living Skeleton and the Punch and Judy man.

One of the best-known showmen was Ned Holt. Originally apprenticed to a baker, Holt became an actor playing in the penny gaffs (laughs); he acted Hamlet in Connor's geggie (travelling theatre) off the High Street, rolling home drunk to his home in the White Horse Inn. In his booth in the Grassmarket he displayed the Fat Lady, the Living Skeleton and the Petrified Mummy. This last was supposed to be a thousand years old: it was encased in a roughly-made wooden box in the shape of a coffin with a glass top, and people paid a penny to view this 'Relic of the Pharaohs'. After many years Holt confessed that the relic was a fake: he had bought the skeleton for a few shillings and covered it with pliable india-rubber and bark from the West Port tannery. Holt was also endowed with a gift for drawing character portraits: his sketches, cruder than the sophisticated etchings of John Kay, are nevertheless masterpieces of their kind and valuable social documents.

Halfway down the High Street at the Tron Kirk the New Year festivities were always the occasion for public entertainment: Ginger Jock, for instance, with his lung-testing machine, or Carrots with his seat-type weighing machine. A regular feature at the foot of the Mound was Patrick Feeney, otherwise known as 'Old Malabar'. He had been born in Sligo, Ireland, in 1800: his particular feat was to toss a solid rubber ball high into the air and catch it in a leather cup strapped to his wrinkled forehead. He wore a red and yellow striped coat, and after many years of entertaining, died in 1883. He was followed by Joe Miller, who, as well as doing the cup and ball stunt, juggled with swords. Later still there appeared an escapologist who tied himself up in ropes in King's Stable Road; a juggler of plates in Infirmary Street; a lace-seller who swung twenty-pound weights on each lace; and an Indian herbalist and fire-swallower in Nicolson Square.

One of the most violent entertainments in the City was the cockfight. Although banned from the streets in 1702, cock-fighting took place regularly in the cockpit at the Grassmarket from 1780; this was also the scene of meetings of the outlawed Jacobites and sympathisers with the French Revolution.

Less bloodthirsty excitement was to be had at Leith Races. On race days a public holiday would be declared with a procession from the Council Chambers to Leith carrying the City Purse decorated with ribbons, led by a file of the City Guard, bayonets fixed, a drummer beating them down Leith Walk. Once at Leith, people crowded among the tents and booths covered with canvas: recruiting-sergeants with drummers, sailors ashore, servant girls and apprentices. In and out of the drinking-places they went, and to the shows: the roley-poley, hobby-horses and wheels of fortune. Afterwards came the scrum as the crowds returned to the City up Leith Walk. Then in 1816 the races were transferred to Musselburgh.

The Poor

The resident and visitor alike may often be tempted to marvel at the bizarre and eccentric figures who stalk the streets of a major city such as Edinburgh: they have their curiosity value and their stubborn individuality, but their independence is sometimes bought at the price of health and security.

The care of the homeless poor was always one of the principal virtues of a Christian society which monasteries, religious orders and monarchs undertook as well as industrial or commercial groups such as the craft guilds or the merchants. Trinity College Hospital was founded by Mary of Gueldres, wife of James II, in 1461 at the corner of Leith Wynd. At the time of the Statistical Account of 1845 it still provided care and shelter for fifty old people and pensions for around one hundred others. William Dunbar, the poet, was scathing about the number of beggars in fifteenth-century Edinburgh, calling the burgh a nest of beggars – the crooked, the blind, the lame – shouting ceaselessly, and molesting honest folk with their heartrending cries, their roaring and their whimpering.

In the following century the Town Council made repeated attempts to cope with the influx of wandering and resident poor. By 1557 only beggars born in the burgh would be allowed in, and the only ones permitted to beg were those 'old, crooked, lame or debilitated by great sickness' and incapable of work. Two years later came a Statute to deal with the 'great multitude and daily confluence of masterful, strong beggars to this burgh'. Those who were tolerated were distinguished from undesirables such as vagabonds, fiddlers, pipers, minstrels and others without masters, 'not having houses within this town nor some honest shift to uphold themselves with', who were ordered to leave 'under pain of branding on the cheek'.

From the time of the establishment of the Reformed Kirk in Scotland and its First Book of Discipline, the responsibility for poor relief lay squarely on the shoulders of the local Kirk Sessions, and this duty remained until 1740 when the Charity Workhouse sytem came into force. Parishes were, understandably, anxious to avoid having to support wandering beggars. To qualify for poor relief men and women had to be born in the parish or have lived there for three years; they had to be genuinely unable to work because of old age, illness or disability. Provided these conditions were met, the person in question would either have his or her name put on the Parish Poor Roll and receive financial support from the Poor Box, or be licensed to beg.

This last method of dealing with the poor dated from the reign of James VI: lead badges would be issued with the name and number of the beggar and the name of the parish he was licensed to beg in. Such beggars would be given blue gowns and often carried pouches for oatmeal which resulted in the nickname of 'gaberlunzie' (literally 'a wallet that hangs on the loins').

In 1743 the Edinburgh Charity Workhouse opened, built with money raised by public subscription. Standing near the Bristo Port, it accommodated about 700 persons. By 1845 it provided for 420 adults, more than a hundred lunatics and around 260 children in a nearby Children's Hospital. The Charity Workhouse was demolished in 1871. The Canongate Charity Workhouse followed in 1765: by 1844 it held one hundred inmates, half of them children. Another workhouse, the St Cuthbert's, had opened in 1761.

Private determination to deal with widespread public begging came in 1813 with the foundation of the Society for the Suppression of Beggars. The eighteenth-century Stevenson's Hotel in the Grassmarket was taken over by the Lodging House

Association from 1840, and in the same year Dr William Alison published his book, *Observations on the Management of the Poor in Scotland and its Effects on the Health of the Great Towns.* Alison's contention was that very little had been done to help the unemployed poor, the aged or the disabled poor and the widows and orphans of the poor. He disagreed with Dr Thomas Chalmers' view that the relief of poverty was best carried out by voluntary societies. For Dr Alison, it was the State which should be obliged to care for the poor with one central authority.

The Statistical Account of 1845 underlines the way in which a large city like Edinburgh fed on poverty: 'In Edinburgh there is always a great number of poor in a very wretched condition, chiefly owing to the want of employment for women and young persons – there being no manufactures, and hand spinning of linen yarn, which was once a regular occupation, being now completely superseded by mill machinery. There are also many Irish always resident in it, who subsist in a mean and filthy state, with large families, chief hawkers of fish, fruit, etc or rearers of pigs. A great deal of private charity is given in Edinburgh, which, it is said, has the effect of drawing the poor to it from a very wide circle of the country, with the view, also, of making out a three years' residence'.

After a Commission of Inquiry into the Poor Laws in Scotland had reported in 1844, a Poor Law Amendment Act for Scotland was passed in 1845 which provided for the setting up of a Central Board of Supervision in Edinburgh for the administration of the Poor Law, for Parish Boards to be set up and Inspectors of the Poor appointed. It was recommended that Poorhouses should be built in all big cities and that money for poor relief should be raised by assessment. In 1849 the Lodging House Association opened the former Stevenson's Hotel as a hostel. It became known as the Victoria Hostel for homeless women, many the victims of violence and broken marriages, who had slept rough in railway stations and disused offices. in 1889 the Castle Trades Hotel opened for men down on their luck and for alcoholics. There were 400 cubicles of wood, with wire mesh on the ceiling, an iron gate at the staircase, and blackened floorboards. In 1891 the following report appeared in the *Scotsman:* 'A tattered and battered fellow whom we got into conversation with some time ago, belonged to this class of tramps. He was one of those cool, brazen-faced individuals who could stare a sheriff-officer out of countenance; one of those calm, self-satisfied persons who are never disconcerted and never in a hurry. "I have been a fortnight in Edinburgh", he said. "Have been in it often before. It is a capital place for resting my feet, and I generally stay in it a fortnight at a time, for there are any amount of "skippers" (places for passing the night in) all round about. I get as good a living as if I was working. By a little mouching I can get as much grub as I need, and I can rest myself whenever I like. But a man would be better off if he could fiddle or whistle or do anything of that kind. I made the price of my "doss" (bed) with a tin whistle yesterday on the High Street and Bank Street; made sixpence in ten minutes, and that got doss, tea and sugar. I do work occasionally to give myself a fresh start. I have been in two or three regiments and deserted. In the winter, when I was hard up, I gave myself up, but soon deserted again, and set off on the road in a fresh rig. I was a militiaman for four years, and that kept me from settling down, having to leave my work every year to go up for training. I have been on tour for two years; during winter get into skippers; in summertime travel through the night and sleep anywhere during the day, under a hedge or on the roadside, only occasionally getting a bed by singing "The Highlandman's Toast" and "Flora Macdonald's Lament". I have got many a copper by singing them during the past six years. I learned them from a song-book. I am quite happy and contented with my lot. I could do like other folk, but don't care to work." When a tramp shuffles into Edinburgh, from whatever point of the compass he comes, he usually makes his way at night to the Night Asylum in Old Fishmarket Close, adjoining the Police Office. There he takes his place among a waiting crew of poor wretches, who, like himself, are without place to lay their head.'

Almost one hundred years later, similarities remain. It is estimated that around a hundred people sleep in cemeteries, factory yards or in Holyrood Park. Some one thousand spend the night in single homeless accommodation of one kind or another, in the renovated former Castle Trades Hotel, in the premises of the Salvation Army or in the People's Palace (the Church of Scotland's night-shelter in the Cowgate where forty homeless persons crowd each night and sleep on benches or on the floor). This is the grim reality behind the daytime facade of the often entertaining street characters of Edinburgh.

A more cheerful subject is games children played. Robert Louis Stevenson remembers proudly that 'I was the best player of hide-and-seek going; not a good runner, I was up to every shift and dodge, I could jink very well, I could crawl without any noise through leaves, I could hide under a carrot plant: it used to be my favourite boast that I always walked into the den'. Scott, in *Guy Mannering*, writes, 'I must come to play Blind Harry and Hy-Spy'. James Clerk Maxwell, the scientist, did not enjoy the ordinary school games at the Edinburgh Academy. He did revel in bools and peeries. Bools were marbles: they would be made of clay, glass or steel. Clerk Maxwell's mind was far from Virgil's *Arma virumque cano;* he wrote his own version, beginning: 'Of pearies and their origin I sing'. Peeries were tops, pear-shaped and whipped by a leather thong. A humming-top was called a French peerie. Diabolo or Diavolo (the Devil) was also a favourite of Clerk Maxwell, and he wrote in 1848 that he had played 'a game of the Devil of whom there is a duality and a quaternity of sticks (a pun on the River Styx) so that I can play either conjunctly or severally. I can jump over him and bring him round without leaving go the sticks. I can also keep him up behind me'. Like most Edinburgh children, he enjoyed Cats Cradles and wrote a (Cats) Cradle Song:

Clear your coil of kinkings
Into perfect plaiting
Locking loops and linkings
Interpenetrating.

It's monstrous, horrid, shocking
Beyond the power of thinking
Not to know interlocking
Is no mere form of linking.

Children's games in the City were not slow to reflect every aspect of life: the One O'Clock Gun, for example:

SKIPPING SONG
One o'clock the gun went off
I dare not stay no longer
If I do mother will say
Playing with the boys up yonder

Stockings red, garters blue,
Trimmed all round with silver:
A red red rose upon my head
And a gold ring on my finger.

Sometimes children in the street would play Mary Queen of
Scots. They chanted:

Mary Queen of Scots
Got her head chopped off
Got her head chopped off
Got her head choped off
Mary Queen of Scots
Got her head chopped off
OFF!

and then chopped the head off a dandelion flower,
watching the white gossamer float away on the wind.

Dr John Brown, in *Rab and his Friends,* records that Pet
Marjorie tested Walter Scott in 1810 with his knowledge of
the following rhymes:

Ziccotty dicotty dock
The mouse ran up the clock
The clock struck wan
Down the mouse ran
Ziccotty dicotty dock

Wunnery tooery tickery seven
Alibi crackaby ten and eleven
Pin pan musky dan
Tweedle-um twoddle-um twenty-wan
Eeerie orie ourie –
You are out!

Another popular street game for many years was Peevers
(Hopscotch). A pattern of chalked beds or boxes was marked
out on the ground over which the peever was pushed by the
hopping foot. Peevers would be made out of a round tin box, a

piece of tile, a small marble chip, slate, wood or even glass. A glass peever can still be seen in Huntly House Museum in the Canongate. Edinburgh is still a repository of children's games of the past and the present. This is mainly due to the efforts of the late Patrick Murray (1908-81). Edinburgh-born and resident all his life, apart from his schooldays at Stonyhurst in Lancashire, he was an optician before his election to the Town Council. While he was chairman of Edinburgh Corporation's Libraries and Museums Committee he started the Museum of Childhood, first in Lady Stair's House in the Lawnmarket and, after eighteen months, in a new site in the High Street at Hyndford's Close. He began the collection with a number of his own toys, 'a pitiful handful of soldiers, building blocks and railway stuff of my own'. The Museum was the first of its kind in the world, dealing not just with toys, but with the customs, hobbies, health, upbringing and education of children from birth to around the age of twelve. His idea has since been copied in many countries.

Edinburgh has always had a sweet tooth. In 1587 the Provost and Baillies celebrated the coming-of-age King James VI by putting a table laden with bread and sweets beside the Mercat Cross. Some years later when the King brought back his bride Anne of Denmark, the Council arranged for sweets to cascade over the steps of the West Bow as the Royal Couple entered the City, a piece of generosity which cost the Council three pounds, two shillings and sixpence in the money values of that time. When James VI's Danish brother-in-law, the Duke of Holstein, visited Holyrood in 1598, the Royal Confectioner, Jacques de Bousie, was paid one hundred and eighty-four pounds for supplying sweets at the banquet in the Palace.

The first manufacturing confectioner to set up in business in the City was an Italian who received permission in 1665 to 'use his trade in making of confits within this burgh, Leith, and Canongate for six months time'. In the same year Robert Mein was appointed to be 'confit maker and confectioner to the good Town', an appointment he was to hold for twenty years. In 1684 the people of Edinburgh were again given the opportunity of eating sweets at the expense of the Council when the latter ordered that a table covered in sweets was to be set up just below the Mercat Cross to celebrate Charles II's birthday.

By 1677 the demand for sweets was so great that street sellers began to adulterate them, and the Council were forced to order that trades description should be accurate and that sweets were no longer to be sold in the streets by fruit women but only in shops.

Where sweets in the seventeenth century had consisted of sugar biscuits, tablet and a kind of pan drop, the eighteenth century introduced gingerbread also, and in the nineteenth century the sweet shops of Edinburgh had black liquorice, peppermint, bull's eyes, and a variety of sweets made from gundy which was akin to glue in its toughness. Gibraltar rock was popular for many years: Jib John was a favourite with the High School boys who crowded into his shop in High School Wynd.

The nineteenth-century sweetie shops were mainly run by gossipy women who stored the sweets in tall glass bottles. The sweets were produced in the back shop: conversation lozenges, humbugs, Cupid's whispers and acid drops. The pedlar still came to town, however, such as Colter who sold a celebrated form of gundy. And into Edinburgh in the nineteenth century came the famous sweetie inventors: Sandy Ferguson from Doune who came in 1822 with his world-famous Edinburgh Rock; James Keiller from Dundee who opened his Princes Street shop in 1824; and William Duncan, also from Dundee, who first started selling sweets from a wheelbarrow in the High Street.

Taverns and Coffee Houses

Drinking-houses have long served a useful function in the history of society, and Edinburgh is no exception in this respect. Inns and taverns were indispensable, not least because travellers wishing to stay a night in the City were forbidden by law from lodging with their friends and had either to sleep in an inn or in the guesthouses of the monastery of Holyrood or in those of the Black or Grey Friars. For more than two hundred years this was the rule in Edinburgh, from 1230 to 1447. Every night the curfew bell of the Tolbooth's Bellhouse Tower signalled that the doors of all inns and taverns must be closed, and the Burgh gates were locked until five the next morning.

It was not until well after the Reformation, however, that the heyday of the drinking-house began. By 1750 there were two kinds of establishment for the good folk of the City to carry on their business, argue or gossip: the ale-house and the coffee-house. The Old Town could boast no fewer than 240 drink licences in 1740 compared to the 100-odd today. Almost everyone seems to have been eligible for a licence, from grocers and bookshops to ironmongers. The main area for taverns was Parliament Close and in the Royal Exchange (later the City Chambers).

Among the booksellers' booths and the toyshops stood **Peter Williamson's** pub *cum* coffee-house: three or four box-like

Peter Williamson

279

apartments, very fragile, some of brown paper. 'Indian Peter', as he was known, had been kidnapped as a boy in his home town of Aberdeen at the age of eight and sold as a slave in Philadelphia. He was captured by Red Indians and made a prisoner by the French. Discharged as unfit because of his injuries, he returned to Edinburgh where he eventually set up the first penny post and published the first Edinburgh street directory.

It is Peter Williamson's *Directory*, published in 1773-4, that definitively records the pecking-order of Edinburgh society, which ran as follows: Lords of Session, Advocates, Writers to the Signet, Lords' and Advocates' Clerks; Physicians, Noblemen and Gentlemen (including Clergymen and the Professions); Merchants, Grocers; Ship Masters; Surgeons; Brewers, followed by various trades. Far down the list come School and Writing Masters, Milliners and Room Setters (persons who let out rooms). Among the interesting features of this list is the difference in prestige between surgeons and physicians, the position of noblemen halfway down the scale, the supreme importance given to the legal profession, and the relative lack of status given to professional educators.

Beside the gallows in Libberton's Wynd, John Dowie dispensed ale brewed by Archibald Younger. This was the haunt of the poet Robert Fergusson, Sir Henry Raeburn the painter and the philosopher David Hume. The largest room held only fourteen people, the 'Coffin' six at a squeeze. On the menu was toasted cheese, tripe, ham, peas, eggs, herring, whiting, beefsteak, skate, Nor' Loch trout (stuffed haddock fried in breadcrumbs), Welsh rarebit and eel pie.

In Craig's Close lay Currie's Tavern. Currie specialised in pap-in (beer and whisky, curried with oatmeal). At Yuletide het-pin was on offer (port, sherry or madeira mulled with cardamom, cloves, nutmet, ginger, cinnamon, and coriander, flavoured with sugar, and frothing with whipped eggs).

Dawnay Douglas's establishment in Anchor Close had the inscription 'Be merciful to me' over the entrance to its turnpike stair. The visitor would go up a few steps, and, in the words of Robert Chambers, 'found himself in a pretty large kitchen – a dark, fiery Pandemonium, through which numerous ineffable ministers of flame were continually flying about'. There Mistress Douglas was to be seen in her towering headdress and her silk gown with daisies upon it like sunflowers and tulips as big as cabbages.

An ever-popular event was the oyster party. Guests would arrive by invitation at the laigh shops below street level. Once down in the vaults, they would find fresh oysters and flagons of beer set on tables lit by tallow candles. The ladies wore black velvet masks kept on by a glass button or jewel held by the teeth. Brandy, rum punch or some other potent concoction followed, and then the dancing began to the harp, the fiddle or bagpipes. The oyster lassies would be called in to share in the festivities and the dancing. At this point the ladies would return home, leaving their menfolk to drink themselves on to the floor.

What of that special breed of women, the 'Lucky'? The dictionary says a Lucky is 'an elderly woman; a midwife; the mistress of an ale-house; a landlady; a witch'. The definition says it all. Ramsay wrote a substantial elegy on Lucky Wood, Fergusson enjoyed the oysters and gin provided by Lucky Middlemass, and Lord Provost William Chambers gives this picture of Lucky Laing: 'The inmates and their visitors, if they felt inclined, could treat themselves to refreshments in a cosy little apartment, half tavern, half kitchen, superintended by a portly female styled 'Lucky Laing' from whose premises issued the pleasant sounds of broiling beef-steaks and the drawings of corks from bottles of ale and porter'.

In Potterrow sat Mrs Flockart in her fifteen square feet of shop, an inner room and her dwelling-house. She sold everything from tea, sugar, beer, herrings, potatoes, stationery, yellow sand and nails to whip-handles. In her striped blue gown, her white lappets tied under her chin, she watched her customers eat stew at her window-seat where only one customer could dine at a time.

Jenny Ha's in the High Street served claret from the butt and capie ale (so called from the quaich or caup used), laced with brandy for Jacobites or Episcopal clergymen.

Lucky Middlemass' patrons marked up their bill with chalk on the table. They could have rizzarded haddock, oysters, lobsters, crab or skate and beer from a 'tappit hen' (a quarter measure jug tapped straight from the barrel).

The Royal Exchange sported three coffee houses, one run by an extraordinary character called Lieutenant John Oswald. Having fought in the Royal Highlanders in North America, he served in India and lived among the Kurds and Turcomans and adopted many Brahmin customs, including vegetarianism. During the French Revolution he crossed to Paris, where he commanded an infantry regiment before finally disappearing. In the years that followed, many curious resemblances in appearance and personality led people to believe that the newly arrived French leader, Napoleon Bonaparte, was in fact old John Oswald!

It was the custom of gentlemen of every walk of life to join together in clubs of various sorts. In 1712 Allan Ramsay founded the Easy Club whose aim was the 'mutual improvement in conversation' of its members. Robert Fergusson was made a member of the Cape Club in 1772. Its membership comprised painters, printers, musicians, tradesmen, advocates and naval officers. Other clubs included the Feast of Tabernacles (for lawyers and men of letters), the Poker Club and the Select Society. Clubs gave men of the world a chance to relax in good company away from the prying eyes of the fairer sex. There were no such privileges for women.

As the Capital of the nation, Edinburgh was the thoroughfare for a constant steam of travellers on business or pleasure, from the north and from the south. Stablers' inns were located principally around the two points of departure for the south: the Water Gate which marked the exit of the Great North Road and the Cowgate Port which gave access to Greenlaw, Blackshiels, Kelso and Lauder.

At the Water Gate was the famous White Horse Inn. In 1712 a stage-coach left every Saturday for London at 6 am. It took thirteen days to make the journey at a cost of £4.50. Alternatively the traveller in a hurry could board a 'new genteel two-ended glass machine hung on steel springs, exceedingly light' which did the trip in ten days in summer and twelve in winter.

The Sheep's Head Tavern at Duddingston has been a popular hostelry since the fourteenth century and is now Edinburgh's oldest pub. King James VI used to drop in when riding between Craigmillar Castle and Holyrood Palace. He is believed to have tasted the delicacy of the house (sheep's head with trotters) on many occasions. To signify his satisfaction he presented the tavern with a ram's head which stood inside the building till the end of the eighteenth century, when it was sold and replaced by a sheep's head. In the snowy season skaters on Duddingston Loch or the Lord Provost and Magistrates of Edinburgh playing the 'roarin' game' (curling) on the Loch often dropped in after their exertions on the ice. Sir Walter Scott was a frequent visitor as well as James Hogg (the Ettrick Shepherd), Christopher North, Dugald Stewart and Robert Louis Stevenson. Other famous men who entered its portals were the artists of J. M. W. Turner and Sir David Wilkie. A further attraction of the tavern was the ancient skittle alley which still exists today.

Another of Edinburgh's oldest hostelries is the Golf Tavern beside Bruntsfield Links. It is believed that its origins lie as far back as 1399 or at least 1456. Between 1792 and 1877 the Golf Tavern was the meeting-place of the Royal Burgess Golfing Society, and even today it provides a safe haven for those who have enjoyed the intricacies of pitch and putt on the Bruntsfield Links.

In 1613 Bernard Lindsay, Groom of the Royal Chamber, was given possession of the imposing King's Wark at Leith by King James VI. The building is close to the waterfront, and Lindsay soon added a tennis court 'for the recreation of His Majesty, and of foreigners of rank resorting to the kingdom, to whom it afforded great satisfaction and delight'. One of the conditions of the King's gift was that one of the building's four cellars should be reserved for the storage of royal wine. Today the King's Wark still stands, overlooking the water and its white swans.

In Kay's wine-coloured autograph album were the signatures of many of the stars who appeared at the Lyceum and at the Usher Hall: the Terry family (Fred and Julia, Phyllis Neilson-Terry and Michael Terry-Lewis); George Bernard Shaw in 1921; Dame Clara Butt; Harry Lauder; Dame Melba and Madama Tetrazzini (who both bought sherry from Mr George Adams, the proprietor); Sir Frank Benson, Sir John Forbes-Robertson, Beerbohm Tree, Sybil Thorndyke, Sir John Barbirolli, and the Norwegian explorer Nansen. There is a story that Joseph Hislop, Edinburgh's world-famous operatic

K

tenor, went to see a throat specialist in Edinburgh before he was due to sing in the Usher Hall. The specialist advised him to buy the well-known Italian wine, Mariana. Hislop tried every wine shop and licensed grocer in town to get this special wine for gargling (it contained cocaine to soothe the vocal chords and throat). He was unable to find it till he tried Kay's who supplied it and thus enabled him to sing as finely as ever without discomfort or injury. Sadly, however, Kay's of Grindlay Street is now no more.

Flinging things out of the window was a good old Edinburgh custom. At 10 am the Town Drummer beat the signal for housewives to fling their slops out of their windows into the gutter below to the cry of 'Gardy-loo' (Gardez l'eau). As the stench drifted into the taverns, the drovers would look up from their potatoes and whisky to light pieces of paper, hoping that the smoke would kill the nauseating smell of the slops.

In the twentieth century the coffee-house tradition survived the passion for tea, although the building of the New Town and the invention of the railway killed off the old inns after 1850. One of the best-known modern coffee-house owners was the late **Moultrie Kelsall.** Trained as a lawyer, he gave up the legal profession of the advice of Tyrone Guthrie, who had been impressed by his acting ability as an amateur with the Scottish National Players, whose business manager Kelsall eventually became. In the late 1930s he was a pioneer of television as one of the first producers at Alexandra Palace in London. He exuded an air of sober and lugubrious pessimism which concealed a well-developed sense of the absurd. He excelled in character parts and appeared in a number of very successful films such as *The Lavender Hill Mob, The Master of Ballantrae, The Man Who Never Was* and *The Maggie.* He was also a long-time campaigner for the preservation of historic buildings. His Laigh coffee-house had a high reputation for good food and service.

The late **Armando Sebastian Alonzo Margiotta** was born in Edinburgh's Royal Mile. Like Eduardo Paolozzi and Richard Demarco, he was educated at Holy Cross Academy but left school at 14. As he recalled it, 'The headmaster said I'd come to no good. Maybe he was right'. He was the self-styled 'Fudge King' who from his small factory in St Mary's Street off the

Armando Margiotta

Royal Mile turned out literally millions of pieces of fudge in over 400 varieties. He began his career in catering as an assistant to his sister who ran 'The Sweet Shop' in the Canongate during the last War. After 1945 he took over the business and later opened the Fudge Shop in the Canongate. Through the winter of 1962, when trade was slow, he and the chief played chess and he built up his collection of 1,000 LPs and 14,000 '78s. He claimed to know sixty operas by heart. He put this boast to the test when he appread on Hughie Green's television quiz, 'The Sky's the Limit'. He beat the panel answering questions on opera and won 15,000 miles of free travel and £400. He was also Scottish Television's TV Chief and appeared on Eammon Andrews' 'What's My Line?' where his avuncular good humour and encyclopaedic knowledge made him an instant favourite.

Although he weighed 21 stones, he announced that 'I ignore the medical profession's advice about my 21 stones. Eating is one of the most fantastic pastimes, believe me'. He was a born teacher and once said, 'Give me two or three weeks with the bloke who says he can't cook and I'll turn him into a chef'.

Jim McGuffie, who died in 1982, ran the ever-popular Doric Tavern in Market Street from 1956 where the obscure rubbed shoulders with the eminent in all branches of the professions, the churches, government and the world of communication and entertainment. Born in Galloway, Jim was the perfect host and had learned his craft the hard way, starting in Glasgow in his own fish restaurant, then on to Gleneagles and Edinburgh's Café Royal. He treated every customer with courtesy and was on first-name terms with most, having an ability to talk on a wide variety of subjects.

Although the Café Royal has long been a favourite meeting-place, with its Oyster Bar and elaborate tiled and stained-glass décor, a trend over the last few years has been the emergence of wine bars. Reflecting another trend, for those who want wholesome vegetarian fare grown without the aid of artificial fertilisers, Henderson's in Hanover Street has for many years been the first eating-place. And, reflecting yet another trend, for which CAMRA (the Campaign for Real Ale) can take the credit, an increasing number of Edinburgh's 680-odd pubs serve a decent pint, many of them – following liberalisation of opening hours – throughout the day and late into the night, a phenomenon which comes as a surprise still to many a visitor from south of the Border.

The Café Royal, Circle Bar

Theatre, Film and Television

Finlay Currie, one of Scotland's best-loved actors, was born in Edinburgh in 1878. He was educated at George Watson's and Edinburgh University, where he studied music. While a student at the University, he was engaged to play the organ at the Theatre Royal for a performance of Shakespeare's *Henry IV*. This was the beginning of his career in the theatre. His musical training had included being a choirboy at Christ Church, Morningside and later at St Peter's, Lutton Place. He had also been organist at the Free Church in Inverkeithing and at Newington Free Church.

In 1898 he joined a stock theatrical company playing at the Pavilion Theatre in Grove Street, Edinburgh. He played leads, gave voices off, sang (doubling as baritone and soprano). This ability to sing falsetto earned hmim the stage nickname of 'the boy with the double voice'. During this period of his life he met and married an American music hall performer and composer, Maud Courtenay, and as Currie and Courtenay they toured India, Australia and the United States. It was his knowledge of American accents which gave him his first West End part, that of a gangster in Edgar Wallace's *Smoky Cell*. Two other Edgar Wallace thrillers followed, and Currie became a close friend of the writer. His career in films began to develop, and he played the part of Captain Billy Bones in Walt Disney's *Treasure Island,* St Peter in *Quo Vadis.* and the convict in *Great Expectations*. His last major role was that of the Blind Seer in the television version of *The Flight of the Heron*. He died in 1968.

One of the best-known and best-loved actors to emerge from Edinburgh was **Alastair Sim,** who was born in Edinburgh in 1900, and educated at James Gillespie's, then Heriot-Watt and Edinburgh University. At the outbreak of the First World War he abandoned his studies for military service. After the War he was appointed Fulton Lecturer in Elocution at New College, where his job was to improve the sermon delivery of trainee Church of Scotland ministers. He also ran a School of Dramatic

Alastair Sim

Training at Palmerston Place and founded an Edinburgh Children's Theatre. His debut as a professional was as a messenger in *Othello* at the Savoy Theatre in 1930. He excelled in roles such as the Mad Hatter in *Alice in Wonderland* and Captain Hook in *Peter Pan*. He was also outstanding as Dr Angelus in *The Anatomist*, where his brand of eccentric menace was particularly telling. He made a number of memorable films including *The Belles of St. Trinians* where he played the shady headmistress. What made his playing the role even more appropriate was the fact that the fictional St. Trinian's was derived, through the cartoons of Ronald Searle, from the real-life Edinburgh private school of St. Trinnean's (Gaelic for Ninian), of which Searle knew indirectly. Sim best summed up his philosophy as an artist in the remark he made early in his career: 'Could I play the fool and know that I was one? Could I wring laughter even from throats unused to laugh? That is the fool's peak of achievement'.

Born in Edinburgh in 1909, **Lennox Milne** was educated at St Oran's School and subsequently trained at the Edinburgh College of Drama and at RADA. After a short spell as a BBC producer she joined the Perth Theatre Company, then the Wilson Barrett, and later the Citizens Theatre, Glasgow. She was a founder member of the Gateway Company and appeared in all of Tyrone Guthrie's productions of *The Three Estates* at the Edinburgh Festival. At the 1953 Festival she performed thirteen characters in *The Heart is Highland*, which had been especially written for her by Robert Kemp. Her greatest role was as Jean Brodie in *The Prime of Miss Jean Brodie*, which she played on Broadway in 1967/68 and repeated at the Lyceum Theatre, Edinburgh in the stage adaptation of the Muriel

Spark novel. She wrote radio scripts in collaboration with her husband, Moray McLaren, and was awarded the first Scottish Arts Council Drama award. She became one of the first directors of Radio Forth, the local radio station for Edinburgh. Acknowledged as the leading lady of Scottish theatre, Lennox Milne spent her last years at Haddington, in East Lothian, where she put all of her considerable energies into the development of the Lamp of Lothian Collegiate Trust. As an actress she had the happy facility of being equally at home in Scots, English and French. She died in 1980.

A Baptist lay preacher, **Tom Fleming** was born in 1927 in Adelaide, Australia, the son of a minister. When his father took up the charge at Dublin Street in Edinburgh, his son was sent to Daniel Stewart's College where he was eventually to win the elocution prize and study privately with Anne Turner Robertson, the co-principal of the Edinburgh College of Drama.

After two years' national service in the Navy, which included performing in an ENSA play in India and the Far East with Dame Edith Evans, Tom Fleming had become the youngest ever announcer on the BBC Light Programme and began to write radio scripts. At the age of twenty-five he began a ten-year period as a Director of the Gateway Theatre in Edinburgh and later spent three years with the Royal Shakespeare Company for whom he played Prospero in *The Tempest* and the Duke in *Measure for Measure*. In 1965 he was appointed Director of the Edinburgh Civic Theatre at the Royal Lyceum, where he was particularly remembered for an outstanding performance as Brecht's Galileo.

In the course of his long career, Tom Fleming remembers very vividly the time when he played in *Julius Caesar* at Stratford on the night of President Kennedy's assassination:

Tom Fleming and Patricia Neal as Bothwell and Mary Stuart in Bjørnson's play 'Mary Stuart in Edinburgh'

the contact with the audience was electrifying. In later years he played Lear on a tour of Eastern Europe and then began a series of major roles including Jesus of Nazareth on television, Robert Burns, Weir of Hermiston, William Wallace and Vincent van Gogh in W. Gordon Smith's play. He also performed Hugh McDiarmid's *A Drunk Man Looks at the Thistle* at the Traverse Theatre, Edinburgh.

Cast in the heroic mould as an actor, and able to convey great moral strength, Tom Fleming is nevertheless as well known today in his role as a BBC commentator at royal and state occasions, following in the steps of the late Richard Dimbleby.

Fleming's view of the role of the actor is one of total commitment: it is a way of life in which acting, he believes, has chosen the actor: 'Acting demands a commitment comparable to that of an international athlete or swimmer'. 'The performance you see on the stage is not the heaven-sent inspiration of that moment; it is the distillation of weeks of concentrated study, exploration, experiment, ruthless re-examination, repetitive perfection-seeking, elation, dejection, creation and drudgery.'

Despite his Icelandic name and the fact that his father was Icelandic consul, **Magnus Magnusson,** born in 1929, is an Edinburgh man, educated at the Edinburgh Academy. After a journalistic career with the *Scottish Daily Express* and the

Magnus Magnusson

Scotsman, he turned to television, which has proved to be very much his element. Many popular and critical successes such as *Chronicle, Mastermind,* and *BC: The Archaeology of the Bible Lands* followed. In 1974 he was named Scottish Television Personality of the Year, and the following year was elected Rector of Edinburgh University. He has published extensively, showing an especial interest in archaeology.

Ludovic Kennedy was born in Edinburgh in 1919. Educated at Eton and Christ Church, Oxford, he married the dancer and film star Moira Shearer. In 1953 he became an Editor on the BBC Third Programme and two years later was a lecturer with the British Council in Scandinavia. From 1965 to 1967 he was on the Council of the Liberal Party and in 1968 became President of the Sir Walter Scott Club in Edinburgh. A spell followed as a columnist for *Newsweek International* and as Chairman of the Royal Lyceum Theatre Company in Edinburgh. Ludovic Kennedy's particular skill lies in pointing out the moral dilemmas in controversial contemporary issues. His publications reflect this: *The Trial of Stephen Ward* (1964) or *The Amazing Case of Patrick Meehan* (1975). The public interest aroused by the latter and Ludovic Kennedy's active pursuit of the issue led to Paddy Meehan's sensational release from prison, and a pardon with compensation.

Sean Connery is probably the actor who of all Edinburgh-born performers has the widest international audience. Born in 1930 and brought up in a 'single-end' in Fountainbridge, he was educated at Darroch's and worked his way through a bewildering variety of jobs: in McEwan's brewery; as a milkman with the Co-op; as a steelworker; a navvy; a French polisher; a

Sean Connery

coalman; and as a male model at the Edinburgh College of Art. In his spare time he took up bodybuilding at the Dunedin Amateur Weight Lifting Club. He was a lifeguard at Portobello Pool in 1950 and a bouncer at the Palais dance hall. He was runner-up in a Mr Universe contest. His acting career began in *Glorious Days* with Anna Neagle at the Empire. Then came a chorus part in *South Pacific* in London. Television viewers first saw him in *Requiem for a Heavyweight* in 1957. He is of course best known for his virile performances as James Bond, secret agent, a part which he made his own and where his fitness and co-ordination, allied to his brooding sex appeal, secured him universal recognition.

Ronnie Corbett has carved himself a special niche in the affections of the British public. In an age when the live theatre struggles to survive the lure of film and television Ronnie Corbett has endeared himself to millions in their homes in a

Ronnie Corbett

way that was never available to that great Edinburgh entertainer, Sir Harry Lauder. Ronnie was born in the City, the son of a MacVitties Guest baker. He was educated at Gillespie's and the Royal High School and then spent six months in the Department of Agriculture working with animal feeds. After National Service in 1949, he started in show business through cabaret in a number of London clubs. Having worked with Danny La Rue, he graduated to television in *The Frost Report*. Subsequently he joined forces with Ronnie Barker to star in the long-running series *The Two Ronnies*.

It was in 1930 that the Edinburgh Film Guild was founded, a year after the Glasgow Film Society. Eight years later the first Films of Scotland Committee was formed, and in 1947 the first

Edinburgh International Film Festival was held, becoming an annual event. In 1968 the Edinburgh Film Theatre was opened as the National Film Theatre, and in the following year the Edinburgh ABC became the first triple cinema in the UK. The Edinburgh International Film Festival was first held in 1976, and the conversion of the Lothian Road Church into a new Filmhouse was completed in 1982. Edinburgh is now securely on the international film and television map, and many first-class films have been premiered there. Edinburgh also has two film companies enjoying a growing reputation: Edinburgh Film Productions outside the City, and Sidharta Films just off the Royal Mile. With the emergence of the new television Channel Four, both companies have been able to take advantage of a new television audience. In 1984 Sidharta Films merged with another Edinburgh company, Turnstile, to form Skyline, the biggest Scottish independent programme-maker for television.

The name of the 7:84 Company of Scotland refers to the proportion of the wealth of Scotland held by seven per cent of the population. The Company was founded in Edinburgh in 1973 by some Scots who had already founded 7:84 Theatre Co England. The Scottish Company's first show was *The Cheviot, the Stag and the Black, Black Oil* by **John McGrath.** This toured the Highlands and Islands and was shown on BBC Television. Next came *The Game's a Bogey* by John McGrath, about the Glasgow socialist John MacLean (who incidentally spent some time in Edinburgh's Calton Prison). The 7:84 Theatre Company attempts to present the realities of working-class life and history directly to working-class audiences without translating it into the language of middle-class theatre.

John McGrath

Visitors

Edinburgh has been a thoroughfare and a bustling capital city for centuries. Countless travellers and visitors (some more welcome than others) have come and gone, some recording their observations of life in Edinburgh. The Romans under Agricola established a fort at Cramond in AD 80 and stayed till about the year 400. The second-century Egyptian geographer Ptolemy knew enough about south-east Scotland to be able to list the tribes which lived there, including the Votadini whose region lay between the Tyne and the Forth. The sixth-century Welsh-speaking poet Aneirin wrote about Dineidin, which means Hill Fortress; he almost certainly visited what is now the Castle Rock.

Until Edinburgh was captured by the Scots in the mid-tenth century the city was part of English-speaking Northumbria. In 1018 Malcolm II finally captured the kingdom of Lothian from the English and brought it and Edinburgh into the Scottish fold.

In 1291 the English King Edward I seized Edinburgh Castle. Five years later he spent two nights in Edinburgh and looted the Castle and some years later took away the Stone of Destiny on which many Scottish kings had been crowned and which was kept in the Castle. It remains in Westminster Abbey in London.

In 1361 the French chronicler Jean Froissart arrived with a French army, France then being Scotland's ally against England. He reported that with only four hundred houses in Edinburgh the French knights had to be billeted in the surrouding villages, such as Dunbar. He found the Scots to be wild and savage and hostile to French gentility, the country barren and the inhabitants scarcely able to grow enough food to feed themselves.

A notable visitor of 1435 was Aeneas Silvius Piccolomini (later Pope Pius II), who called on James I at Edinburgh in 1435. He was not impressed by Scotland or its climate, which he claimed had given him rheumatism. The King he found to be fat but healthy. About the Scottish people he writes: 'They eat flesh and fish to repletion, and bread only as a dainty. The men are small in stature, bold and forward in temper; the women fair in complexion, comely and pleasing, but not distinguished for their chastity, giving their kisses more readily than Italian women their hands'. Aeneas found that the Scots he met took a great delight in criticising the English. He was shocked by the poverty he saw: 'In this country I saw the poor, who almost in a state of nakedness begged at church doors, depart with joy on their faces on receiving stones as alms. This stone, whether by reason of sulphurous or some other matter which it contains, is burned instead of wood, of which the country is destitute'. He was, of course, referring to coal.

In the 1490s the Spanish ambassador, Don Pedro de Ayala, reported to his masters that the Scots were neither hard-working nor capable of working together in peace. He was impressed by the Scottish army when he saw it assembled. He was struck by the vanity of the Scottish nobility and their strength. He repeats the criticism of Aeneas that the Scottish women were overly affectionate even to strangers, but he admired their sense of dress. Unlike Froissart, de Ayala had a high opinion of the husbandry of Scotland, its produce, its sheep and the large quantities of fish which it exported. The houses were often of stone with windows of glass and numerous chimneys. There were sixty monasteries and a good number of abbeys.

A century later the English student Fynes Moryson commented on the prosperity of the Scottish burgesses. He admired Edinburgh's High Street but spoke of 'the rest of the side streets and alleys being of poor buildings and inhabited with very poor people'. He adds: 'The houses are built of unpolished stone, and in the fair street good part of them is of freestone, which in that broad street would make a fair show, but the outsides of them are faced with wooden galleries, built upon the second storey of the house; yet these galleries give the owners a fair pleasant prospect into the said fair and broad street, when they sit or stand in the same'. Moryson also notes that the High Street around St Giles was often heaped with filth of one kind or another and cluttered with market stalls.

Another visitor to the Capital towards the end of the century was the Frenchman, the Duc de Rohan, who agreed with Moryson in most respects, adding that in his opinion the City was overpopulated. There were some compensations, however, for he found the country 'truly generous in the production of virtuous persons. For, besides the nobility whom I found full of civility and courtesy, the country possesses a multitude of learned men, and a people of such courage and fidelity that our kings of France chose from among them the soldiers who formed the special guard of their person'.

Daniel Defoe, author of *Robinson Crusoe,* was in Edinburgh in 1706 to encourage popular support for the Union of the Parliaments (he was also to edit the *Edinburgh Courant*), and reported regularly to his masters in London, giving a lurid account of rioting in Edinburgh against the Union: 'We have had the last two nights a worse mob than this and that was in the street, and certainly a Scots rabble is the worst of its kind'. He continues: 'I had not been long there but I heard a great noise and looking out saw a terrible multitude come up the High Street with a drum at the head of them shouting and swearing and crying out all Scotland would stand together, 'No Union, no Union,' 'English Dogs' and the like'.

The night entry of Bonnie Prince Charlie's army into Edinburgh in 1745 has many of the ingredients of a Whitehall farce: four hundred volunteers of the College Company under the future Lord Provost, Captain George Drummond, paraded in the College Yards, their relations crowding round them and pleading with them not to fight. The Town Council tried to stall the Prince by sending letters back and forth. However, when the Netherbow Port was opened to let the carriage out with the Town Council delegation, Cameron of Locheil, who had been waiting outside with a detachment of soldiers, forced his way in, and the Town Guard (most of whom were Highlanders) dispersed. So the Prince took Edinburgh without shedding a drop of blood. The Prince and his army, writes Lord Elcho, were 'met by vast multitudes of people, who by their repeated shouts and huzzas, expressed a great deal of joy to see the prince'. Lord Elcho rode on the Prince's left: 'In the steepest part of the park going down to the Abbey he was obliged to alight and walk, but the mob out of curiosity, and

some out of fondness to touch him or kiss his hand, were like
to throw him down, so, as soon as he was down the hill, he
mounted his horse and rode through St Anne's Yards into
Holyroodhouse amidst the cries of sixty thousand people, who
filled the air with the acclamations of joy'.

Flora MacDonald (1722-90) was the daughter of Ranald
MacDonald of South Uist. Dr Johnson, who was never eager to
praise anything Scottish, said of her that 'Hers is a name that

Flora MacDonald

will be mentioned in history, and if courage and fidelity be
virtues, mentioned with honour'. He was, of course, referring
to her protection of Prince Charles Edward Stuart after his
defeat at Culloden and of her loyalty to him and his cause. Yet
Edinburgh also has a claim to some connection with her. She
first came there at the age of eighteen in 1740 in the household
of Sir Alexander MacDonald of Sleat and was enrolled in the
exclusive school for young ladies run by a Miss Henderson in
Old Stamp Office Close. She proved to be a hard-working and
clever pupil; she was a fine spinet player and was often in
demand in the drawing-rooms of the Capital to sing Gaelic
songs. She spent three years at school in Edinburgh and had
the opportunity to enjoy the fashionable life of the City under
the care of the mother of her guardian, the beautiful Countess
of Eglinton. In 1745 Flora was visiting her friends Lady Bruce
of Kinross and Bishop Forbes at the Citadel in Leith when she
was summoned to join Sir Alexander and Lady MacDonald,
news having come that the Prince was contemplating a landing
in Scotland. They sailed in a fishing-boat from Leith making
for Inverness, and so began the adventures of Flora MacDonald. A year later she was again in Leith as a State prisoner on
board the troopship *Bridgewater* in Leith Roads, where she
remained for many weeks, visited by her friends.

After her release in London in 1747, she again returned to Edinburgh and decided to improve her writing, taking lessons from the writing-master, David Beatt, who had officially proclaimed the Prince as King James VIII in front of Holyrood House after Charles Edward's capture of Edinburgh. Beatt commented in a letter that Flora needed 'very much to be advanced in her writing'. Flora, for her part, married Allan MacDonald of Kingsburgh in 1750, and emigrated to America in 1774, but returned in 1779, eleven years before her death.

Edward Burt, who published his impressions of Edinburgh in 1754, was struck by the magnificence of the High Street lands (tenements) and the quality of their stonework. However, there were other aspects of Edinburgh life he did not find quite so congenial: 'Being a stranger, I was invited to sup at a Tavern. The cook was too filthy an object to be described . . . another English gentleman whispered me and said, he believed, if the fellow was to be thrown against the wall, he would stick to it'. Burt seems, however, to have eaten well, for he continues: 'We supped very plentifully, and drank good French claret, and were very merry till the clock struck ten, the hour when everybody is at liberty, by beat of the City Drum, to throw their filth out at the windows. Then the company began to light pieces of paper, and throw them upon the table to smoke the room, and, as I thought, to mix one bad smell with another'.

Benjamin Franklin, the American scientist and politician, visited Edinburgh on two occasions: in 1759 and 1771. Dr Alexander Carlyle, in his *Autobiography,* records that 'we supped one night in Edinburgh with the celebrated Dr Franklin at Dr Robertson's house, then at the head of the Cowgate. Dr Franklin had his son with him; and besides Wight and me, there were David Hume, Dr Cullen, Adam Smith, and two or three more. Wight and Franklin had met and breakfasted together in the inn without learning one another's names, but they were more than half acquainted when they met here'. Carlyle describes Franklin as 'a silent man', and goes on to say that 'Franklin's son was open and communicative, and pleased the company better than his father; and some of us observed indications of that decided difference of opinion between father and son which in the American war, alienated them altogether'. On his second visit Franklin wrote to his friend William Strahan: 'Thro' storms and floods I arrived here on Saturday night, late, and was lodg'd miserably at an inn; but the excellent Christian David Hume, agreeable to the precepts of the Gospel, has received the stranger, and I now live with him at his house in the New town most happily. I purpose staying about a fortnight'. Franklin was one of the signatories of the American Declaration of Independence in 1778.

A more caustic commentator arrived in 1771 in the shape of **Dr Samuel Johnson,** accompanied by his faithful biographer **James Boswell.** Dr Johnson was predisposed to be critical: Edinburgh and Scotland were guilty until proved innocent. Boswell leased his residence in James Court from its former occupant, David Hume, and it was there that he brought the good Doctor for four days in 1773. 'Mr Johnson and I,' writes Boswell, 'walked arm-in-arm up the High Street, to my house in James's Court. It was a dusky night; I could not prevent his being assailed by the evening effluvia of Edinburgh.' Upon his arrival in an inn at the head of the Canongate 'the Doctor had unluckily had a bad specimen of Scottish cleanliness. He then drank no fermented liquor. He asked to have his lemonade made sweeter; upon which the waiter, with his greasy fingers, lifted a lump of sugar, and put it into it. The Doctor, in indignation, threw it out of the window'. Johnson, however, did amire the breadth of the High Street and the noble height of the buildings on each side, although he is better remembered for his remark to Boswell: 'I smell you in the dark!'

During the years 1786 and 1787 **Robert Burns** was in the

Robert Burns with the (Edinburgh) Burns Monument

City. Aged twenty-seven, Burns made the two-day journey from Ayrshire on a borrowed pony and entered by the West Port and along the Grassmarket. He shared a room with a friend in the Lawnmarket. His visit was primarily a business one: to discuss the publication of a new edition of his poems with William Creech, the bookseller and publisher. Burns visited Robert Fergusson's grave in the Canongate Kirk and wrote to the Baillies of Canongate, asking permission to erect a monument to his predecessor poet. He wrote the inscription on the stone. And there was a near-meeting with the young Walter Scott, who writes: 'I was a lad of fifteen in 1786-1787, when he came first to Edinburgh, but had sense and feeling enough to be much interested in his poetry, and would have given the world to know him. As it was, I saw him one day at the late venerable Professor Henderson's, where there were several gentlemen of literary reputation. His person was strong and robust; his manners rustic, not clownish; a sort of dignified plainness and simplicity. There was a strong sense of shrewdness in all his lineaments; the eye alone, I think, indicated the poetical character and temperament. It was large, and of a dark cast, and glowed (I say literally *glowed*) when he spoke with feeling or interest. I never saw such another eye in a human head, though I have seen the most distinguished men of my time . . .'

When the composer **Felix Mendelssohn** came to Edinburgh in 1829 he was charmed with the City and the view from Arthur's Seat: 'Below on the green are walking the most variegated people, women, children, and cows; the city stretches far and wide; in the midst is the castle, like a bird's nest on a cliff; beyond the castle come meadows, then hills, then a broad river'. There was more, though, than the countryside: 'the great blue sea, immeasurably wide, studded with white sails, black funnels, little insects of skiffs, boats, rocky islands, and such like. Why need I describe it? When God Himself takes to panorama-painting, it turns out strangely beautiful'.

Charles Dickens first came to Edinburgh in 1834 as the representative of the *Morning Chronicle* (the daughter of whose proprietor he was to marry). In 1841 he stayed at the Waterloo Hotel. As a member of the Scott Monument Committee he disapproved of the final result: 'I am sorry to report the Scott

Monument a failure. It is like the spire of a Gothic church taken off and stuck into the ground'. He came back in 1848 to play the part of Slender in *The Merry Wives of Windsor* (an amateur production) at the Theatre Royal in order to raise money to pay for a curatorship of Shakespeare's house at Stratford. Already in 1841 he had received the Freedom of the City; and an Edinburgh Pickwick Club had been formed as early as 1837. He came north in 1858 for a reading of *A Christmas Carol* and observed: 'Coming back to Edinburgh is like coming home'. He returned to five further readings in 1861, 1867 and 1868. On this last he notes: 'Such a pouring of hundreds into the place already full to the throat, such indescribable confusion, such a rending and tearing of dresses, and yet such a scene of good humour on the whole. I never saw the faintest approach to it. I read with the platform crammed with people'. He observed also: 'My old likening of Boston to Edinburgh has been constantly revived within these last ten days. There is a certain remarkable similarity of *tone* between the two places. The audiences are curiously alike, except that the Edinburgh audience has a quicker sense of humour and is a little more genial. No disparagement to Boston in this, because I consider an Edinburgh audience perfect'.

On her arrival in Edinburgh in 1842 a day late (much to the consternation of the waiting dignitaries) **Queen Victoria** raced off to Dalkeith Palace and the hospitality of the Duke of Buccleuch, returning to the City another day to enable her loyal subjects to greet her. Edinburgh was as fine was she had been led to believe. 'The view of Edinburgh', she wrote in her journal, 'from the road before you enter Leith is quite enchanting; it is, as Albert said, 'fairy-like', and what you would only imagine as a thing to dream of, or to seen in a picture'. She noted that the people were 'most enthusiastic, and the crowd very great. The Porters all mounted, with curious Scotch caps, and their horses decorated with flowers, had a most singular effect; but the fishwoman are the most striking-looking people, and are generally young and pretty women – very clean and very Dutch-looking, with their white caps and bright-coloured petticoats'. Referring to the close-knit fishing community of Newhaven, she adds: 'They never marry out of their class'.

George Eliot, the novelist, twice visited Edinburgh in 1845 when she saw Holyrood and the Borders, and in 1852 when she announces: 'here I am in this beautiful Auld Reekie'. She visited Francis Jeffrey at Craigcrook and was entranced: 'Between the beauty of the weather and the scenery, and the kindness of the good people, I am tipsy with pleasure. I have a beautiful view from my room window – masses of woods, distant hills, the Forth – not an ugly object to be seen. When I look out in the morning, it is as if I had waked up in Utopia'. She had good cause to love Edinburgh, as it was Blackwood's, the Edinburgh publisher, who brought out her first book and most of her other novels.

When **Hans Christian Andersen** stayed in Edinburgh, at the home of the banker Joseph Hambro in Trinity, he compared Edinburgh to Naples set in Greek scenery. He also visited Jeffrey at Craigcrook and was shown round the City by Sir James Young Simpson. What he saw disconcerted him: 'It was Sunday, and that means something in Scotland, I can tell you. Everything is then at rest, even the railway trains dare not run. All the houses are closed, and the people sit inside and read their Bibles or drink themselves blind drunk, for so I was everywhere told'. Andersen's experience echoes that of Bismarck, the German Chancellor, who sailed into Leith one Sunday on his yacht and was walking up towards the centre of town whistling happily when, to his amazement, a well-dressed workman approached him and scolded him for whistling on the Sabbath. Andersen was a little nonplussed by the design of the New Town: the only Scottish element he thought he could see in it was that the grid-like criss-crossing of the streets bore a resemblance to the pattern of Highland tartan. He was charmed by the unspoiled waterfront at Leith and the costumes of the Newhaven fishergirls. But back in Sir James Young Simpson's residence, he was horrified at the ether-inhaling sessions during house-parties at which the ladies who had had a whiff of the gas laughed with 'open lifeless eyes'.

Frederick Chopin, the celebrated Polish pianist and composer, came to Edinburgh in 1848 and stayed at 10 Warriston Crescent, the home of Dr Lyschinski. Chopin had recently broken with his friend, the French woman novelist George

Sand: and Revolution in France had upset his concert schedule. It was October, and he felt the cold, spending much time huddled round the fire, and suddenly crossing to the piano and playing to warm his hands. Sometimes he went out for a drive round the City. He was filled with melancholy: 'I cannot become sadder than I am; a real joy I have not felt for a long time. Indeed I feel nothing at all; I only vegetate, waiting patiently for my end'. Edinburgh, it would seem, did nothing for him.

John Ruskin was a frequent visitor. He had been born of Edinburgh parents and had spent his early years in Midlothian. The *Edinburgh Review* had published most of his work. His family had been wine merchants in the High Street and his father had been educated at the Royal High School. Ruskin was of the opinion that the Scott Monument should have been placed on Salisbury Crags. In the course of a lecture to the Edinburgh Philosophical Institute he attacked the 'vandals' who were even then extending the classical New Town. He was convinced that all the natural advantages of Edinburgh's magnificent viewpoints (Calton Hill, the Castle Rock, Arthur's Seat) had been thrown away. He abhorred the plainness of Edinburgh's new architecture and recommended a return to decorative Gothic.

Henry James wrote this description of Edinburgh after his visit in 1878: 'The night of my arrival here was a superb one; the full moon had possession of a cloudless sky. There is no street in Europe more spectacular than Princes Street, where all the hotels stand in a row. Princes Street was absolutely operatic. The radiant moon hung right above the Castle and the ancient houses that keep it company on its rocky pedestal, and painted them over with a thousand silvery, ghostly touches. They looked fantastic and ethereal, like the battlements of a magician's palace'.

Since the visit of George IV in 1822 and that of Queen Victoria in 1842, Royal Visits to Edinburgh have become something of a family tradition. Not only has the monarch attended the General Assembly of the Church of Scotland, but an annual Visit takes place later in the summer, with an opportunity for the monarch to meet a wide cross-section of the Scottish people.

King Edward VII, especially when he was Prince of Wales, liked to come to Edinburgh as an antidote to the formalities of court life in London. The present **Duke of Edinburgh** has a close social and working relationship with Scotland's Capital. Among his many official positions are the Chancellorship of

The Duke of Edinburgh

Edinburgh University, and he has also held the office of Master of the Merchant Company (1967), besides being a Fellow of the Royal College of Surgeons, an Honorary member of the Royal Scottish Academy, and an Honorary Fellow of the Royal Zoological Society of Scotland.

Edinburgh has had many honorary burgesses. Once the decision had been made to grant the Freedom of the City, the proclamation was read from the Mercat Cross. In 1618 the playwright and poet, Ben Jonson, was elected a burgess and entertained at a public banquet. In 1682 Samuel Pepys came to Edinburgh with the Duke of York and received the Freedom. Benjamin Franklin followed in 1759 and the author Tobias Smollett in 1760. In the next century Dr Edward Jenner (who discovered a smallpox vaccine) was made a Freeman in 1804, Dr Livingstone in 1857, and Giuseppe Garibaldi in 1864. General Ulysses Grant, President of the United States, was made a Freeman in 1877, Jan Smuts (South African statesman and soldier) in 1917, David Lloyd George in 1918, and Field-Marshal Montgomery in 1946.

Two great statesmen and Freemen of the City of Edinburgh have given, in their speeches of acceptance, their own assessment of Edinburgh. **General Eisenhower** in 1946 said: 'This ancient city, in its more than a thousand years of recorded history, has witnessed man's emergence from the Dark Ages . . . Cities like Edinburgh, far from being mere structures of brick and stone, are living symbols of mankind's fundamental need of faith in co-operative action'. Four years previously **Winston Churchill** had this to say: 'It seemed to me that Edinburgh, the ancient capital of Scotland, enshrined in the affection of the Scottish race all over the world, rich in memories and tradition, immortal in its collective personality, stands by itself'.

Others to have come and gone are **George Bernard Shaw** in 1950 (who asked to have his photograph taken below the statue of John Knox – 'he has a better beard than I have'); **Laurel and Hardy** in 1954; **Bulganin and Kruschchev** in 1956 (they were presented with a facsimile of the commission from Peter the Great given to the Scot, Captain Thomas Gordon, as Admiral of the Russian Navy); **Pope John Paul II** in 1982 (giving new meaning to the Murrayfield roar and packing Princes Street on his way to meet the Moderator below the statue of John Knox); and **Mr Gorbachev,** the new Soviet leader, in 1984.

Also in 1985 the Roman Catholic Primate of Poland, **Cardinal Jozef Glemp,** arrived at Edinburgh Airport to begin a two-day visit to Scotland. The Cardinal, who is of Scottish ancestry, celebrated Mass in a packed St Mary's Cathedral in Edinburgh, staying the night (as Pope John Paul II had) as guest of Cardinal Gordon Gray. Cardinal Glemp addressed hundreds of expatriate Poles, thanking them for the 'human solidarity' of the Scottish Polish community who had sent food and medical equipment to Poland. Among those expatriates was the doyen of the Edinburgh Polish community, General Stanislaw Maczek, who, as commander of the First Polish Armoured Division, had contained the elite Second SS Panzer Corps at the Chambois Bottleneck in August 1944, and so contributed greatly to the victory of the Allied Forces in Normandy.

Reciprocal links between Edinburgh and Poland go at least as far back as 1714 when a Scottish merchant living in Poland, Robert Brown, offered Lord Provost George Warrender funding for the education of Polish Protestant students. The first student to benefit from this arrangement arrived to study at Edinburgh University in 1719; and during the Second World

War the Polish School of Medicine (founded in 1941) trained many Polish students as medical graduates of the University of Edinburgh.

And lastly, perhaps the strangest visitors of all, and the most popular – seen by 220,000 people – the Emperor's Warriors. From the tomb of Chinese Emperor Qin Shihuang (c. 259-210 B.C.) at Xian, out of a 7,500-strong guardian army of life-sized terracotta figures (each one an individual portrait) came probably Edinburgh's most sensational exhibtion ever, silently but eloquently spanning continents as well as three thousand years: 'The Eighth Wonder of the World'.

Index